On the Way to Heidegger's
Contributions to Philosophy

On the Way to Heidegger's
Contributions to Philosophy

Parvis Emad

THE UNIVERSITY OF WISCONSIN PRESS

The University of Wisconsin Press
1930 Monroe Street
Madison, Wisconsin 53711

www.wisc.edu/wisconsinpress/

3 Henrietta Street
London WC2E 8LU, England

1   3   5   4   2

Printed in the United States of America

Library of Congress Cataloging-in-Publication Data
Emad, Parvis.
On the way to Heidegger's *Contributions to philosophy* / Parvis Emad.
        p.   cm.
Includes bibliographical references and index.
ISBN 0-299-22220-9 (cloth: alk. paper)
1. Heidegger, Martin, 1889–1976. Beiträge zur Philosophie.
2. Philosophy.   I. Title.
B3279.H48B44534   2007
193—dc22   2006031477

For
SELENE JONNA
with all my love

Denn das Ereignis ist, eignend-haltend-ansichhaltend, das Verhältnis aller Verhältnisse.

[For enowning is owning-sustaining-holding back; it is the relation of all relations.]

Heidegger

Contents

Preface

With the appearance of *Beiträge zur Philosophie (Vom Ereignis)* in 1989 and a decade later its English translation, *Contributions to Philosophy (From Enowning),* philosophy faces the task of a renewed appropriation of Heidegger's thought. It is toward this appropriation that the essays collected in this volume intend to make a contribution.

The elucidation undertaken in these essays is based on the realization that thinking in *Contributions to Philosophy* unfolds in a nonlinear manner, and that the inconclusive character of this work does not diminish its status as Heidegger's second major work after *Being and Time.* The misleading assumption that *Contributions to Philosophy* represents Heidegger's working notes disregards that the thinking unfolding in this work needs no note taking, because at each step of its unfolding it remembers the attunement speaking to it.

The earlier versions of these essays appeared for the first time between 1991 and 2006 in various journals and anthologies in the United States and abroad. In compiling the present volume, I considered two factors and thoroughly revised and rewrote these papers accordingly. First, the general topics of the anthologies in which some of the essays appeared, and into which they had to fit, no longer determine the limit and scope of what I want to say. This realization freed my hand to broaden the topic under discussion in these essays. Second, I realized that I cannot broaden the discussion without incorporating into it what I had learned since I first wrote them.

As the title of this volume indicates, these essays are explicitly concerned with the thinking that shapes Heidegger's *Contributions to Philosophy.* Ever since I took part in the task of translating this work into English, I realized that the thinking unfolding in it, much as the thinking that shapes *Being and Time,* is without precedent in the history of Western philosophy. Thus the thinking at work in these essays presents an alternative to the views on Heidegger held by deconstructionists, by Anglo-American analytic philosophers, by those in pursuit of the "genesis" of the thinking of being, by those who assume that this thinking can be used as a measure of comprehensibility or incomprehensibility of reality, and by those who distort this thinking as they misconstrue Heidegger's early and temporary entanglement in Germany's National Socialism.

Be it the deconstructionists' striving to make Heidegger's writings deconstructable; the analysts' distorted views of Heidegger's thought; the attempt to invent a "genesis" for the thinking of being (as though its "genesis" lies in something other than being); the view that interprets this thinking as a measure for the comprehensibility or incomprehensibility of reality; or the method that uses the biographical as the sole criterion for interpreting Heidegger's philosophy, *all* these approaches share the fundamental inability to project-open the thinking of being. Far easier than undertaking the task of projecting it open is submitting this thinking to the illusion that this thinking is available wholesale to theoretical disputation.

In these essays I have tried to project-open the being-historical thinking of *Contributions to Philosophy* and in so doing to show that this thinking comes into its own only when it is enacted and not when it is treated unquestioningly as a specific variety of theory. My concern with projecting-open being-historical thinking required me to work with Heidegger's words and phrases as they appear in *Contributions to Philosophy* rather than replacing them. Thus in reading this collection the reader should bear in mind that what may seem at first glance to be a repetition of Heidegger's language is actually the first condition that any projecting-opening of his being-historical thinking must meet. By working with Heidegger's language rather than replacing it, the interpretation that is presented in the following pages acknowledges its *underway* character, which is in part reflected in the title of this collection.

Being underway toward *Contributions to Philosophy*, the thinking unfolding in these essays as projecting-opening raises no claim to having rendered Heidegger's being-historical thinking totally transparent. Closely connected to relinquishing this claim is my concern with a question of paramount importance for projecting-opening and coenacting being-historical thinking: whether this thinking, once projected-open, can be used to resolve the perennial problems of life and to explain and justify its pressing practical situations, concisely put, the question of whether one can live by Heidegger's thought at all.

This question is at the center of one of Tolstoy's stories, which attests to the fact that not only philosophers but also novelists of rank are concerned with the age-old connection between life and thought. In our time Alexander Solzhenitsyn takes up this question in his novel *Cancer Ward*, in which he confronts the protagonists, who are more or less aware of their mortality because of their illness, with Tolstoy's question "What do men live by?" Solzhenitsyn elicits responses from his characters that range from "men live by their rations, uniform, supplies" to "men live by their pay, professional skill, or by love." At the end Solzhenitsyn gives the forum to the apparatchik Rusanov, who without hesitation unsurprisingly delivers the doctrinaire Marxist reply: "There is no difficulty about that. Remember: people live by their ideological principles and by the interests of their society."[1]

Would Solzhenitsyn's characters in *Cancer Ward* have responded to the question "What do men live by?" in the same way had they been familiar with Heidegger's thought in general or with the thinking that unfolds in his *Contributions to Philosophy* in particular? Would these characters be prepared to say that people can live by Heidegger's being-historical thinking? I think not. For had they been sufficiently familiar with this thinking, they would have had to admit that people cannot live by this thinking since it does not *immediately* offer any means for dealing with and resolving the problems people face in concrete situations of life. But having nothing *immediately* to offer for resolving the perennial and pressing problems of life is one thing; having *nothing at all* to say about these problems is quite another. Although Heidegger's being-historical thinking has *nothing immediately* to offer for resolving such problems, it has a great deal to say about responses to the question "What do men live by?" delivered as philosophical, theological, scientific, or technological precepts and explanations. Indeed, Heidegger's being-historical thinking has such fertility and generative power that although it has nothing immediately to offer by which we may live our lives, it can place philosophical, theological, scientific, and technological precepts in a new and hitherto unconsidered perspective. This thinking thus renders these precepts transparent in a way that completely transforms them. I touch on this aspect of being-historical thinking in the essays that deal with the question of God in the last part of *Contributions to Philosophy*; that address the inception of being-historical thinking; and that discuss the mastery of be-ing vis-à-vis the coercive force of machination.

When in a letter to Hannah Arendt dated January 10, 1926, Heidegger talks about their relationship, he seems acutely aware of the unavoidable and all-pervasive question, "What do men live by?" Why else would he be prompted to say:

It is not because of indifference or external circumstances that came in between that I have forgotten you, but because I had to forget you, and I will forget you as often as I enter the path of concentrated work. This is not a matter of hours or days but a process that takes weeks and months for preparation, and then again fades away. And when I look at philosophical achievement from the point of view of abandoning and breaking off all human relations, I find this achievement to be the most overwhelming thing that I know of in human experience.[2]

It is clear from this letter that he is prompted to take a frank, honest look at his relationship with Hannah Arendt since he is aware of the unavoidable question "What do men live by?" And what he lives by is the demands of philosophical achievement that overwhelm and take hold of him—one might say with the irresistibility of an attunement—as soon as he engages in concentrated philosophical work. Thus he lives neither by indifference, which might have prompted him to forget Hannah Arendt, nor by external circumstances, which might lead to that forgetting; rather, he lives by the inescapable demands of philosophy to achieve what is humanly possible to achieve.

These essays engage Heidegger's *Contributions to Philosophy (From Enowning)* in order to explicate aspects of Heidegger's thinking of enowning and thereby elucidate something of the enlightening power that I find in this thinking. I wish to demonstrate that although thinking of enowning does not immediately resolve the practical problems of life, it nevertheless does not nihilistically reject or discard the prevailing responses that purport to resolve these problems. Rather than rejecting such responses, thinking of enowning transforms them in light of what is withdrawn from them. In this vein, it is perhaps not far-fetched to say that Heidegger's being-historical-enowning thinking is the most potent modifier and elucidator of the hitherto given and tested moral, ethical, and theological responses to the question "What do men live by?"

Based on their specific focus, the essays in this volume are divided into two groups.

The first group consists of essays that specifically deal with *Contributions to Philosophy*. The second group consists of those that also address other issues.

Bibliographical information on the earlier versions of the essays and on other works specifically devoted to Heidegger's *Contributions to Philosophy* may be found in the bibliography. Full bibliographical information for cited works not appearing in the bibliography is given in the respective endnotes.

Throughout this volume, *Contributions* enclosed in parentheses and followed by page number(s) refers to the English translation of *Beiträge zur Philosophy (Vom Ereignis): Contributions to Philosophy (From Enowning)*, translated by Parvis Emad and Kenneth Maly (Bloomington: Indiana University Press, 1999). *Mindfulness* enclosed in parentheses and followed by page number(s) refers to the English translation of *Besinnung: Mindfulness*, translated by Parvis Emad and Thomas Kalary (London: Continuum Books, 2006). All other citations of Heidegger's work refer to his *Gesamtausgabe*, cited as *GA* enclosed in parentheses followed by volume and page number. All quotations, including those from *Sein und Zeit*, are my own translation. Both the Macquarrie-Robinson and Stambaugh translations of this work carry the German pagination in their margins, and this pagination is also reproduced in the *Gesamtausgabe* edition of *Sein und Zeit*, from which I quote; thus readers wishing to compare passages quoted from *Sein und Zeit* against the Macquarrie-Robinson or Stambaugh translations can readily locate them by following the German pagination. For bibliographical information regarding the volumes of the *Gesamtausgabe* from which I quote, as well as the English translations of these volumes, the reader is referred to the "Update on the *Gesamtausgabe*" (*Heidegger Studies* 22 [2006]: 235–46).

For English renderings of the keywords of being-historical thinking as they appear in these essays, especially the different spellings of the word *being*, the reader should consult the translators' foreword in *Contributions to Philosophy (From Enowning)* (xv–xliv), as well as the translators' foreword in *Mindfulness* (xiii–xlii).

My indebtedness to Gertrude Emad is immeasurable, and I thank her from the bottom of my heart for her support as well as her invaluable and conscientious help in typing the manuscript and preparing the bibliography.

Acknowledgments

Grateful acknowledgment is made to the following publishers for permission to use previously published works of the author:

State University of New York Press (New York, N.Y.) for permission to use pages 51–71 of *The Presocratics after Heidegger,* edited by David C. Jacobs (1999)

Indiana University Press (Bloomington) for permission to use pages 229–49 of *Companion to Heidegger's Contributions to Philosophy,* edited by Charles E. Scott et al. (2001)

Kluwer Academic Publishers (now Springer, Netherlands) for permission to use pages 129–46 of *From Phenomenology to Thought, Errancy and Desire,* edited by B. E. Babich (1995)

Humanitas (Bucharest), the publisher of *Studia Phaenomenologica,* in which the author's "Translating *Contributions to Philosophy* as an Hermeneutic Responsibility" appeared in 2006

Duncker & Humblot (Berlin), the publisher of *Heidegger Studies,* for permission to use pages 15–35, vol. 7 (1991); pages 55–71, vol. 16 (2000); and pages 197–207, vol. 22 (2006)

Duncker & Humblot (Berlin) for permission to use pages 73–90 of *Vom Rätsel des Begriffs,* edited by Paola-Ludovica Coriando (1999)

Beck Verlag (Munich) for permission to use pages 115–32 of *Heidegger und die Antike,* edited by Hans-Christian Günther and Antonios Rengakos (2006)

On the Way to Heidegger's
Contributions to Philosophy

Introduction

And more erroneous still would be the view that in the epoch of
asthenia for and lack of joy in foundational word one could ever
eliminate this state of affairs overnight by publishing a "book."

Mindfulness, 60

The essays collected in this volume enter into the "dialogue" that
throughout Heidegger's long and productive preoccupation with
hermeneutic phenomenology is shaped within the thinking of being
by the onefold of "what shows itself in itself, the manifest" *(Phä-
nomen/das Sich-an-ihm-selbst-zeigende, das Offenbare)* and "interpretation" (ἑρμηνεύειν, *Auslegung*) (*GA* 2:38 and 50). We must enter into this
"dialogue" if hermeneutic phenomenology is to remain the only guide
for understanding and appropriating the being-historical thinking of
Contributions to Philosophy. Since this understanding and appropriation
are ventures, I characterize the essays in this volume as being underway to this second major work of Heidegger's.

The "dialogue" within the thinking of being is shaped by the thrust
of hermeneutic phenomenology, that is, by the self-transforming onefold of "what shows itself in itself, the manifest," and "interpretation." Accordingly, one of the premises of these essays is that the
transcendental-horizonal thinking of *Being and Time* as well as the
being-historical thinking of *Contributions to Philosophy*, each in its own
way, originates from within this self-transforming onefold.

To let the being-historical thinking of *Contributions to Philosophy*
speak for itself, these essays enter into the "dialogue" within the thinking of being, which is shaped by the onefold of "what shows itself in itself, the manifest" and "interpretation." With *this* "dialogue" in mind, I
adopt a dialogical approach, as distinguished from a monological one.

I

Let us first briefly consider the place these essays occupy in the hermeneutic situation surrounding Heidegger's thought in the United States. With few exceptions, this situation is dominated by discussions which do not take their orientation from the "dialogue" within the thinking of being which is shaped by the onefold of "what shows itself in itself, the manifest," and "interpretation." Appearances notwithstanding, these discussions are monologues because the thinking of the participants does not return to "stillness" *(Stille)*—not to be mistaken with the absence of sound—which Heidegger sometimes calls being *(Sein)* and sometimes be-ing *(Seyn)*. As a monologue it returns the participants to their starting point: the deconstructability of the thinking of being, its invented "genesis," and the applicability of this thinking to reality as a criterion for its comprehensibility or incomprehensibility.[3] Thus what transpires *in* and *as* such a discussion implicates a returning that ipso facto is monological and reductive. In contrast to this monological reductive returning, the returning that takes its orientation from the "dialogue" within the thinking of being is a return to "stillness"—a return which according to *Contributions to Philosophy*, is a matter of returnership *(Rückkehrerschaft)*, not of hours, days, or years.[4]

At the risk of oversimplifying this returnership, I consider Heidegger research in its light and suggest that in almost all cases this research occurs outside returnership because it is indifferent to the "dialogue" within the thinking of being which is shaped by the onefold of "what shows itself in itself, the manifest" and "interpretation." This research does not take its orientation from the "beginning" inherent in that "dialogue" and consequently fails to do justice to the thinking of being. In almost all cases such research follows associative thinking, that is, it begins and ends with historical influence, with what is extraneous to the "beginning" inherent in that "dialogue." By and large Heidegger research today employs historical theorizing and imposes the notion of historical influence on the thinking of being.

It makes little difference whether this theorizing draws on Aristotle, or on Dilthey or Husserl; or whether for good measure it adds reflections on Nietzsche, or Jünger without ignoring Plato or forgetting Kant or Hegel, to mention only a few examples. What is important is that historical theorizing takes its orientation not from the aforementioned

"dialogue" within the thinking of being but from the notion of historical influence.

To put the essays in this volume into proper perspective, we must
critically address the issue of historical influence. While the monological
reductive approach to Heidegger's thinking of being takes for granted
and does not question the notion of historical influence, the dialogical
approach carefully examines this notion and unmasks its unquestioned
superiority. The monological reductive approach fails to appropriate
the thinking of being because of its counterproductive orientation to
the notion of historical influence. Heidegger draws attention to the
counterproductive character of this notion when he says: "Whoever
without hesitation reads and hears the lecture-courses only as a 'historical' presentation of some work and whoever then compares and
reckons up the interpretation [*Auffassung*] with the already existing
views or exploits the interpretation in order to 'correct' the existing
views, *he has not grasped anything at all*" (*Mindfulness*, 372).

Certain insights of Plato, Aristotle, Kant, Hegel, Dilthey, Husserl,
Nietzsche, and Ernst Jünger (to mention only a few) are doubtless
present in Heidegger's lecture courses and, mutatis mutandis, in his
thinking of being. The assumption that Heidegger's thinking of being
is also present and preserved intact in the philosophies of these thinkers, however, must be denied. The relationship between Heidegger and
philosophies of the past must be understood only in terms of what the
thinking of being draws out of these philosophies, demonstrating that
philosophical doctrines and teachings of the past offer unique *occasions*
for Heidegger to *break through to* new insights into the thinking of being.
What follows this breakthrough is altogether different from the philosophies and doctrines of the past. Totally unaware of the uniqueness and
novelty of the outcome of that breakthrough, a monological reductive
approach to the thinking of being focuses on comparing Heidegger's
interpretations of the philosophies of the past with views currently expressed about them, and sometimes on exploiting his interpretations to
"correct" the existing views.

The monological reductive approach to the thinking of being derives chiefly from perceiving *similarities* between earlier philosophical
thought and certain insights of Heidegger's as these insights come to
fruition in the thinking of being. This approach does not examine these
similarities to determine how they *differ* from Heidegger's insights. Although this failure is at work in and shapes most instances where a

monological approach reduces Heidegger's thinking of being to the doctrine of an earlier philosopher, for my purposes it suffices to briefly address one such assessment, namely, that involving Heidegger's relationship to Nietzsche.

Although a monological reductive approach does indeed recognize *similarities* between Nietzsche's and Heidegger's views on science and technology, it does not attempt to detect the *differences* between those views. It thus hurriedly concludes that Heidegger simply takes his views on science and technology from Nietzsche. By contrast, a dialogical approach also identifies the differences and finds that Nietzsche's insights into science and technology become unique *occasions* for Heidegger to achieve a novel understanding of science and technology in light of "what shows itself in itself, the manifest," which Heidegger addresses in *Contributions to Philosophy* under the rubric *machination*. A monological reductive approach interprets machination as Heidegger's way of summarizing Nietzsche's insights into science and technology. But strictly speaking, machination is not at all a summary, since it refers to "what shows itself in itself, the manifest." What Heidegger calls machination is "*a* manner of the swaying of be-ing," and as such it is "*a* manner of what shows itself in itself, the manifest." Thus Nietzsche's view on science and technology, augmented by Greek ποίησις and τέχνη, become for Heidegger *occasions* for new insight—but insight found in neither Nietzsche nor the Greeks—namely, that science and technology are sustained by machination, that is, by *a manner* of the swaying of be-ing.[5]

II

A brief discussion of Heidegger's own views on the issue of understanding his work is in order. At two significant junctures in his philosophical career, Heidegger looks back at his work and addresses this issue. The first coincides with his transcendental-horizonal thinking, immediately after the appearance of *Being and Time*. The second coincides with his being-historical thinking and appears several years after the writing of *Contributions to Philosophy*.

Heidegger's position at the first juncture makes it clear that to achieve an understanding of his work, one must begin with the central perspectives and impulses shaping it. His position at the second juncture illuminates his thoughts on the elucidation of philosophical texts in general.

The first juncture appears in Heidegger's response to a letter from

Karl Löwith in which for the first time in his philosophical career Heidegger states that to understand his work one must abandon the approach that seeks his development in "the sequences of lecture courses and what is communicated in them alone. This short-winded view forgets backwards and forwards the central perspectives and impulses at work."[6] Heidegger leaves no doubt that one cannot understand his work through a chronological approach to his writings. It is central perspectives and impulses operating in his work, not chronology, that are significant. In Heidegger's view, the central perspectives and impulses are *the only* reliable guide for understanding his work. He highlights this point in this letter when he notes: "[I]t is no accident that I constantly occupied myself with Duns Scotus, and the Middle Ages and always came back to Aristotle."[7] Here he makes it clear that the thoughts of Aristotle, Duns Scotus, and medieval philosophers shape—*but are not identical with*—the central perspectives and impulses operating in his work and that these perspectives and impulses account for his constant return to these philosophers.

That is, his studies of Aristotle, Duns Scotus, and medieval philosophy do not merely represent a passive reception of a historical influence. Since the letter to Löwith was written right after the publication of *Being and Time* and thus belongs to the transcendental-horizonal perspective, it shows that the key to understanding his works deriving from this perspective is precisely a recognition of the absence of any passive reception of these thinkers. Instead, their teachings serve as *occasions* for new insights into the thinking of being—insights that form the central perspectives and impulses operating in his work.

In contrast to a monological approach that reduces *Being and Time* to the historical influence of Aristotle and thus views this philosopher as the actual originator of the fundamental ontology of the transcendental-horizonal perspective, we should view Aristotle as the originator of certain insights that serve Heidegger as the occasion for achieving new insights, which come to fruition in the transcendental-horizonal thinking of *Being and Time*, that is, in a thinking that can *nowhere be found in Aristotle*.

We come to the second juncture in Heidegger's essay "Nietzsche's Word God Is Dead" (1943). Heidegger's elucidation of Nietzsche's proclamation on the death of God includes a significant passage in which he outlines the tasks that we must tackle if we are to understand Heidegger's work, tasks that have guided my work in the essays collected in this volume.

His interpretation of Nietzsche's text on the death of God includes remarks on reading and explicating a philosophical text. Whether we read and explicate Nietzsche's or Heidegger's text, we are engaged in elucidating a text. To succeed, this elucidation must tackle the tasks that Heidegger outlines in the following passage:

> To be sure, every elucidation must ascertain not only the matter that is at issue in the text; it must also, unnoticeably and without boasting, add something of its own concern to the text. The layperson, who measures this addition by what he holds to be the content of a text, always perceives this addition as reading something into the text. And with the right that the layperson claims for himself, he castigates this addition as arbitrary. However, a proper elucidation of a text never understands it better than its author understood it but surely differently. And yet, this different understanding must be such that it touches *(trifft)* the same issue that the elucidated text itself is pondering. (*GA* 5: 213–14)

The hermeneutic import of these tasks appears to be virtually *conditio sine qua non* for grasping Heidegger's works devoted to elucidating the texts of earlier philosophers. Whether it is a fragment of Anaximander or Nietzsche's *Will to Power,* Hegel's introduction to the *Phenomenology of Spirit* or Kant's *Critique of Pure Reason,* Heidegger always ascertains the matter at issue in a text, adds his own concern to the elucidated text, and thereby understands the text differently from the way its author understood it; at the same time this different understanding touches the "same issue" that the elucidated text itself is pondering. Of paramount importance for understanding Heidegger's writings, however, is that one cannot elucidate a text in the manner described unless one is mindful of the aforementioned onefold of "interpretation" and "what shows itself in itself, the manifest."

To see how Heidegger's views on elucidating texts are squarely lodged within this onefold, let us briefly consider his elucidation of Nietzsche. From 1936 to 1943, Heidegger's elucidation ascertains that the matter at issue in these texts is the will to power and eternal return. He introduces his own concern to these texts by outlining "machination," which as *a manner* (not *the* manner) of the swaying of be-ing is the "clearing" *(Lichtung)* within which Nietzsche discloses beings as quanta of the will to power that eternally return. Thus Heidegger understands Nietzsche's text differently from the way Nietzsche himself understood the text. Yet this different understanding touches the "same issue," that is, the will to power and eternal return that Nietzsche's text ponders. Thus the doctrines of the will to power and eternal return become *occasions* for Heidegger to achieve a new insight into the swaying of be-ing that he calls machination.

Regarding the onefold of "interpretation" and "what shows itself in itself, the manifest," Heidegger uses Nietzsche's doctrines of the will to power and eternal return as occasions for the thinking of be-ing to achieve new insights. According to these insights, the will to power and eternal return, along with the specific statements each doctrine makes about the appearing of beings, are indisputable indicators that Nietzsche enters the domains of "what shows itself in itself, the manifest," and "interpretation." Hence to grasp properly and assess Heidegger's elucidations of Nietzsche's texts, one must—instead of taking those elucidations as indications of historical influence—orient oneself toward the onefold of "interpretation" and "what shows itself in itself, the manifest."

Understood thus and applied to the prevailing approaches to Heidegger's texts, the tasks that the elucidation of a philosophical text faces—as outlined here—are systematically ignored by the monological reductive approach to Heidegger's texts. This approach does not ascertain the central issue in Heidegger's texts and therefore does not enter into the domain of the onefold of "interpretation" and "what shows itself in itself, the manifest." It fails to do so because the addition it makes to Heidegger's text is the assumption of historical influence, that is, something that does not touch the "same issue" that Heidegger's own text is pondering. It does not touch the "same issue" because it takes the *similarities* between what Heidegger's text is pondering and the thoughts of earlier philosophers as the reason for its historical theorizing—for advancing the thesis of historical influence. This approach disregards *the differences* between what Heidegger's text is pondering and the thoughts of past philosophers. We can clarify these critical points by examining some cases in which a monological reductive approach bypasses the central issue in Heidegger's texts.

Until recently this approach paid lip service to the central issue in Heidegger's texts by mentioning "the question of being" *(Seinsfrage)* as an important one for understanding Heidegger's thought and acknowledged this importance without working out the structure and hermeneutic import of the question of being. Now, however, the monological reductive approach no longer attaches any importance to this question and does not hesitate to dismiss it as an outright "ethereal question."[8] When it comes to adding its own concern to its elucidation of Heidegger's texts, the monological approach ignores what Heidegger's text is pondering by quickly pointing to Aristotle, Nietzsche, Kant, or another philosopher as the begetters of historical influences determining what Heidegger's texts ponder. More specifically, the monological reductive approach is quick to add something of its own to the elucidation of Heidegger's texts, but what it adds derives from an unawareness of the difference between what is a historical influence and what is merely an occasion for Heidegger's thinking of being to achieve new insights.

Accordingly, the havoc created by the monological reductive approach in understanding Heidegger's writings stems from its failure to ascertain the central issue in his texts, a result of its failure to be mindful of the aforementioned onefold of "interpretation" and "what shows itself in itself, the manifest."

III

The issues of transferability and translatability of the language of the thinking of being are crucial for grasping the premises of these essays. The monological and dialogical approaches to Heidegger's thought not only determine the outcome of the hermeneutic efforts devoted to his writings but also the understanding of the issues of transferability and translatability of the language of the thinking of being. As I shall presently show, the dialogical approach is guided by an understanding of translation that is fundamentally different from the understanding of translation that leads the monological approach.

Besides these two approaches to the issue of translation, a third approach to this issue is not given—*tertium non datur*. Even if we consider the thesis of deconstruction on the issue of translation, we still have to maintain that there are only two approaches to the issue of translation and transfer of the basic words of the language of the thinking of being: monological and dialogical. The thesis of deconstruction does not constitute a third approach because this thesis maintains that translation in general and translation of Heidegger in particular has come to an end. With this thesis deconstruction cuts itself off from the task of translating and transferring the basic words of the language of the thinking of being.

From the beginning and regardless of the direction it takes, a monological reductive approach takes lightly the issues of transferability and translatability of the language of the thinking of being. This approach is blind both to the fact that for Heidegger earlier historical doctrines are occasions to reach new insights and to the questions that ultimately determine the transferability and translatability of the language of the thinking of being. This blindness is manifested primarily in two closely related assumptions: either a monological reductive approach unquestioningly and a priori assumes that the language of the thinking of being is absolutely transferable from German into English, or it takes the dictionary as the ultimate authority and arbitrator for resolving the uncertainties that arise in that process.

The first assumption is the motivating and determining force behind the monological reductive approach to the language of the thinking of being: it presumes the basic words of this language to be exhaustively transferable and translatable into English. According to this assumption, basic words of the language of the thinking of being can be rendered in English without a residue of untranslatability. Hence this approach ignores the need for a translation that approximates the German original rather than aspiring to substitute and replace it. With its *absolute faith* in the thesis of *the absolute transfer,* monological reductive approach turns these issues into nonissues. The foremost expression of this absolute faith is the demand that, against the accepted practice today, the basic word *Dasein* be rendered in English exactly, instead of retaining this word in this language.

The second assumption underlies renderings of the basic words of the language of the thinking of being made on the authority of the dictionary. This assumption is at work, for instance, when a monological reductive approach unquestioningly and a priori accepts such renderings as "essence" for *Wesen* and "event" or "event of appropriation" for *Ereignis.* The obstinacy with which this approach clings to these renderings reveals that it is closed off to the thinking of being and to the ways in which this thinking, out of the depths of what is ownmost to language, alters the meaning of common German words such as *Wesen* and *Ereignis.* If this alteration is given its due, then one can understand why in the language of the thinking of being *Wesen* and *Ereignis*—central words of Heidegger's being-historical thinking—do not retain their familiar meaning.

To be open to the ways in which the thinking of being alters the meaning of common German words, one must recognize that the thinking of being exclusively takes place within what is ownmost to language, that is, within *das Wesen der Sprache,* which is neither the exclusive property of a *particular language* nor common to *all languages.* Were we to think of the ownmost of language as the exclusive property of a particular language, then remaining languages would be deprived of this ownmost and hence would cease to be languages. Were we to conceive of the ownmost of language as a property common to all languages, then all languages would have the same "essence" and thus would be identical. But the monological reductive approach does not concern itself with these alternatives because it disregards the fact that what is ownmost to language sustains the alteration of the meaning of common German words.

Since what is ownmost to language is not accessible through the dictionaries of a given language, and since the alteration of the meaning of common German words originates from within that ownmost, when monological approach appeals to the dictionary as the exclusive arbiter in matters of transferability and translatability of the words of the language of the thinking of being this approach only shows that it is not fit for grasping that alteration. It thus demonstrates its unawareness that the thinking of being has altered the familiar meanings of words such as *Wesen* and *Ereignis* and its lack of even a rudimentary grasp of the basic words of the thinking of being. Consequently, this approach clings to the dogma of absolute transfer and strives for the semantic equivalency of words such as *Wesen* and *Ereignis* with their English counterparts.

When we realize that what is ownmost to language is neither the exclusive property of a given language nor the selfsame essence of language that all languages share, we can understand the role that a particular language plays in transferring and translating the language of the thinking of being. If a particular language plays a significant role in transferring and translating the words of the language of the thinking of being, it plays this role *not* because it happens to be the mother tongue. In other words, the ownmost of language is not confined within a given language and therefore does not exclusively reside in the mother tongue. Thus the mother tongue is not what determines the issues involved in the transferability and translatability of the basic words of the language of the thinking of being.

However, the monological reductive approach to these issues is determined solely by the significance it attaches to the mother tongue. For both the dogma of absolute transfer and the authority of the dictionary are rooted in the assumption that the mother tongue is ultimately the sole arbitrator in matters of transfer and translation of the words of the language of the thinking of being. Because the words of the mother tongue are immediately familiar and transparent, the monological reductive approach submits the issues of transferability and translatability of the words of the language of the thinking of being to the authority of the mother tongue. This submission understands the words of the thinking of being as thoroughly transferable and inexhaustibly translatable because its standard is the familiarity and transparency of the words of the mother tongue.

In contrast to the monological reductive approach, the dialogical approach does not begin with the familiarity and transparency of the words of the mother tongue. And this is not without precedence. The first thinker who disputes and rejects the supremacy of the mother tongue in matters of transfer and translation is the Russian poetess Marina Tsvetayeva. Aptly but quite cautiously called "Martin Heidegger's secret twin sister," Tsvetayeva experiences in her own poetic way the illimitability of what is ownmost to language when she addresses the issues of transferability and translatability of the poetic word and refuses to submit these issues to the authority of the mother tongue.[9]

Addressing the significance and the authority of the German language, which *is* Rainer Maria Rilke's mother tongue, in relation to French, which *is not* his mother tongue and in which he writes some of his poems (his *Vergers*, for example), Marina Tsvetayeva states:

No language is the mother tongue. . . . I am not a Russian poet and am always astonished to be taken for one and looked upon in this light. The reason one becomes a poet (if it were even possible to *become* one, if one *were* not one before everything else!) is to avoid being French, Russian, etc., in order to be everything else. Or: one is a poet because one is not French. Nationality—segregation and enclosure. Orpheus bursts nationality, or he extends it to such breadth and width that everyone (bygone and being) is included.[10]

By vigorously dislodging from Rilke's poetry the central authority of the mother tongue, Marina Tsvetayeva clearly demonstrates that something other than the mother tongue sustains it. Without calling this "something other" *das Wesen der Sprache*—as Heidegger will call it a few decades later—Marina Tsvetayeva dislodges the central authority of the mother tongue and opens the way for a novel approach to the issues of transferability and translatability.

She herself, however, neither traverses this path nor shows that transfer and translation take place within what is ownmost to language and not primarily within the mother tongue. By contrast, Heidegger looks away from the mother tongue, takes his orientation from what is ownmost to language, and does indeed traverse the path to a novel approach to the transferability and translatability of the language of the thinking of being.

As early as 1924, Heidegger has in mind what is ownmost to language when he addresses the issues of the transferability and translatability of the basic words of the language of the thinking of being. He focuses on what is ownmost to language when he differentiates the terminological meaning of a word from its common meanings. Speaking of the Aristotelian concept of οὐσία, he begins with this differentiation and says:

> [A]ccording to its common and familiar meanings οὐσία means "wealth," "property," "one's belongings," and "possession." If we probe into these familiar meanings, we would perhaps discover what being as such meant to the Greeks. But we must be careful not to infer the terminological meaning of οὐσία from its familiar meanings. What is at stake here is understanding the familiar meanings in such a way as to discern *directives* from these meanings for understanding the terminological meaning of οὐσία. (*GA* 18:24)

By differentiating the familiar from the terminological meanings of the word and the concept of οὐσία, Heidegger presents a model for understanding the terminological meaning of the words central to the language of the thinking of being. If we apply this differentiation to the basic words of the language of the thinking of being, such as *Dasein, Wesen, Ereignis,* and *Ab-grund,* we realize that the transfer and translation of these words from German into English must be guided by the directives inherent in their familiar meanings without, as Heidegger puts it, making the mistake of assuming that *"the terminological meaning emerges directly out of the familiar meanings"* (*GA* 18:24, italics added).

In keeping with this differentiation, the terminological meaning of the word *Dasein* does not emerge directly from any of its familiar meanings, that is, *Anwesen* (presence), *gegenwärtig* (present), *vorhanden* (extant), *Existenz* (being), and *Leben* (life). Yet these familiar meanings hold within themselves directives for understanding the terminological meaning of the word *Dasein.* For even though the terminological meaning of the word *Dasein,* as a word central to the language of the thinking of being, entails the first two meanings, that is, *Anwesen* and *gegenwärtig,* and even though the terminological meaning has a prohibitive relation to the last three familiar meanings, that is, to *vorhanden, Existenz,* and *Leben, Dasein* as understood within the language of the thinking of being is *not identical with any one of these meanings.* For within this language *Dasein* is the word for the *Da* of *Sein,* that is, the *t/here* of being.

Does English have a word that could satisfy the dogma of absolute transfer and translate this central word of the language of the thinking of being without leaving a residue of untranslatability? I think not. For even the construction *There-being* fails to transfer absolutely the component *Da* insofar as "there" and the sense of presence it conveys do not absolutely transfer what is at stake in the *Da* of *Dasein:* this *Da* does not mean the sheer presence of being.[11] Also the other component, *Sein* (being), which is another central word of the language of the thinking of being, cannot be absolutely transferred into English with the help of words such as *presence* or *absence* or even with the aid of the naively constructed *pres-absentiality,* because only a being is present or is absent but not being as such.

To cite another instance, the terminological meaning of the word *Wesen* does not emerge directly out of any of its familiar meanings, that is, *Sosein* (essence), *vorhandensein* (to be extant), *tätigsein* (to be active), and *wirksamsein* (to be effective). Yet these familiar meanings function as directives for understanding the terminological meaning of the word *Wesen* even though the terminological meaning is *not* identical with *any one of these meanings.* Put differently, even though meanings such as "essence," "extant," "active," and "effective" point to the terminological meaning of the word *Wesen,* this terminological meaning is not the aggregate of any of these meanings.

Using the familiar meanings of the word *Wesen* as directives, Heidegger arrives at the terminological meaning of this basic word. Referring to a central characteristic of *Dasein* in *Being and Time,* namely, "Das Wesen des Daseins liegt in seiner Existenz" (*GA* 2:56), he differentiates the terminological meaning of *Wesen* from *one* of its familiar meanings, that is, *Essenz,* or "essence," by noting that terminologically *Wesen* must not be taken in the sense of essence but in the sense of "ownmost inner possibility" (*GA* 9:141). Thus he shows that the dictionary-based rendering of *Wesen* as "essence" distorts the terminological meaning of *Wesen,* insofar as "essence" is merely *one* of the several meanings of *Wesen* and so cannot account for the wholesale presence of a being called *Dasein.*

How do we explain the widespread and entrenched mistranslation of the phrase *das Seiende im Ganzen* with "beings as a whole"—a mistranslation that at first glance does not seem derived from the supremacy attributed to the mother tongue and from faith in the dogma of absolute transfer? Appearances to the contrary, this mistranslation too comes from the supremacy that is unjustifiably attributed to the mother tongue. Disregarding the connection between this phrase and the compound "being-in-the world"; without taking into account the German word *im* in the phrase *das Seiende im Ganzen;* without considering the fact that Heidegger speaks of *das Seiende* im *Ganzen* and *not* of *das Seiende* als *Ganzes,* the monological reductive approach perpetuates a misconception and suggests that with *das Seiende im Ganzen* Heidegger has in mind *das Seiende als Ganzes,* that is, "beings as a whole." Why does the monological reductive approach choose this mistranslation rather than the correct rendering, "beings in a whole"? It does so because the mother tongue demands smooth readability of the translated terms and resists opening itself to the unfamiliar words and phrases of the language of the thinking of being. Thus it makes for a smoother reading to take the crucial phrase *das Seiende im Ganzen* as meaning "beings as a whole" instead of coming to terms with its terminological meaning, "beings in a whole." The monological reductive approach prefers to distort the terminological meaning of this phrase because it is committed to the supremacy of the mother tongue.

The monological reductive approach does not want to abandon either the certainties inherent in the mother tongue or the authority of the dictionary and the dogma of absolute transfer, so it distorts the meaning of the basic words and phrases of the language of the thinking of being. In the final analysis this refusal stems from the failure of this approach to gain access to the thinking of being.

IV

By heeding the ownmost of language and by not losing sight of the onefold of "interpretation" and "what shows itself in itself, the manifest," the elucidation of Heidegger's texts in the following pages begins with ascertaining the matter at issue in these texts. This ascertainment cannot be achieved without transferring and translating the basic words and phrases of the language of the thinking of being from German into English, which in turn requires that Heidegger's words and phrases be carefully preserved.

If not properly understood, this requirement could be mistaken for a propensity to repeat Heidegger's own words, what an untutored eye perceives as "rehearsing" Heidegger. However, preserving Heidegger's own words to elucidate his texts involves neither repeating nor rehearsing Heidegger and is instead the first necessary step to broaching Heidegger's texts as *his* texts instead of concocting a text of our own making. An appropriate transfer and translation of the basic words of the language of the thinking of being cannot be separated from the decision to preserve Heidegger's own words. Insofar as the elucidations of Heidegger's text attempted here do not take their orientation from the supremacy and security of the mother tongue or from the authority of the dictionary, they are directed by Heidegger's own words.

The elucidator of Heidegger's texts must be distinguished from the commentator who is presumptuous enough to believe he has mastered the thinking of being with the help of historical theorizing or to have overcome the difficult task of *thinking along with Heidegger*. The elucidator of Heidegger's texts in this collection of essays does not claim to have mastered the thinking of being, not only because in *Mindfulness* and elsewhere Heidegger himself denies the very possibility of such mastery but also because the thinking of being cannot be mastered at all. One can only be on the way toward this thinking. Perhaps the role of the elucidator is that of trying his hand at elucidating Heidegger's texts, ascertaining the central issue in these texts, and then putting the fruits of this labor at the disposal of others so that they may try the same procedure. This seems to be in keeping with Heidegger's manner of dealing with the texts of historical figures of Western philosophy. He puts the fruits of his labor at our disposal after dispassionately judging the works of a historical figure, always granting that figure the right to be himself, always considering what each figure stands for, and never assuming that he can triumphantly overcome a figure and remove him from the purview of philosophical thinking.

In a letter to Marie von Thurn und Taxis (June 1, 1911, see note 12 below), Rilke expresses his admiration for the work of his friend the philosopher Rudolf Kassner, titled *Die Elemente der menschlichen Größe* (The Elements of Human Greatness). He describes what Kassner achieves in this work with words that could easily be applied to what Heidegger accomplishes in his:

[T]his incredible way in which certain concepts are made mindful of themselves—certain concepts that one is inclined to say have been slumbering for centuries—this unparalleled elucidation of entire regions; this first-time acquittal of mistrustful forces and the unperturbed manner of accepting the guilty ones; this . . . court of justice that leaves us a little time while itself has time, does not *press*, does not *convert*, but only *enacts itself*.[12]

Today, long after Kassner has been forgotten and Rilke and Heidegger occupy their indisputable places in the pantheon of thought, these words have special resonance. They remind us that elucidation of Heidegger's texts is elucidation of a thinking that judges but is not judgmental, presses but is not upsetting, persuades but does not want to convert. For Heidegger's thinking thrives only in enactment. It is toward an appropriation of Heidegger's thinking as one awaiting enactment that I hope to make a contribution in the essays collected in this volume.

I

Translating Heidegger's
Contributions to Philosophy as
a Hermeneutic Responsibility

From the vantage point of cultural history, the translation into English of Heidegger as a German philosopher seems based on one important assumption, namely, that this translation is essentially an *inter*lingual transfer of words between the two languages, German and English. According to this assumption of cultural history, the *inter*lingual translation of Heidegger is unavoidable in cultural exchange and the translator of Heidegger is a cultural translator and his or her work is an *inter*lingual and *inter*cultural means of exchanging cultural goods.

Two consequences follow from this assumption: First, "Heidegger in translation" is less important than "Heidegger in German" because reading and interpreting him in German do not involve the risks and uncertainties of *inter*lingual translation. Intimately tied to this is, second, the lack of awareness of the very existence and the need for an *intra*lingual translation of Heidegger's keywords.

But a basic familiarity with what Heidegger's thought—the unmistakable corollary of *Seinsfrage*—has established about translation is enough to undermine the assumption at work in cultural history. By differentiating *intra-* from *inter*lingual translation, by demonstrating the intersecting and the coalescing of translation and interpretation and their ultimate indistinguishability, Heidegger's thought regarding being not only undoes the assumption of cultural history but also puts forth intralingual translation as the domain wherein *all* interpretations of Heidegger—including interpretations in German—begin and end. To meet the hermeneutic responsibility of translating the keywords of Heidegger's *Contributions to Philosophy*, one must be mindful of the coalescing of translation and interpretation and attend to the differentiation between *intra-* and *inter*lingual translations.

The thesis of the following discussion is that Heidegger himself is engaged in an intralingual translation wherein interpretation and *this* translation coalesce, and an interlingual translation of the keywords of *Contributions to Philosophy* should thus take its orientation from this coalescing. My argument is guided by the de facto intersecting and coalescing of interpretation with intra- and interlingual translations in Heidegger's work.

Thus instead of wandering from one dictionary to another in the hope of finding words that exactly replace the German original, instead of speculating on the end of translation in general and that of Heidegger's work in particular, and finally instead of adding another theory to the familiar stock of theories on interlingual translation—advanced from Goethe all the way to Walter Benjamin—I begin by closely examining the coalescing of interpretation with intra- and interlingual translations in Heidegger's work.

This approach allows me to take the path of hermeneutic phenomenology rather than submit to the comfortable distractions of associative thinking, which seizes the first opportunity to avoid enacting Heidegger's thought itself. This route alone leads one to an appreciation of the contributions that thinking of being as hermeneutic phenomenology makes toward understanding the task of translating interlingually the keywords of *Contributions to Philosophy*.

Of the many texts in Heidegger's work that warn against the claims and pretensions of associative thinking, one passage from his 1952 lecture course titled *Was heißt Denken?* (What Calls Thinking Forth?) is especially revealing. Alluding to the transcendental-horizonal and being-historical paths of his thought, Heidegger in this passage summarily dismisses associative thinking as one that does not traverse the paths of his thought but only chats about them. He says:

Thinking itself is a path. We are in accord with this path only when we continue to be underway. It is one thing to be underway in order to build the way. It is an entirely different thing to position oneself on the way from somewhere and to strike up a conversation about whether the earlier [meaning transcendental-horizonal path] and the later [meaning being-historical] stretches of the way are different and in their difference are perhaps even incompatible—incompatible, namely, for those who never traverse the path and never set about traversing it but position themselves outside the path in order to constantly only imagine it and to chat about it. (*GA* 8:173)[13]

If the work of thinking that is translating the keywords of *Contributions to Philosophy* is to succeed, it must follow the path that this translation inherits from Heidegger's thinking; otherwise it ignores the coalescing of translation and interpretation and overlooks the differentiation between intra- and interlingual translations. The result is a notion of translation that has nothing to do with Heidegger's work.

Whether the translator of Heidegger acknowledges it or not, his translation inherits the paths of hermeneutic phenomenology. But inheriting is one thing; appropriating the inherited is something entirely different. Ignoring this inheritance and failing to appropriate it positions the translator outside the paths, outside the differentiation between intra- and interlingual translations; one chats about translation, and as far as Heidegger's thinking and the translation of his keywords are concerned, accomplishes nothing.

If a translation of Heidegger's keywords does not appropriate what it inherits from the paths of hermeneutic phenomenology, it risks unquestioningly aspiring to the ideal of an absolute transfer of these words from German into English, that is, of a translation that purports to produce a total and irrevocable replacement—an exact substitute—of the original German words. However, instead of aspiring to the ideal of absolute transfer, translation of the keywords should be guided by Heidegger's own labor of translation, by his explicit concern with the coalescing of translation and interpretation, his reflections on intra- and interlingual translations, his renderings of the basic words of philosophical tradition, his views on the status of the mother tongue and the untapped richness of the originary philological roots, and his expressed rejection of the authority of the dictionary. By following this path, the translator relinquishes the need for the absolute transfer of the keywords by realizing that this need is unappeasable.

Heidegger accounts for the incessant working of the intralingual translation when he observes: "Initially we grasp the process of translation from the outside as a technical-philological procedure. We believe that translation is the transfer of a foreign language into another language or, conversely, the transfer of a mother tongue into another language. However, we fail to see that we constantly translate our own language, the mother tongue, into its own words" (*GA* 54:17). He further highlights the incessant working of the intralingual translation when he says: "Speaking and saying are in themselves a translation whose fundamental unfolding is by no means exhausted by the fact that translated words and the words to be translated belong to different languages. An originary translation prevails in every conversation and every monologue" (*GA* 54:17). Thus the *intralingual* translation is more originary than the *interlingual* because it is ongoing. As we shall see, Heidegger is engaged in the intralingual translation of the mother tongue into its own words when he translates the word *Ereignis* into the prefix *Er-* and the construct *eignis*.

If my consideration of the status of keywords within the earliest shapings of Heidegger's hermeneutic phenomenology and within his transcendental horizonal thinking as well as within *Contributions to Philosophy* demonstrates that these keywords are not automatically transparent within the German language itself but rather emerge from and unfold within the coalescing, in the hermeneutic phenomenology, of interpretation with intra- and interlingual translations, then we may relinquish the possibility of an absolute transfer of the keywords into English. Rather than striving for the absolute transfer of these keywords, we should aim for the more modest but obtainable goal of using words that do not purport to replace the German originals but merely approximate them. In short, we should abandon the notion of an absolute transfer in favor of an approximate translation.

We will see that as early as 1919 interpretation and intralingual translation intersect and coalesce in Heidegger's thought. This process begins with the earliest shapings of hermeneutic phenomenology that precede Heidegger's transcendental-horizonal thinking and continues with the coalescing of interpretation and intralingual translation within the transcendental-horizonal thinking. Finally, this process reaches one of its high points in the coalescing of interpretation and intralingual translation occurring within *Contributions to Philosophy*.

The earliest shapings of hermeneutic phenomenology are the War Emergency lecture course of 1919, *Die Idee der Philosophie und das Weltanschauungsproblem (The Idea of Philosophy and the Problem of Worldview)* (*GA* 56–57) and the first Marburg lecture of the winter semester 1923–24, *Einführung in die phänomenologische Forschung (Introduction to Phenomenological Research)* (*GA* 17). The coalescing in these lecture courses of interpretation and intralingual translation is manifest in the keywords *es weltet, Erleben, Entleben, Vorgang,* and *Ereignis*. As the transcendental-horizonal path opens up and as Heidegger accounts for the coalescing of phenomenon and interpretation in *Being and Time*, this coalescing gives rise to the keywords *Dasein, Existenz,* and *Wesen*. Finally, the coalescing of interpretation with intralingual translation in *Contributions to Philosophy* gives rise to words such as *Ereignis* and *Abgrund* that are central to being-historical thinking.

I

In the War Emergency lectures of 1919, interpretation and intralingual translation coalesce, the result being that familiar German words such as *Welt, Entleben,* and *Ereignis* acquire new meanings. This occurs as Heidegger seeks to differentiate hermeneutic phenomenology from Husserl's transcendental phenomenology of reflection. We can see this in three decisive junctures of this lecture course.

In the first juncture Heidegger's critical stance toward Husserl's understanding of the object comes to the fore. Heidegger makes a number of incisive observations on lived-experience, or *Erlebnis,* all of which refer to the familiar object in a lecture hall called a *lectern.* These observations are incisive because they unravel the prereflective and pretheoretical status of the lectern, one in which the lectern shows itself by itself before it is reduced to an eidetic object via Husserl's transcendental reduction. Heidegger makes this clear in the following passage:

Let us bring to mind the lived-experience of the environing world, that is, my seeing the lectern. As I hold my comportment of seeing the lectern in my regard while the lectern gives itself environmentally, do I find in the pure meaning of the lived-experience something like an I? In this lived-experience . . . my I . . . resonates *along with* this "seeing." . . . Only through the co-resonance of the own and the given I does the I experience something of the environing world, that is, it worlds [*weltet es*]. And wherever and whenever it worlds [*es . . . weltet*] for me I am somehow fully thereby. (*GA* 56–57:73)

Here we have the first instance of the coalescing of interpretation of the word, *die Welt,* world and its intralingual translation, *es weltet.*

The second juncture in the War Emergency lectures occurs when Heidegger shows that objectification through transcendental reduction impoverishes the lived-experience of the environing world and obfuscates the prereflective, pretheoretical status of the object. As soon as objectification occurs, "the worldly [*das Welthafte*] is extinguished. . . . Then the object, objectness as such do not concern *me. I* am not at all the 'I' that ascertains. Ascertaining as a lived-experience [*Er-lebnis*] is still merely a leftover of the live-experience [*Er-leben*]—it is a de-living [*ein Ent-leben*]" (*GA* 56–57:73–74). Here we have another instance of the coalescing of interpretation of ascertaining the *Er-lebnis* (the lived-experience), and its intralingual translation, *Ent-leben, de-living.* This coalescing requires Heidegger to translate the German language into its own words with the result that now *Entleben* no longer means killing *(vita privare)* but impoverishment of the living quality of the experience, its de-living.

At the third juncture in the War Emergency lectures, Heidegger shows that the lived-experience of ascertaining that resonates along with the "I" is not a process—a *Vorgang*—but an *Ereignis*. He says: "In seeing the lectern I am fully thereby with my I, which . . . resonates along with this seeing as a lived-experience specifically for me. . . . However, this lived-experience is not a process but a making one's own [*ein Ereignis*]. . . . The lived-experience does not pass by in front of me like a thing that I place before myself as an object. Rather, I myself make it my own [*er-eigne es mir*] as it comes to pass according to its ownmost" (*GA* 56-57:75). Here we have another instance of the coalescing of interpretation and intralingual translation. Interpretation of the lived-experience of seeing the lectern coalesces with the intralingual translation of the word *Ereignis*. This interpretation requires Heidegger to translate the German language, the mother tongue, into its own words with the result that *Ereignis* here no longer retains its familiar meaning, "event." It now means "making one's own," which happens when as I see the lectern, I make this experience my own in accord with what is its ownmost. (I shall return later to this early usage of the word *Ereignis*.)

II

In his first Marburg lecture of 1923–24, *Introduction to Phenomenological Research*, Heidegger has *Dasein* in full view, albeit without the systematic treatment that *Dasein* will receive in *Being and Time*. Here Heidegger's critique of Husserl is intertwined with the coalescing of his interpretation of the word *Dasein* and the intralingual translation of this word. I shall forego a detailed analysis of Heidegger's critique of Husserl in this lecture except to say that by interpreting *Dasein* as *Sorge* (care), Heidegger rejects Husserl's epistemological and theoretical orientation in the treatment of "intentionality," "evidence," and "certainty" as well as his eidetic reduction. Heidegger rejects the latter because it operates with ontological determinations that apply to the extant such as genus *(Gattung)*, class *(Art)*, specific difference, and categories, that is, with determinations that "have their own definite basis but *do not say anything about a being like consciousness*" (*GA* 17:274). Heidegger proposes to go "back to things themselves" by taking his lead from "the care" that inheres in *Dasein*—"the care" that, unbeknown to Husserl, also sustains intentionality, evidence, and certainty.

Here we have another instance in which interpretation and intralingual translation coalesce. In *Dasein* (translated intralingually as *Sorge*) intralingual translation and interpretation coalesce. Within this coalescing, *Dasein* no longer retains its familiar meanings such as *Anwesen*, *gegenwärtig*, *vorhanden*, and *Leben*. The introduction to *Being and Time* provides a fuller view of this coalescing.

III

In his introduction to *Being and Time*, Heidegger follows through with the programmatic announcement he makes toward the end of the first Marburg lecture that he must obtain a basic stance from *Dasein* itself if he is to wrest the genuine ontological character of life from prevailing theorizations. To obtain this basic stance is to obtain a science of phenomena, that is, to grasp "the objects of this science in such a way that everything about these objects . . . is exhibited directly and demonstrated directly" (*GA* 2:46). Both direct exhibition and direct demonstration are defining moments of hermeneutic phenomenology, which for Heidegger means neither a philosophical standpoint nor a philosophical trend but "primarily a *concept of method*" (*GA* 2:37).

Phenomenology designates a method that entails a definite "kind of treatment" (*Behandlungsart*) and a definite "kind of encounter"(*Begegnisart*). Both require and condition each other since both are called for by the phenomenon, that is, by that "*which shows itself by itself*, the manifest" (*GA* 2:38). Moreover, the phenomenon not only calls for a definite kind of treatment and encounter but also for the λέγειν of phenomenology, that is, "letting something be seen by exhibiting it" (*GA* 2:44).

It is in the λέγειν of that which shows itself by itself that we encounter the coalescing of interpretation and intralingual translation. To see this coalescing we must bear in mind that the manifest "is such that initially and for the most part it does *not* show itself and vis-à-vis what . . . shows itself is . . . *hidden*" (*GA* 2:47). Thus the λέγειν of hermeneutic phenomenology has the task of letting the hidden be seen and be exhibited. And what "remains *hidden* in an exceptional sense is not a specific being but rather . . . the *being* of beings" (*GA* 2:47). This narrows the task of the λέγειν of hermeneutic phenomenology to exhibiting the hidden being of beings, which in the case of a tool is handiness (*Zuhandenheit*) and in the case of human beings is existence (*Existenz*).

The being of a being such as a tool remains hidden insofar as, in contrast to an extant and handy tool, the being of a tool, handiness, is neither extant nor handy. The being of a human being, existence in the originary sense of *ex-sistere* remains hidden insofar as in contrast to the extant determinations of this being (sex, race, age, etc.) existence is neither extant nor categorizable. However, since "to be" means "to be disclosed," and since being *(Sein)* means disclosedness *(Erschlossenheit)*, handiness and existence, as hidden modes of being, are hidden modes of disclosedness. Initially hidden, these modes of being are phenomenologically exhibitable and demonstrable insofar as the "I," the existing self, is thrown into these modes and can project them open. In other words, the exhibition and demonstration of these initially hidden modes of disclosedness are sustained by thrown projecting-open, *der geworfene Entwurf.*

Once exhibited and demonstrated, that is, projected-open, both handiness and existence prove to be intertwined. We see this when we consider the fact that handiness appears on a horizon *into* which the "I," the existing self, is stretched and *unto* which the "I," the existing self, transcends the extant tool in the direction of handiness. Thus a hidden but discloseable being called the existing transcending self is intertwined with the horizon unto which the existing transcending self transcends the extant tool toward its being, the handiness. This intertwining of the existing transcending self and the horizon makes up what F.-W. von Herrmann aptly calls the self-like *(selbsthaft)* ecstatic horizonal disclosedness.[14] In this self-like ecstatic horizonal disclosedness, the interlingual translation into *"Existenz"* (existence) of the word *Dasein* and the interpretation of *Dasein* coalesce. As a consequence, the word *Existenz* means no longer *Leben, vorhandensein,* and *Wirklichkeit* but the being of *Dasein.*

What do we gain from this excursion into the lecture course texts of 1919, 1923–24, and the introduction to *Being and Time?* We find that the terms *es weltet, Er-leben, Ent-leben, Vorgang, Ereignis,* and *Dasein* claim meanings that are not identical with those they have within the German language. In the case of *Dasein,* it is of paramount importance to note that it refers not to an abstract, static universal *essence* of individual human beings but to the occurrence called the self-like, ecstatic, horizonal disclosedness. To take this occurrence in the sense of the static *essence* of human beings amounts to obfuscating it.

Considering the manner in which *Dasein* appears in the first Marburg lecture course, and given the explication of *Dasein* in the introduction to

Being and Time, can we account in our English translation for the happening called the self-like, ecstatic, horizontal disclosedness by taking our lead from the familiar meanings of the word *Dasein* such as *Anwesen, gegenwärtig, vorhanden, Leben,* and proceed to an absolute transfer of this word via an interlingual translation? Given the fact that this disclosedness is not identical with *Anwesen, gegenwärtig, vorhanden,* and *Leben,* the word *Dasein* clearly cannot be transferred intact, that is, absolutely rendered into English.

Presumably the translators of the two existing English translations of *Sein und Zeit* were aware of the impossibility of an absolute transfer of this word into English, since both translations retain the word *Dasein.* However, this retention is not necessarily based on a clear understanding of the coalescing of the occurrence called the self-like, ecstatic, horizonal disclosedness, and the intralingual translation of the word *Dasein* into *Existenz.* The retention of the word *Dasein* should be based on the differentiation between its familiar meanings and the occurrence of self-like, ecstatic, horizonal disclosedness. That the translators fail to grasp this differentiation becomes clear when we examine their rendering of the word *Wesen.* By translating *Wesen* as "essence," both translations of *Sein und Zeit* neutralize the effectiveness of retaining the word *Dasein* and show that it is merely used as a loan word in these translations.

Regarding *Wesen* and the feasibility of its absolute transfer into English, let us begin with the question whether one of the meanings of this word, *Essenz*—the German rendering of *essentia*—should guide us in settling this issue and whether we should take our orientation from the coalescing of the occurrence called the self-like, ecstatic, horizontal disclosedness with the intralingual translation of the word *Dasein* into *Existenz.* In this regard, we must heed what Heidegger himself says about *Wesen.* Referring to the central characteristics of *Dasein* and noting that *"Das Wesen des Daseins liegt in seiner Existenz"* (*GA* 2:56, italics in the original), Heidegger in *Being and Time* differentiates the terminological meaning of the word *Wesen* from one of its familiar meanings, *Essenz.* He points out that terminologically *Wesen* must be taken not in the sense of *Essenz* but in the sense of "ownmost inner possibility" (*GA* 9:141). He thus makes clear that as used in hermeneutic phenomenology, the word *Wesen* does not have the meaning of the Latin *essentia.*

It is important to note that as early as 1924 Heidegger differentiates the terminological meaning of a basic word of hermeneutic phenomenology from its familiar meaning. Speaking of the Aristotelian concept of οὐσία, he observes:

[A]ccording to its common and familiar meanings, οὐσία means "wealth," "property," "one's belongings," and "possession." If we probe into these familiar meanings, we would perhaps discover what being as such meant to the Greeks. But we must be careful not to infer the terminological meaning of οὐσία from its familiar meanings. At stake here is only understanding the familiar meanings in such a way as to discern *directives* from these meanings for understanding the terminological meaning of οὐσία. (*GA* 18:24)

By differentiating the familiar from the terminological meanings in the word and the concept of οὐσία, Heidegger provides a model for understanding the terminological meaning of the keywords of his philosophy such as *Dasein*. In view of the differentiation between the familiar and the terminological meanings, if the translation is to reflect the terminological meaning of the word *Dasein*, it must relinquish the possibility of an absolute transfer and retain the untranslated word *Dasein*. However, here we must not overlook the danger that, as a consequence of a mistranslation of *Wesen*, we might use the word *Dasein* but misunderstand it in the sense of the essence of human beings.

If the terminological meaning of the word *Dasein* requires that we retain the untranslated word *Dasein*, then the possibility of an absolute transfer of this word proves to be irrelevant to the task of translating this keyword. What speaks against the possibility of an absolute transfer in this instance is the coalescing of the interpretation of *Dasein* as the happening of the self-like, ecstatic, horizonal disclosedness—which is not the same as the static and *vorhanden* essence of individuals—and the intralingual translation of the word *Dasein*.

IV

We cannot address the coalescing of interpretation and intralingual translation in *Contributions to Philosophy* without taking into account the transformation that language undergoes when it becomes the language of this work. Right at the beginning of this work, Heidegger captures this transformation and the emergence of the new language with the word *Sagen*, "saying." He differentiates this *Sagen* from *Aussage*, "assertion," by noting that "[t]his saying does not describe or explain, does not proclaim or teach. This saying does not stand over against what is said. Rather, the saying itself *is* the 'to be said,' as the essential swaying of be-ing" (*Contributions*, 4). Since the coalescing of interpretation and intralingual translation in *Contributions to Philosophy* is one that occurs within language, and because the language of this work is the transformed language called "saying," this coalescing occurs specifically within this "saying."

However, this coalescing is not only that of interpretation and intralingual translation but also the coalescing of interpretation and interlingual translation. When in this "saying" interpretation and *intra*lingual translation coalesce, a group of words emerges, among them *Ereignis* and *Abgrund*. When in this "saying" interpretation and *inter*lingual translation coalesce, then this coalescing results in the rendering into German of the basic words of Western philosophy, of which I should mention ἰδέα, ἐνέργεια, γένεσις, *ratio,* and *cogitare.* Let us first take a brief look at the coalescing of interpretation and intralingual translation as it gives new meanings in *Contributions to Philosophy* to the two words *Ereignis* and *Abgrund*.

The primary outcome of the coalescing of interpretation and intralingual translation in this work is the terminological meaning that the word *Ereignis* receives. In light of this terminological meaning, being-historical thinking unfolds and proliferates from *Contributions to Philosophy* onward. It is essential to keep in mind that on the way to this terminological meaning, the coalescing of interpretation and intralingual translation endows an independent status to the prefix *Er-* and the construct *eignis* in the word *Ereignis*. Henceforth, each functions as a single word requiring a distinct translation. To do justice to the terminological meaning of the word *Er-eignis,* one must take into account this independent status by translating both the prefix *Er-* and the construct *eignis.* Only by being mindful of their independent status can one account for *Er-eignis* as "[the] self-supplying and self-mediating midpoint into which all essential swaying of the truth of be-ing must be thought back in advance. . . . And [from which] all concepts of be-ing must be said" (*Contributions,* 51).

To grasp the intralingual translation of the word *Ereignis* as Heidegger translates this word into the prefix *Er-* and the construct *eignis,* we must bear in mind that this translation does not take its orientation from a dictionary. Thus Heidegger's use of *Ereignis* is not bound by its dictionary-based definition.

The autonomy of the intralingual translation of *Ereignis* vis-à-vis its dictionary-based definition prompts Heidegger to reject the authority of the dictionary. By doing so, he also rejects the idea that the dictionary functions as the undisputed arbiter in matters of translation. He says: "A dictionary can provide an indication for understanding a word . . . but it is never an absolute authority that would be binding a priori. The appeal to a dictionary is always an appeal to an interpretation of language, which is often not grasped at all in its style and limits" (*GA* 53:75). He does not accept the undisputed authority of the dictionary not because with its definitions a dictionary displaces each word into the subsets of other words but because *the openness* inherent in each word eludes these definitions. This openness makes possible the intralingual translation of the word *Ereignis*.

What is this openness? "It is that . . . wherein being allots itself to man such that man preserves the allotted in its ownmost and such that for his part man first finds his ownmost from out of such preserving and retains it" (*GA* 54:115). The "word" does not have the function of *relating* the human to being. Rather, the word appears as that wherein being *allots itself* to the human. Put more precisely, the "word" is not the link between the human and being. The issue here is not *linkage* or *relatedness* but *allotment*. In view of this allotment, Heidegger considers the "word" to be "the essential mark of distinction of man" (*GA* 54:118). And the "word" sustains such an allotment because it is openness through and through. Precisely as this openness the "word" allows for the intralingual translation of the "word" *Ereignis* into *Er-* and *eignis*.

Turning now to the problems that pertain to the translation of *Er-eignis*, the most crucial being-historical word, I should note that my translation of this word is oriented by Heidegger's own stance toward this "guiding word." (He articulates this stance when he points out that *Ereignis* is as untranslatable as the Greek λόγος or the Chinese Tao.)[15] The first thing to be kept in mind is that the prefix *Er-* and the construct *eignis* have an independent status calling for distinct translations of both if the translation is to be hermeneutically responsible to what Heidegger says with *Er-eignis*. In *Er-eignis* the prefix *Er-* has an active character, which places an unmistakable emphasis on the dynamism and the movement inherent in the verb *eignen*. Moreover, the construct *eignis* opens the way to the being-historical word *Eigentum*, "ownhood."

I first considered leaving *Er-eignis* untranslated. But doing so requires an explanation that cannot be given without interpreting *Ereignis*, and such an interpretation ipso facto requires translating the word. Leaving *Ereignis* untranslated also leads to other problems concerning the family of words closely related to *Ereignis* such as *Ereignung, Eignung, Zueignung, Übereignung, Eigentum, ereignen, zueignen, übereignen, eignen*. Accordingly, I translated *Ereignis* as "enowning"—a word "that approximates the richness of the German word *without pretending to replace it*" (*Contributions*, xx).[16]

The English prefix *en-* in *enowning* adequately assumes the same function as the German prefix *Er-* in *Ereignis*. The English prefix *en-*, with its varied meanings of "enabling something," "bringing it into a certain condition," and "carrying thoroughly through," captures the dynamic character of *Er-* in *Ereignis*. When enjoined with *owning, en-* conveys a different meaning of owning, an unpossessive owning with no appropriatable content, as differentiated from an "owning of something."

The rendering of *Ereignis* as "enowning" has several advantages: unlike terms such as *event, appropriation, event of appropriation,* the word *enowning* lends itself readily to hyphenation and thus functions as an approximate rendering of the *Er-* and *eignis* of *Er-eignis;* unlike terms such as *event, appropriation, event of appropriation,* and *befitting, enowning* is not tied to a content whose appropriation or fitting would be an "event"; unlike the aforementioned terms, *enowning* speaks of an "owning" that has nothing in common with hegemonic seizing; and unlike the aforementioned terms, which are hard put to reflect the hermeneutic-phenomenological kinship of *Ereignis* to words such as *Ereignung, Eignung, Zueignung,* and *Übereignung, enowning* reflects this kinship and allows for an approximate rendering of the following words: *Ereignung* with *enownment, Eignung* with *owning, Eigentum* with *ownhood, Eigenheit* with *ownness, Zueignung* with *owning-to, Übereignung* with *owning-over-to, Eigentümliche* with *what is of ownhood.*

The other outcome of the coalescing in *Contributions to Philosophy* of interpretation and intralingual translation is the terminological meaning of the word *Abgrund* that Heidegger captures through hyphenation: *Ab-grund.* This coalescing endows an independent status to the prefix *Ab-* and the noun *Grund.* Henceforth, each functions as a single word that requires a distinct translation. We should not overlook this independent status, if we are to do justice to the terminological meaning of *Ab-grund.* One must translate both the prefix *Ab-* and the noun *Grund.*

In *Contributions to Philosophy,* Heidegger draws attention to the hermeneutic-phenomenological significance of the prefix *Ab-* for grasping what he means by *Abgrund* when he hyphenates this word and alternately italicizes the prefix *Ab-* and the noun *Grund:* "Der *Ab*-grund ist Ab-*grund.*"[17] With this hyphenation Heidegger introduces a new word intended to articulate a ground that prevails while it *stays away* and, strictly speaking, is the hesitating refusal of ground. In other words, the hyphenation of *Abgrund* aims at *a very specific* hermeneutic-phenomenological insight and is thus to be carefully differentiated from a basically insignificant lexicographical device.

The thematically crucial hyphenation and alternating italicization of the prefix *Ab-* and the noun *Grund* lose their intended meaning if *Ab-* and *grund* are not treated as independent words and translated distinctly. If the hyphenation is merely conceived as a lexicographical device, which like a hiccup might interrupt the flow of this word, then one can translate *Ab-grund* as "abyss." But by opting for *abyss* one only reveals a failure to grasp the hermeneutic-phenomenological insight that Heidegger captures with his hyphenation and alternate italicization. One must be phenomenologically blind to overlook this insight and translate *Abgrund* as "abyss" and for good measure hyphenate this word.[18] The proposed hyphenation of *abyss (a-byss)* is pointless because, unlike *grund*, which is stressed when Heidegger hyphenates *Abgrund*, the resulting *byss* is not a word. *Ab-grund* is a ground that remains by staying away. *Abyss never stays away; it always remains.*

When Heidegger interprets *Ab-grund* as the ground that remains while staying away, he is engaged in a renewed appropriation of the word *Abgrund* and in the intralingual translation of it into the prefix *Ab-* and the noun *Grund*. This renewed appropriation is possible because of the openness that *is* the word *Abgrund* and because of the intralingual translation that takes place within this openness. From the preceding discussion, it should be clear that this openness eludes the dictionary-based definitions of *Abgrund* not because the dictionary definitions displace this word into the subsets of other words but because *the openness that is this word* does not allow itself to be constrained by the dictionary-based definition.

The necessity of translating both the prefix *Ab-* and the noun *Grund,* leads to the question of how to translate the word *Ab-grund.* Following Kenneth Maly's suggestion, we translated *Ab-grund* as "Ab-ground." This choice has several advantages: the English prefix *ab-*, meaning "away from," has a similar power of expression as the German prefix *Ab-*; the English word *ground* comes as close as possible to the German *Grund;* the word *abground* easily lends itself to hyphenation with the result that in stark contrast to the contrived *byss* of *a-byss,* the word *ground* is a legitimate English word; *ab-ground* reflects the movement of staying away inherent in *Ab-grund; ab-ground* makes possible the introduction into English of other words related to the German *Grund,* such as *Un-grund* ("unground") and *Urgrund* ("urground"); and finally the intact presence of *ground* in *ab-ground* also allows for thinking through the being-historical verb *gründen,* which speaks of a ground that is simultaneously *ur*ground, *ab*ground, and *un*ground.

At this point it is instructive to contrast Heidegger's use in 1919 of the word *Ereignis* with its being-historically determined terminological meaning of 1936–38. In the War Emergency lecture course of 1919 Heidegger uses the word *Er-eignis* in order to highlight the worldly-character of the pre-theoretical, lived experience of an inner-worldly being like a lectern. After indicating that this "lived-experience is specifically for me" and "I myself make it my own" [*ich selbst er-eigne es mir*], he goes on to say that this "making one's own [*Er-eignis*] is not to be taken to mean that I would appropriate the lived-experience from somewhere outside" (*GA* 56–57:75). It is here that Heidegger uses the word *Er-eignis* for the first time and hyphenates it. However, this hyphenation is not enough to endow the prefix *Er-* and the construct *eignis* with the status of independent words. More importantly, with this hyphenation he does not bring to the fore his insight into *"eignis"* as something capturing the being-historical meaning of *Eigentum*, or *own-hood*. In the War Emergency course, the construct *eignis* indicates that which is one's own in the domain of lived-experience; it does not indicate *ownhood*. By saying "ich ereigne es mir" [I make it my own], Heidegger shows in 1919 that he understands *eignis* in the context of the lived-experience where the experiencing I and the worlding world are grasped as dimensions of the same movement of worlding. In 1919 he does not understand *eignis* in the context of ownhood of be-ing in its enowning relationship to *Dasein*.

So much for the coalescing of interpretation and intralingual translation in *Contributions to Philosophy*. What about the coalescing of interpretation and *inter*lingual translation that also takes place in this work? The outcome of the latter is the rendering into German of the basic words of Western philosophy such as ἰδέα, ἐνέργεια, *cogitare*, and so on. Here I shall only discuss Heidegger's translation into German of Descartes' *cogitare*. To do so I must first deal with Heidegger's treatment of the Cartesian proposition *cogito ergo sum* and with his translation of it.

What distinguishes Heidegger's translation is the coalescing of interpretation of this proposition and its interlingual translation. At its core this interpretation rests on what Heidegger calls the inceptual re-latedness of ψυχή and ἀλήθεια, which first Plato and then Descartes modify: "The relation between ψυχή and ἀλήθεια (ὄν) as ζυγόν, already *prepared* by Plato, turns with Descartes . . . into the connection of subject-object. Thinking becomes *I*-think; the *I*-think becomes: I unite originarily, I think unity (in advance)" (*Contributions*, 139). Heidegger interprets

Descartes' celebrated *cogito,* his "I think," in the light of the inceptual relatedness of ψυχή and ἀλήθεια and consequently takes *cogito ergo sum* as what comes to pass in the interplay of the first and the other beginning. Descartes understands *cogito*—the "I think"—as the unifying activity by which the subject, the "I," "puts before itself" a unified object. At the core of Heidegger's *interpretation* of *cogito ergo sum* in *Contributions to Philosophy*—not at the core of his *translation* of this proposition—lies this "putting before oneself."

But what about Heidegger's *inter*lingual translation—*not* his interpretation—of Descartes' *cogito ergo sum*? We come upon Heidegger's interlingual translation of this Cartesian proposition in a lecture course text on Nietzsche written at the same time as *Contributions to Philosophy*. Taking a close look at the following passage of that text, we see Heidegger's interlingual translation of this proposition in its specificity:

Ego cogito (ergo) sum—I think, therefore, I am. This is word for word correctly translated. This correct translation seems to supply already the correct understanding of Descartes' "proposition." With the assertion "I think," a fact is ascertained, namely, "therefore I am." . . . We translate *cogitare* with "thinking" and thus assure ourselves of knowing clearly what Descartes means by *cogitare* . . . [However,] at important junctures of his work Descartes uses instead of *cogitare* the word *percipere (per-capio)*—to take possession of something, to overpower something in the sense of putting something at one's disposal by way of putting something before oneself, i.e., *vor-stellen.* (*GA* 48:190)

In this passage we have Heidegger's interlingual translation of the Cartesian proposition in its specificity. Heidegger's decision to bring *cogitare* into German with *vor-stellen* (re-presenting) rather than *denken* (thinking) is based on the uncovering of the relatedness of ψυχή and ἀλήθεια and on the interchangeable use that Descartes makes of *cogitare* and *percipere*. This interchangeability opens the way for interpreting *cogitare* as "taking possession of something," "overpowering something," "putting something at one's disposal by putting something before oneself." By focusing on this "putting before oneself," Heidegger enacts the interlingual translation by rendering *cogitare* as *vor-stellen*. More precisely, by uncovering the relatedness of ψυχή and ἀλήθεια and by gaining insights into the interchangeability of *cogitare* and *percipere*, Heidegger arrives at an interpretation of the Cartesian *cogito ergo sum* that coalesces with his interlingual translation of *cogito* with *vor-stellen*.

Looking at Heidegger's interpretation of modernity as the historical period in which beings are unconcealed as objects, we note how deeply this interpretation depends on his interlingual translation of *cogitare* as *vor-stellen.* By bringing to the fore the inceptual relatedness of ψυχή and ἀλήθεια, by indicating that ψυχή is the opening within which beings in modernity are unconcealed as objects, and by drawing on Descartes' interchangeable use of *cogitare* and *percipere,* Heidegger derives from the familiar meaning of *cogitare,* that is, thinking, or *denken,* its terminological meaning, re-presenting or *vor-stellen.*

If the terminological meanings of the words *Ereignis, Abgrund,* and *cogitare* are not identical with the familiar meanings these words have in German (as in the case of the first two words) and within the tradition (as in the case of *cogitare*), then it is counterproductive to assume the possibility of an absolute transfer in translation. Rather than striving for such a transfer, the translator of the keywords of *Contributions to Philosophy* should be directed by what he inherits from hermeneutic phenomenology and attempt an approximate translation.

V

As noted, the translator of the keywords of *Contributions to Philosophy* meets his hermeneutic responsibility by appropriating what he inherits from the path of hermeneutic phenomenology. Here the question becomes whether this appropriation presupposes a decision on the part of the translator. And to respond to this question, we must first examine what Heidegger says in *Contributions to Philosophy* about decision *(Entscheidung).*

To lay out Heidegger's notion of decision in its entirety requires analyzing the account of "de-cision" *(Ent-scheidung)* that he gives in section 43 of the "Preview" of *Contributions to Philosophy* and extending that analysis to the eleven shapes of "de-cision" that he outlines in section 44.[19] Such an analysis is not within the scope of this essay. Fortunately, however, in his recently published work on Ernst Jünger, Heidegger presents the gist of the notion of "de-cision." Concerning "de-cision" he says that it "can neither be grasped in terms of the 'will' nor in terms of 'consciousness.' De-cision neither means reckoning with an either or nor is it an urge-driven affirmation of oneself. Rather, de-cision is the enopening of the truth of be-ing: whether be-ing is experienced and grounded and whether be-ing enjoins the 'in-between' of beings as beings. De-cision is the swaying of be-ing itself and *human* de-ciding is only *the manner of belongingness unto the truth of be-ing*" *(GA* 90:13–14). With this account in mind, we recognize that "de-cision" should not be confused with deciding between alternative things, choosing one thing over another, and preferring one thing to the other. More specifically, we gain an insight into "de-cision" by realizing that it means the en-opening of be-ing itself and its truth, neither of which is accessible to choice, preference, and the like.

The immediate consequence of this insight is that the translator of the keywords realizes he must relinquish the belief that he *can choose* "de-cision," that is, he can opt for the enopening of be-ing and its truth. This enopening is not a matter of choosing because for choosing to be enacted it is referentially dependent on an alternative that in the case of the enopening of be-ing and its truth does not exist. To assume an alter-native to the enopening of be-ing and its truth is to assume what is phenomenologically inconceivable, namely, the total collapse and elimi-nation of all manifesting, disclosing, and so on.

Another consequence of this insight into "de-cision" is that besides inheriting Heidegger's intra- and interlingual translations of *Ereignis*, *Abgrund*, and *cogitare*, the translator also inherits his notion of "de-cision." Thus to approach his task responsibly, the translator of the keywords of *Contributions to Philosophy* must come to terms with "de-cision." A first step in this direction is to inquire into the locus of "de-cision." The immediate result of this inquiry is the realization that the locus of "de-cision"—where it occurs—is language. But how is the translator to approach language in order to articulate this locus?

He should approach it in terms of the distinction between what is the ownmost of language—what is its *Wesen*—and the function of lan-guage as a means of expression. The enopening of the truth of be-ing, that is, "de-cision," occurs within the ownmost of language, which sev-eral decades after *Contributions to Philosophy*, Heidegger characterizes as "the gathered ringing of stillness" *(das Geläut der Stille)*.[20] However, an understanding of language that sees it only as a means of expression fails to recognize what is ownmost to language. By contrast, when Hei-degger enacts the intra- and interlingual translations of words such as *Ereignis, Abgrund,* and *cogitare,* he experiences the ownmost of language and therein the "de-cision."

It goes without saying that because it is Heidegger, and *not* we, who enacts the intra- and interlingual translations of these words, we cannot presume to be the master of these words and effect their absolute trans-fer into English language. If the translator nevertheless has difficulty abandoning the quest for an absolute transfer of these words, it is be-cause of his self-understanding—how he conceives of himself—and how he conceives of translation. Heidegger has in mind the inter-twining of the translator's self-understanding and his conception of translation when he says: "Tell me how you conceive of translation and I'll tell you who you are."[21]

When the translator realizes that it is not he but Heidegger who enacts the intra- and the interlingual translations of words such as *Ereignis*, *Abgrund*, and *cogitare*, and who in enacting these translations experiences the gathered ringing of stillness (the ownmost of language), then the translator abdicates the throne he occupies when he conceives of himself as the master and the lord of language empowered to enact the absolute transfer of these keywords into English. By making *this decision* and by taking his direction from hermeneutic phenomenology, namely, the happening within language's ownmost (within the gathered ringing of stillness) of "de-cision"—of the enopening of the truth of be-ing—*and* the intra- as well as interlingual translations, the translator then seeks an approximate translation.

It is the happening of "de-cision" within language's ownmost that opens for Heidegger a path for the further unfolding of the being-historical thinking from the *Contributions to Philosophy* of 1936–38 to the *Time and Being* of 1962. This happening "opens and makes ways," that is, accomplishes what Heidegger specifies as "way making," *Be-wëgen*. In its simple construction, the word *Be-wëgen* refers to *Weg*, or path, which is used neither as a metaphor in the Heideggerian corpus nor as an indicator of the incomplete and provisional character of the findings of hermeneutic phenomenology, nor does it have any biographical undergirding as is sometimes assumed when one speaks of "Heidegger's life as a journey of thought." Heidegger highlights what happens with "way making" when he notes that it means "Wege allerest ergeben und stiften" (*GA* 12:186), that is, "first and foremost yielding and bringing about paths." The crucial question here is how does the "way-making" that occurs from "de-cision"—how does the yielding of paths—illuminate the task of an approximate translation of the keywords of *Contributions to Philosophy?*

To achieve an approximate translation, the translator of the keywords should heed the *"way making"* that comes about through what we earlier referred to as a "saying" that always highlights the terminological meanings of the keywords of *Contributions to Philosophy*. Heidegger presents such a "saying" in conjunction with the terminological meaning of *Abgrund* when he points out that "Der *Ab*-grund ist Ab-*grund*" (*GA* 65:379) ("*Ab*-ground is ab-*ground*" [*Contributions*, 265]). He presents such a "saying" in conjunction with the terminological meaning of *Ereignis* when he stresses that be-ing as *Ereignis* is "der Ursprung . . . der erst Götter und Menschen *ent-scheidet* und *er-eignet*" (*GA* 65:87) ("the origin that *de-cides* gods and men in the first place and *en-owns* one to the other" [*Contributions*, 60]). Finally, he presents such a "saying" in conjunction with the terminological meaning of *cogitare* when he notes that to grasp its meaning one must take *cogitare* "in dem Sinne des Sich-zu-stellens von der Art des Vor-sich-stellens, des *'Vor-stellens'*" (*GA* 48: 190) ("in the sense of putting something at one's disposal by way of putting something before oneself, that is, *vor-stellen*"). By heeding the "way making" that comes to pass with each "saying," the translator sees the inappropriateness of rendering *Abgrund* as "abyss," *Ereignis* as "appropriation"/"event of appropriation" or "befitting," and *cogitare* as "thinking," that is, with words chosen with no regard for the happening of "de-cision" *and* with no concern for the *intra-* and *interlingual* translations in Heidegger. By contrast, the approximate translations of *Abgrund*, *Ereignis*, and *cogitare*, with "abground," "enowning," and "representing," respectively, take the happening of "de-cision" seriously insofar as these translations never claim to have replaced the words that emerge directly from within Heidegger's experience of "de-cision."

VI

Let me conclude by returning to the terminological meanings of the two pivotal keywords, *Ereignis* and *Abgrund*, in order to address two questions. The first question concerns the loss that might be said to occur when, following the happening of "de-cision" and intra- as well as interlingual translations within the ownmost of language, we enact an approximate translation of the keywords. The second question concerns the extent to which an approximate translation might be said to be faithful to the German original.

Does the interlingual but approximate translation of the keywords *Ereignis* and *Abgrund* as "enowning" and "abground," respectively, unavoidably involve a certain loss of what the original German says, and in this respect does this interlingual translation corroborate the general characterization of interlingual translation as "the art of loss"?[22] Considering the preceding analyses as a whole, I must respond affirmatively to this question: something of *Ereignis* and *Abgrund* is irretrievably and irrevocably lost in *enowning* and *abground*.

But what about the interlingual translation of *cogitare* as *vorstellen*? Does this translation too corroborate the general characterization of interlingual translation as "the art of loss"? Can we say that something of the Cartesian *cogitare* is irretrievably lost when Heidegger renders this word as *vorstellen?* Not at all, for in this case Heidegger articulates what is unthought in this word as its being-historical meaning. No loss occurs in this interlingual translation because it represents essentially the being-historical homecoming of the Cartesian *cogitare.*

What about the faithfulness to the original when we translate *Ereignis* as "enowning" and *Abgrund* as "abground"? Ostensibly, an absolute transfer need not bother with the question of faithfulness because if the translation has totally replaced the original German, the question of faithfulness is irrelevant. But an approximate translation cannot avoid this question. Hence we ask, to what extent is *enowning* faithful to *Ereignis* and to what extent is *abground* faithful to *Abgrund?* For a response let me turn briefly to the so-called neighborhood of thinking and poetizing, that is, to the "Nachbarschaft vom Denken und Dichten," which, considering Heidegger's interpretation of Sophocles in the War Emergency lecture course text, lies within his phenomenological purview as early as 1919.[23] By taking a quick look at Paul Celan's poetic and interlingual translation, which eo ipso takes place within this neighborhood, I can address the question of faithfulness as it concerns the interlingual translation. We should bear in mind that drawing on Celan is not the same as introducing a thematic alien to Heidegger insofar as he considered Celan's poetizing *(dichten)* to be of great import and closely studied it.[24]

We gain a significant insight into the contributions that Celan makes to our understanding of the issue of faithfulness in interlingual translation when we consider what he accomplished with his translation from Russian into German. According to John Felstiner, the perceptive biographer and the able translator of Paul Celan, when Celan translated Osip Mandelshtam from Russian into German he "managed to transpose Mandelshtam into German almost intact. Intact . . . he had said as much in a 1948 love poem: 'Only faithless am I true / I am you, when I am I' *(Ich bin du, wenn ich ich bin).* In love or translation, identifying with an other demands truth to oneself."[25]

To the extent that Celan is faithless to the Russian poems and to the extent that he is true to himself, Celan succeeds, according to Felstiner, in enacting the almost intact transposition of Mandelshtam into German. What is instructive in this assessment of Celan's interlingual translation is the insight that the truer the translator is to himself, the more faithless he becomes to the original.

Would it be fair to extend this estimation of Celan's interlingual translation, with its inherent messages of faithlessness and being true, to the task of translating the keywords of Heidegger's *Contributions to Philosophy?* Because Celan's work of translating Mandelshtam stands at one of the poles within "the neighborhood of thinking and poetizing," that is, at the pole of poetizing, and because embedded in this pole are the criteria of faithlessness and being true to oneself, can we not say that what transpires at the other pole within this "neighborhood," that is, at the pole called thinking, when we translate *Ereignis* as "enowning" and *Abgrund* as "abground" is also subject to these criteria?

If Celan the translator is faithless to Mandelshtam's words at the same time as he is true to himself, could we not say that to the extent that the translator of the keywords of *Contributions to Philosophy* remains true to himself, he is faithless to the original German? But to be faithless to Heidegger's original German while remaining true to oneself—is that not the price the translator must pay for realizing that the interlingual translation of the keywords of *Contributions to Philosophy* is not what cultural history takes it to be, namely, the absolute transfer of cultural goods for the purpose of cultural exchange?

On "Echo," the First Part
of *Contributions to Philosophy*

Nothing seems to tell us more about *Contributions to Philosophy (From Enowning)*—Heidegger's second major work after *Being and Time*—than the twofold aspect of its title and the announcement at the outset of a fundamental distinction between the two parts of this title. The title, Heidegger says, consists of two parts, one presenting the public title or heading and the other the proper one. Significantly, these two parts are not separated by a colon. The form of the title, along with Heidegger's own characterization and distinction between "public" and "proper" strengthen the expectation that *Contributions to Philosophy* is devoted primarily to the elucidation of enowning *(Ereignis)*.

As the work unfolds, however, we make the remarkable discovery that, contrary to this expectation, *Contributions to Philosophy* does not begin with an elucidation of enowning but with an examination of dis-enowning *(Ent-eignis)*. Although the word *dis-enowning* appears neither in the title nor in the text of the first part, use of the words that are derived from *dis-enowning* throughout the work make it abundantly clear that in "Echo" Heidegger addresses the echo of be-ing that resonates in dis-enowning. One soon realizes that "Echo" is the echo of be-ing and must be understood in terms of dis-enowning. We recognize this not just by noting the frequency with which Heidegger uses words that are derived from *Ent-eignis* such as *ent-eignen* and *ent-eignet* but also by following his directives *(Hinweise)* preceding the first part in the opening section of *Contributions to Philosophy*, "Preview." To appropriate the thinking that unfolds in "Echo," we must take our orientation from these directives.

Before turning to the directives that Heidegger presents in "Preview," let me briefly elucidate the nature of the thinking that aspires to appropriate "Echo." We must grasp the fundamental character of this appropriative thinking if we are to appropriate the directives presented in "Preview." What is an appropriative thinking of *Contributions to Philosophy?*

We can appropriate *Contributions to Philosophy* only when our thinking awakens to its potential for acting and is thereby carried out as acting. This acting is quite different from the activity of thinking. Under the pressure of two and a half millennia of practicing the activity of thinking, we risk mistaking thinking that acts for the activity of thinking and of identifying thinking as acting—which *Contributions to Philosophy* calls for—with the activity of thinking. As Heidegger notes in the *Letter on Humanism*, this mistake occurs since we do not "decisively enough consider what is ownmost to acting *(Handeln)*" (GA 9:313). We do not differentiate thinking as acting from a thinking that produces an effect. Thinking as acting differs from the thinking that produces an effect, since *as* acting (not *by* acting) thinking does not partake of a causal nexus. As Heidegger observes in the *Letter on Humanism*, what takes place in thinking understood as acting is, strictly speaking, an accomplishment that is not the same as producing an effect at the end of a causal connection. What thinking accomplishes when it acts is to unfold something into the fullness of its ownmost. In this sense only what already "is" can be accomplished—completed or unfolded into the fullness of its ownmost. Since what already "is" is above all be-ing, accomplishing means unfolding be-ing into the fullness of its ownmost. Seen in this light, accomplishing means opening up and disclosing what be-ing proffers to thinking. But this opening up, this disclosing, never occurs outside language—in a "language-free" zone—but always in and through language. Thus what be-ing proffers to thinking, and what thinking as acting opens up, is proffered through language and its disclosing potentials. From the perspective of language, thinking as acting does not stand over against what be-ing proffers to thinking. In other words, thinking understood as acting does not objectify what be-ing proffers to thinking.

What do we learn from these brief observations on thinking as acting that might facilitate engaging our thinking appropriately with respect to the first part of *Contributions to Philosophy*, "Echo"? We learn that appropriative thinking acts specifically to open up the directives Heidegger presents in "Preview" for understanding "Echo." Without opening up these directives, we have no access to the thinking that unfolds in "Echo," or for that matter in the entirety of *Contributions to Philosophy*. Specifically, when appropriative thinking acts and thus opens up these directives, it grasps what Heidegger discloses in "Echo." By opening up these directives, the thinking that unfolds in this work becomes an accessible *and* co-enactable thinking. And there is no other way to demonstrate this than to awaken our thinking to its potential for acting and thus to open up Heidegger's directives in "Preview."

I

What are the directives Heidegger offers in "Preview"? Let us begin with a brief characterization of the opening section of *Contributions to Philosophy*. Heidegger calls this section "Preview" because it represents a preliminary, preparatory, and anticipatory view of what unfolds in the work as a whole. As such, it differs from an overview or an introduction. For in this section Heidegger presents in a preliminary, preparatory, and anticipatory manner a prospective view of *Contributions to Philosophy* as a whole, hence the title, "Preview."

Heidegger does not call the opening section an overview because it does not survey the themes and topics of the work. He does not call it an outlook because it does not examine the themes and topics of the work from the standpoint of the beginning. Finally, he does not call it an introduction because it does not present a developing discourse that narrates the progression of the work from a lesser to a more complete stage of unfolding. Rather, he calls it "Preview," because it offers a preview of be-ing as enowning. In contrast to an overview, an outlook, or an introduction, "Preview" is, from its inception, already a preview of enowning, that is, of the issue to which Heidegger devotes *Contributions to Philosophy* as a whole. To see this clearly, we need to know more specifically how this opening section is a preliminary, preparatory, and anticipatory preview of be-ing, of enowning.

Heidegger presents a *preliminary* view of enowning in this section insofar as he unfolds enowning in a manner that awaits further unfolding. The presentation here is *preparatory* because it sets the stage for enowning as it unfolds in the work as a whole. Finally, the presentation here is *anticipatory* because what this section says about enowning looks ahead to and thus anticipates the full swaying of be-ing as enowning. Here Heidegger previews enowning and takes an initial look at it that is fundamental for the entire work. In "Preview" Heidegger offers directives that thinking must open up if it is to glimpse be-ing as enowning and hear the echo of be-ing as dis-enowning. Hence the directives in "Preview" are directives to enowning. If considered by themselves, and unrelated to enowning, they cease to accomplish their mission: They become utterly mute.

We find these directives in the remarks Heidegger makes in the opening section on the swaying of be-ing and in what he says about thinking as it traverses a path lighted by the grounding-attunement of reservedness. We also find these directives in his characterization of the structure of presentation peculiar to *Contributions to Philosophy*. To analyze these directives then, I shall begin by addressing be-ing's swaying as Heidegger addresses it within "Preview" and examine the thinking that is thoroughly attuned to the grounding-attunement of reservedness and thus shapes the structure of presentation of *Contributions to Philosophy*. I will then be in a position to address "Echo."

II

We encounter the first directive imbedded in "Preview" when we closely observe the way Heidegger thematizes the appearing of beings within be-ing's swaying. This requires that we focus on the question of being. What distinguishes the thinking Heidegger enacts and which is known as thinking of being is that it is correlated to the question of being. Having dealt with this question from the point of view of fundamental ontology in the transcendental-horizonal perspective of *Being and Time*, in *Contributions to Philosophy* Heidegger addresses it anew from within the be-ing-historical perspective and reformulates it.

In the transcendental-horizonal perspective the question of being reads: "What is the meaning of being?" In the being-historical perspective Heidegger reformulates this question to read "[h]ow does be-ing sway?" (*Contributions*, 5). Because this reformulated question of being functions as the first directive that thinking as the thinking of being must follow, we must ask how does Heidegger arrive at this reformulation.

Heidegger arrives at the question "how does be-ing sway?" by focusing on the coalescing of be-ing and beings in be-ing's fundamentally historical swaying. He alludes to this coalescing when he says: "[w]henever a *being is,* be-ing must sway" (*Contributions*, 5). But rather than asking what is a being? as the tradition before him did, Heidegger focuses on the coalescing of be-ing and beings and asks how does be-ing sway? He thus arrives at a question which functions as the first directive for thinking as the thinking of be-ing, that is, of enowning, and of the echo of be-ing, that is, disenowning. To understand this directive we must be clear about two points: the specific character of the question, how does be-ing sway? and how this question relates to the question, what is a being?

Regarding the first point, it will not do merely to repeat this question. The question, how does be-ing sway? originates from within an attunement that holds be-ing's swaying in reserve and is therefore called the grounding-attunement of reservedness. The question presupposes this attunement. Reserved and preserved in this attunement, the question, how does be-ing sway? initiates "a questioning that belongs neither to the purposeful activity of an individual nor to the limited calculation of a community. Rather, it is above all the further hinting of a hint which comes from what is most question-worthy and remains referred to it" (*Contributions*, 4).

To sum up we can say that the question, how does be-ing sway? neither belongs to the goal-directed activity of an individual nor does it serve the restricted calculation of a community. *It is the further hinting of a hint.* As such, it is concerned with what is most question worthy, that is, with be-ing, and thus reaches far into the past and deep into the future.

Regarding the second point, it is through the question, what is a being? that the 'first beginning' is implicated in the question, how does be-ing sway? In *Contributions to Philosophy* the expression the 'first beginning' (*der erste Anfang*) stands for the beginning that the Greeks made when they asked "What is a being?" In asking, "What is a being?" (τί τὸ ὄν), the Greeks thus addressed the question of being by focusing on beings. An element of necessity attached to this way of dealing with the question of being because the question came to the Greeks via the attunement they called awe (θαυμάζειν). The Greeks were amazed that beings *are*, because they were guided in their thinking by the attunement of awe. This attunement unabatedly guided the Greek inquiry concerning being. The Greeks' thinking and questioning were so attuned to awe that ultimately their thinking acted by opening up, that is, accomplishing what already "is," namely, the beingness of beings. But the Greeks' thinking as an acting attuned to awe did not lead them to the question, how does be-ing sway? that is, to the question that is a further hinting of a hint at the swaying of be-ing. We must be clear about this question if we are to understand the manner in which it functions as a directive to be-ing, that is, to enowning, and to the echo of be-ing, that is, to dis-enowning.

Heidegger calls the thinking of *Contributions to Philosophy* inceptional thinking, because it is grounded in the inceptional question, how does be-ing sway? This thinking is inceptional because it opens up and readdresses the question that transpires and shapes the 'first beginning,' the question, what is a being? In "Preview" Heidegger carefully distinguishes these two questions. He calls "How does be-ing sway?" the grounding-question to stress its grounding power. And he calls "What is a being?" the guiding-question to stress its guiding power. The guiding-question, what is a being? leads the thinking of being to the determinations of the beingness of a being. By contrast, the grounding-question, how does be-ing sway? ultimately brings into view be-ing's swaying, that is, enowning.

These two questions are thus intimately related to each other. When the question, what is a being? is examined in light of the historical unfolding of be-ing, it becomes an occasion for the grounding-question, how does be-ing sway? to come to the fore. Heidegger addresses this occasion in specific terms when he notes that "[t]he question of being . . . [w]hen accomplished and grasped as it historically unfolds . . . becomes the *grounding-question*—over against the hitherto 'guiding-question' of philosophy, which has been the question about beings" (*Contributions*, 5). Here we have in brief Heidegger's account of the historical unfolding of the question of being. The question, what is a being? unfolds historically when the being-historical element hidden in this guiding-question places philosophical thinking in the crossing to the 'other beginning.' And what is this being-historical element? We find the answer in a lecture that Heidegger wrote at the same time as *Contributions to Philosophy* under the title *Basic Questions of Philosophy: Selected "Problems" of "Logic."* This text is important because in it Heidegger works out the being-historical element hidden in the guiding-question, what is a being? And this being-historical element is none other than *one* of the five Greek determinations of the beingness of beings. After a penetrating analysis, Heidegger demonstrates that *one* of these determinations has the historical power to function as a hint at the 'other beginning.' What is this historically loaded determination, and how does it hint further at the 'other beginning'?

Prompted by awe (θαυμάζειν), Greeks' philosophical thinking in the 'first beginning' of philosophy responds to the question, what is a being? by disclosing and opening up the determinations of beingness, namely, constancy (*Ständigkeit*), presence (*Anwesenheit*), shape (*Gestalt*), and boundary (*Grenze*) (*GA* 45:130). As constant, a being stands out and resists disintegration (*Zerfall*). As present, a being does not dwindle away but perseveres in presence. The shape of a being is what presses it forth and resists its dissolution into shapelessness. Finally, the boundary of a being protects it from boundlessness and from the unbounded pull *(bloßer Fortriß)*. However, the Greeks' thinking does not reveal the further hinting of a hint in the determinations such as constancy, presence, shape, or boundary. Rather, the determination that is historically loaded and proves to be the further hinting at the 'other beginning' is what the Greeks call the unconcealed, τὸ ἀληθές. And this determination directly points to unconcealment, ἀλήθεια, which is why Heidegger notes that the Greeks "always name ἀλήθεια, unconcealment when they name a being" (*GA* 45:122).

By delving into the guiding-question, what is a being? and by examining the determinations of the beingness of a being, Heidegger concludes that the unconcealed, τὸ ἀληθές, is the only determination of beingness that hints further at unconcealment, ἀλήθεια. Heidegger arrives at this conclusion because "in Plato and Aristotle a being and truth—ἀλήθεια καὶ ὄν—are always mentioned together. . . . That here καὶ should be understood in the sense of 'that is to say' is unequivocally borne out by the fact that Plato and Aristotle instead of ὄν often simply say ἀλήθεια or τὸ ἀληθές" (*GA* 45:117–18). This shows that although the unconcealed, τὸ ἀληθές, is the last of the five determinations of beingness, it highlights the other four. This allows Heidegger to say that "[u]nconcealment—ἀλήθεια—is the one determination—last-named, but really belonging first—that radiates and prevails throughout all the other determinations of the beingness of a being, namely, the ambiguous constancy, presence, shape, and boundary" (*GA* 45:130). Here Heidegger makes clear that the unconcealed, τὸ ἀληθές—one of the determinations of the beingness of a being—is the hint that hints further at unconcealment, ἀλήθεια. Heidegger comes to this realization because in contrast to the Greeks, who set out from the guiding-question, what is a being? he sets out from the grounding-question, how does be-ing sway? From this point of departure, he can ascertain that the last determination, the unconcealed, τὸ ἀληθές, is the hint that hints at unconcealment, ἀλήθεια. Thanks to this unconcealment, the other four determinations of the beingness of a being appear as unconcealed and are maintained in unconcealment, ἀλήθεια.

This brief excursion into the lecture course text that Heidegger wrote at the same time as *Contributions to Philosophy* enables us to understand that the analysis of the appearing of a being as presented there is the key for understanding the coalescing of beings and be-ing's historical swaying and the manner in which the question, how does be-ing sway? functions as a directive to be-ing, that is, to enowning, and to the echo of be-ing, that is, dis-enowning. If the unconcealed, τὸ ἀληθές, is the hint that hints at unconcealment, ἀλήθεια, then we must ask who enacts the unconcealing of a being? Heidegger's response highlights the directive to enowning and to the echo of be-ing, that is, to dis-enowning, by observing that this unconcealing is enacted by those who go under and are thus *en-owned* by be-ing. And if we wonder how to understand this en-ownedness, Heidegger responds by alluding to be-ing's need. If we continue our questioning and ask how to understand be-ing's need, then Heidegger responds by saying: "Be-ing . . . needs those who go under; and, wherever beings appear, it has already *en-owned* these founders who go under and allotted them to be-ing. That is the essential swaying of being itself. We call it *enowning*" (*Contributions*, 6). In short, the unconcealing of beings is a matter of going under, enownment and allotment, and those who unconceal beings are those who go under, are enowned by be-ing, and who are allotted to be-ing.

What Heidegger says in this passage enables us to specify the "who" that enacts the unconcealing of beings. This who is none other than *Dasein*, which is en-owned by be-ing. That is why Heidegger speaks of *Dasein* as the founder who is allotted to be-ing. As beings appear, that is, as they are unconcealed, be-ing's need for the founder, for *Dasein*, which is allotted to be-ing, manifests the swaying of be-ing as enowning. In "Preview," therefore, enowning appears in the light of be-ing's need for *Dasein*, and *Dasein*'s allotedness to be-ing. Thus Heidegger's account of who enacts the unconcealing of beings places in the foreground be-ing's need and allotedness of *Dasein*. To take a closer look at this need and allotedness, we must draw upon "thrown projecting-open" (*geworfener Entwurf*), that is, that basic conception of *Dasein* that occupies center stage in the fundamental ontology of the transcendental-horizonal perspective.

What light can this conception cast on the thinking that shapes the 'first beginning'? Insofar as this thinking projects-open the beingness of beings, we have to say that it is thrown into the coalescing of beings and be-ing's swaying. Since the thinking of the Greeks takes place within that coalescing, it proves to have been allotted to be-ing and in this manner to have been a response to the need of be-ing. And philosophical thinking in the 'first beginning' is thrown into and projects-open this coalescing because this coalescing comes to Greek thinking from be-ing's turning relation to this thinking. Thus we understand the allotedness of thinking (*Dasein*) and be-ing's need in light of be-ing's turning relation to thinking (to *Dasein*).

In the aforementioned lecture course text, Heidegger shows that in the 'first beginning' beings appear, that is, are unconcealed in the light of the attunement, awe, and that their beingness consists of constancy, presence, shape, and boundary, all of which make up the unconcealed, that is, τὸ ἀληθές. Thus by projecting-open the beingness of beings, the Greek philosophical thinking, unbeknown to itself, demonstrates its character of being thrown into ἀλήθεια, the unconcealment. Moreover, by projecting-open the beingness of beings in terms of constancy, presence, shape, and boundary, this thinking, unbeknown to itself, shows that by projecting-open the unconcealed, τὸ ἀληθές, it also opens the way for projecting-opening ἀλήθεια. However, this thinking stops short of projecting-open ἀλήθεια because it is guided by the question, what is a being? and *is not* grounded in the question, how does be-ing sway?— is not grounded in enowning.

If we recall the magnitude of the historical achievements of the Greek philosophical thinking that are inconceivable without this thinking taking place within the coalescing of beings and be-ing's sway—a coalescing that comes to this thinking from be-ing's turning relation— then we understand why in "Preview" Heidegger can say that "[t]he riches of the turning relation of be-ing to Dasein, which is en-owned by be-ing, are immeasurable. The fullness of the enowning is incalculable" (*Contributions*, 6). Heidegger speaks of the riches of be-ing's turning relation because this relation sustains the historical achievements of philosophical thinking from the pre-Socratics to Nietzsche.

To conclude this attempt to explicate the first directive Heidegger presents in "Preview," let me summarize the main points. The first directive, namely, the being-historically reformulated question of being, how does be-ing sway? implicates the question, what is a being? and thereby relates to the appearing of beings, to the interconnectedness of the unconcealed and unconcealment, and to thrown projecting-open— all of which we examined in the historical context of the 'first beginning'. To appropriate the thinking that unfolds in the first part of *Contributions to Philosophy*, we must follow this directive. We can do so only when we cross from the guiding-question, what is a being? toward the grounding-question, how does be-ing sway? And we can do so when we follow the second directive, namely the grounding attunement of reservedness *(Verhaltenheit)*.

III

No sooner does Heidegger allude to the necessity of crossing from the guiding-question of the 'first beginning,' what is a being? toward the grounding-question of the 'other beginning,' how does be-ing sway?

than he presents the second directive, the grounding attunement of reservedness. As we know, attunement does not appear for the first time in *Contributions to Philosophy;* it also plays a significant role in the treatment of the question of being in the fundamental ontology of the transcendental-horizonal perspective. In this work, however, attunement has an epochal-historical dimension that it did not have in fundamental ontology.

Beginning from within the 'first beginning' and crossing to the 'other beginning,' being-historical thinking at each stage is attuned by the attunement of the 'other beginning,' reservedness. When in "Preview" Heidegger enacts being-historical thinking, he leaves no doubt that this thinking accomplishes what it does because it is attuned by reservedness. This shows that attunements in general and the grounding-attunement of reservedness in particular are the sine qua non of being-historical thinking. This prompts Heidegger to say that "if the grounding-attunement stays away, then everything is a forced rattling of concepts and empty words" (*Contributions,* 15-16). The perspicacity of being-historical thinking, the fact that it is not a forced rattling of concepts and empty words, derives from its being attuned by the history-building grounding-attunement called reservedness. Heidegger's negative description of a thinking bereft of grounding-attunement can conveniently be applied to the thinking that sustains epistemology. What he says with this description—without thematically analyzing it—is that the attunement-bereft thinking epistemology puts forth is historically barren. Epistemological thinking is historically barren because it is bereft of, and hence is deprived of, disclosive capabilities and grounding potentials inherent in attunement. By contrast, the grounding-attunement called reservedness empowers being-historical thinking and illuminates its course and direction. Thus we can say that the grounding-attunement of reservedness, being-historical thinking, and the matter to which this thinking is devoted are inseparable.

We recall from Heidegger's account in the lecture course text mentioned earlier that the thinking in the 'first beginning' is attuned by the attunement called awe (θαυμάζειν). Considering that here the unconcealing of beings depends on this attunement, we understand why this thinking only discloses and opens up the determinations of beingness, one of which, as we saw, is the unconcealed—τὸ ἀληθές. We also understand why this thinking does not follow the lead of this last determination as a hint at unconcealment, or ἀλήθεια. But the being-historical thinking of *Contributions to Philosophy* unfolds the hint at unconcealment because it is empowered by the grounding-attunement called reservedness. This empowerment comes from the turning relation of be-ing which is reserved and preserved in that grounding-attunement. In brief, being-historical thinking unfolds the hint at unconcealment because it is empowered by the reserved turning relation of be-ing. In the aforementioned lecture course text that is written at the same time as *Contributions to Philosophy*, Heidegger reiterates the reservedness of the turning relation of be-ing when he notes that "[r]eservedness is the grounding-attunement of the relation to be-ing" ("Verhaltenheit ist die *Grundstimmung des Bezuges zum Seyn*" [*GA* 45:2, Heidegger's itlaics]).

When in "Preview," Heidegger addresses reservedness and along with it being-historical thinking, he makes clear that because this thinking is attuned by the grounding-attunement called reservedness, it should not be confused with a thinking that proceeds in successive stages and progressively accumulates and supplies knowledge. Although it is preparatory, being-historical thinking does not unfold progressively. However, it is not preparatory in the sense in which preparation implies that the prepared stage lacks actual cognition. It is preparatory in a different way. We might illustrate this point by looking at Kant's *Critique of Pure Reason*, in which "Transcendental Aesthetic" and "Transcendental Analytic" prepare for "Transcendental Dialectic." In the first two sections, Kant's thinking does not yet deliver actual cognition: it is the third section, "Transcendental Dialectic," that does so. By contrast, being-historical thinking is preparatory in the sense that in *Contributions to Philosophy* preparation "does not consist in acquiring preliminary cognitions as the basis for the later disclosure of actual cognitions. Rather, here preparation is: opening the way, yielding to the way—essentially, *attuning*" (*Contributions*, 60). Perhaps it is difficult to read the words *preparation* and *preparatory* and not associate them with processes of development and progression. This difficulty emerges because we tend to take words such as *preparation* and *preparatory* in their usual sense. But as laid out in "Preview" preparation does not refer to a preliminary and introductory stage of the discussion that should lead to actual knowledge; it means opening the way, bringing onto the way, yielding to the way, and attuning. In brief, with the word preparation Heidegger refers to way-making and opening of the way.

In "Preview" preparation assumes the role already described because it is shaped by the grounding-attunement called reservedness.

We must not take the word *preparation* in "Preview" in the sense of manufacturing a steppingstone, as it were, but in the sense of opening the way and way-making, each of which comes to being-historical thinking from the grounding-attunement called reservedness. In the context of this thinking, preparation as opening the way and way-making intimately belongs to language and its ownmost. This is as it ought to be because being-historical thinking takes shape within language and the latter's way-making. And this way-making is nowhere clearer than in the preparation that takes shape when Heidegger's being-historical thinking opens the way—makes a way—from the unconcealed, from τὸ ἀληθές, to the unconcealment, to ἀλήθεια.

However, the way-making move that being-historical thinking makes and so opens the way from the unconcealed to unconcealment is not solidified into a modern and randomly repeatable methodology. As way-making this thinking is underway and belongs to the future. Heidegger alludes to this thinking when he says that "[f]uture thinking is a thinking that is *underway,* through which the domain of be-ing's essential swaying—completely hidden up to now—is gone through, is thus first lit up, and is attained in its ownmost enowning-character" (*Contributions,* 3).

To be underway, to open the way, is what differentiates being-historical thinking from a thinking that submits itself to the modern conceptions of method. Whereas in modern philosophy and modern science, method dominates the subject matter, being-historical thinking, as a thinking that is underway and opens the way, does not at all dominate the domain of be-ing's epochal-historical unfolding. By going through this domain, being-historical thinking realizes its own enowned and allotted character. When in "Preview" Heidegger addresses the issues of "way" and "method," he notes that the path of being-historical thinking and the domain of be-ing's epochal-historical unfolding are not separated by what is called "method" in modern philosophy. One of the most instructive instances of this inseparability is the "way" that being-historical thinking "makes" from the unconcealed, τὸ ἀληθές, to unconcealment, ἀλήθεια.

Heeding the hint that hints at unconcealment, at ἀλήθεια, is a far cry from submitting to modern metaphysical methodologies. This heeding is attuned by the grounding-attunement of reservedness. We must not forget that *reservedness* translates *Verhaltenheit,* which not only means "holding back" and "keeping in reserve," but, considering the important element of *Verhalten,* also means "comportment." Heeding the way, opening the way from the unconcealed, τὸ ἀληθές, to unconcealment, ἀλήθεια, means comporting toward be-ing's swaying, which is held back and kept in reserve. And it is precisely this element of comporting that differentiates the metaphysical methodologies dominating modernity from the "way-making" "method" of being-historical thinking and its character of being underway. Rather than aspiring to dominate the domain of be-ing's swaying—an aspiration recalling metaphysical methodologies—the "way-making" "method" of this thinking submits itself to the hint and thus comports itself toward be-ing's swaying, which is held back and kept in reserve. In short, the "way-making" "method" of being-historical thinking has a comporting relationship to be-ing's swaying.

Because of this relationship, the path traversed by being-historical thinking—Heidegger at times calls the latter enthinking of be-ing—differs further from the methods of modern philosophy in that its course does not follow the secure and foreseeable direction laid out by those methods. Heidegger contrasts the "way-making" "method" of being-historical thinking—of the enthinking of be-ing—with the methods of modern philosophy when he says: "But the pathway of this enthinking of be-ing does not yet have a firm line on the map. The territory first comes to be *through the pathway* and is unknown and unreckonable at every stage of the way" (*Contributions,* 60). What is of paramount importance for understanding this thinking is that it perseveres in being underway; it gives up all calculative posture and expectation. This thinking does not calculate ahead because as enthinking of be-ing, as being-historical thinking, it is solely sustained by be-ing's incalculable turning relation. This is why in "Preview" Heidegger alludes to be-ing's incalculable turning relation when he characterizes the path of being-historical thinking—the path of the enthinking of be-ing—as one ultimately attuned and determined by be-ing: "The more genuinely the way of enthinking is the way to be-ing, the more unconditionally is it attuned to and determined by be-ing itself" (*Contributions,* 60). As attuned and determined by be-ing itself, the path of being-historical thinking brings a rigor and stringency to this thinking that protect it from being mistaken for the unmethodical and haphazard thinking that fabricates something. Thus protected, being-historical thinking is capable through questioning of placing itself before be-ing: "Enthinking is not thinking-out and haphazard invention but rather [is] that thinking that through questioning places itself before be-ing" (*Contributions,* 60). The enthinking of be-ing—being-historical thinking—is the most rigorous and stringent thinking because of its path which enables this thinking, through questioning, to place itself before be-ing. Heidegger thus intimates that this path originates from within be-ing's turning relation—from within a relation marked by comportment and reservedness. Originating in this manner, the path of enthinking enables this thinking to place itself before be-ing and demand that be-ing attune its questioning: "Enthinking . . . is that thinking that . . . demands of be-ing that it attune the questioning, all the way through" (*Contributions*, 60). By alluding in "Preview" to the intricate connections between path, being-historical thinking, enthinking, and grounding-attunement, Heidegger alludes to be-ing itself as that which attunes questioning.

Summarizing the main points of our discussion of grounding-attunement as another directive that Heidegger presents in "Preview," we can say that this attunement comes from be-ing itself, determines the path of enthinking, and places this thinking as being-historical thinking before be-ing so that be-ing attunes questioning. In view of this attunement, the "way-making" "method" of enthinking of be-ing differentiates itself from the modern, metaphysical methods. For a thinking that seeks to appropriate *Contributions to Philosophy* and intends to co-enact being-historical thinking, the enabling power of the grounding-attunement and its impact on the "method" of this thinking are paramount. Equally paramount in this context is that this enabling attunement necessitates a particular structure of presentation for *Contributions to Philosophy*. It is in this structure that we find a third directive for understanding "Echo."

IV

Let me note first that language assumes a unique role in shaping the structure of the presentation of *Contributions to Philosophy*, but language understood as attuned by the grounding-attunement of reservedness, which reserves and preserves be-ing's turning relation. Because it is attuned to this reserved, turning relation, the language of this work reflects the ownmost of language. Long before in *Unterwegs zur Sprache* of 1959 Heidegger works out the enowning of "the ringing of stillness" as the ownmost of language, he states in an essay on Hölderlin (written at the same time as *Contributions to Philosophy*) that language is enowning: "Language is not a tool at one's disposal, but the enowning that as such promotes the highest possibility of being human" (*GA* 4:38).[26] In this essay Heidegger calls language enowning based on the view on language that he presents in "Preview" of *Contributions to Philosophy*. In the essay on Hölderlin, he calls language enowning because in *Contributions to Philosophy* he takes language to be shaped by an en-owned "saying." This "saying" is unlike the familiar modes of language-articulation, specifically, unlike assertion *(Aussage)*. Unlike assertion, this en-owned "saying" does not stand over against, does not objectify what is said: "[r]ather, the saying itself *is* the 'to be said,' as the essential swaying of be-ing" *(Contributions, 4)*. In view of such "saying"—itself be-ing's swaying—that is, in view of a specific mode of language-articulation, Heidegger, in the essay on Hölderlin, calls language the enowning that promotes the highest possibilities of being human.

We obtain more clarification about what Heidegger calls "saying" from his further differentiation of "saying" from assertion. Whereas assertion is a mode of language-articulation that describes, explains, proclaims, or teaches, "saying" does none of these: "This saying does not describe or explain, does not proclaim or teach . . . does not stand over against what is said. Rather, the saying itself is the 'to be said,' as the essential swaying of be-ing" *(Contributions, 4)*. Since it is shaped by the language-articulation called "saying," the structure of presentation of *Contributions to Philosophy* turns out to be of a particular kind. By preserving "saying" intact, this structure protects the language of this work from willful manipulation, simplification, and reduction that often prevail the academic discourse in philosophy. What is this structure?

Contributions to Philosophy consists of 281 sections that must be carefully distinguished from chapters. If we read these sections superficially, if we fail to see that each section is a sustained presentation of "saying," we fail to perceive the intimate interrelatedness—jointedness—of these sections. When we read these sections in the light cast on them by Heidegger's rigorous determination of "saying," we understand why the 281 sections constitute what he calls six "joinings."

We must be careful not to mistake a "joining" for a poetic metaphor or a more imaginative substitute for what is usually called a chapter. A "joining" is that part of *Contributions to Philosophy* in which what is "said" therein is said in such a way as to join in what is "said" elsewhere in this work. (Needless to say, the word *said* here refers directly to "saying.") Thus rather than being connected to one another by the ironclad theses that tie one chapter to another, each of the six "joinings" fits into other "joinings" not by any thesis but by the *sameness*—not the identity—of what each "joining" says, a sameness that must be distinguished from the sameness of a thesis. And it is with respect to this sameness that we can say that each "joining" of *Contributions to Philosophy* fits into other "joinings" and makes up a jointure.

What distinguishes the structure of this work from the structure that modern philosophy calls system is precisely this jointure. As a constitutive part of a jointure, a "joining" is not an incomplete segment of a system, nor are all "joinings" together the completed whole of a system. That is why in addressing the structure of presentation of *Contributions to Philosophy*, Heidegger reminds us in "Preview" that the "time of 'systems' is over" (*Contributions*, 4).

Contributions to Philosophy does not represent a system because a system is structured in accordance with assertion, whereas this work is structured by "saying." It does not represent a system because, unlike assertion, "saying" itself *is* the swaying of be-ing, enowning—"saying" is not an assertion made about the swaying of be-ing. Thus "saying" cannot fulfill the function that rightly belongs to assertion. This is clearly reflected in the very first paragraph of "Preview," where Heidegger unequivocally states that *Contributions to Philosophy* "must avoid all false claim to be a 'work' of the style heretofore" (*Contributions*, 3). Avoidance of this previous style—the traditional style of the system—does not mean that Heidegger again decides to differ from what everyone else usually does. This avoidance is necessitated by the en-owned "saying," that is, by enowning. It is in consideration of enowning that, in speaking of the structure of presentation of *Contributions to Philosophy*, Heidegger stresses its "enowning character" (*Contributions*, 3).

But how are we to grasp the outline that the structure of this work presents as "Echo," "Playing-Forth," "Leap," "Grounding," "The Ones to Come," and "The Last God"? Heidegger anticipates this question when he explicitly addresses the outline: "This outline does not yield an arrangement of various observations about various objects. It is also not an introductory ascent from what is below to what is above" (*Contributions*, 5). In this vein he alerts us to the fact that although the six "joinings" of *Contributions to Philosophy* appear in and present an outline, this outline is not to be confused with one that presents a developmental hierarchy. There is no hierarchy in this outline because "[e]ach of the six joinings of the jointure stands for itself, but only in order to make the essential onefold more pressing. In each of the six joinings the attempt is made always to say the same of the same, but in each case from within another essential domain of that which enowning names" (*Contributions*, 57). To say the same of the same is not to repeat the same thing. Each of the six "joinings" of the one jointure that is titled *Contributions to Philosophy* says the same, but in view of another essential domain of that which be-ing's essential swaying, enowning, names. Thus

in the sixfold "joining" structure of this work, Heidegger does not intend each "joining" to be a stage in the hierarchical development of a
doctrine or a system. What takes place in each of the six "joinings" is
the actual history that, "since the end of metaphysics must be always
more decisively owned up to, namely that thinking of be-ing is not a
'doctrine' and not a 'system,' but rather must become actual history
and thus what is most hidden" (*Contributions,* 59). This actual history
emerges in the relationship between the title of each "joining" and the
texts of the six "joinings."

If, structurally speaking, "Echo" stands for what goes on in the entirety of the first "joining," then how is this title related to the entirety of
this "joining"? Is it fair to suggest that what is presented as the text of
this "joining" is Heidegger's "narrative" of this "Echo"—a narrative
composed of the *assertions* he makes *about* it? If we recall what we ob-
served earlier about "saying" and the way it differs from an assertion,
then we cannot simply assume that the title "Echo" contains the nu-
cleus of the "narrative" Heidegger lays out in this "joining." Thus the
sentences constituting the text of this "joining" are not to be confused
with the assertions constituting a "narrative." And this is the case because every sentence in this "joining"—even the seemingly insignificant or the grammatically incomplete ones—reflects the "saying" and
should be read, interpreted, and understood in light of Heidegger's rigorous determination of "saying." Heidegger presents the gist of this determination when he notes that "[t]his saying gathers be-ing's essential
sway unto a first sounding, while it itself [this saying] sounds only out
of this essential sway" (*Contributions,* 4). To see the simplicity and the
rigor of this determination, we recall the way unconcealed, τὸ ἀληθές,
relates to unconcealment, ἀλήθεια. The unconcealed, τὸ ἀληθές, is not
what is said *about* a being; it is not an assertion made about a being, because the unconcealed, τὸ ἀληθές, gathers the unconcealment, ἀλήθεια,
into a first sounding, thereby bringing history to the fore.

To summarize, any thinking seeking to appropriate *Contributions to
Philosophy* must not only follow the directives of the question, how does
be-ing sway? and of the attunement that grounds thinking but also the
directive summed up in the mode of language-articulation called "saying." Besides following the two former directives, appropriative thinking must also let itself be guided by the "saying," that is, the mode of
language-articulation that shapes the structure of presentation of this
work. As shaped by "saying," this structure brings the gathering of
be-ing's swaying to a first sounding, which is the occurrence of actual

history. This is what happens when, for example, the unconcealed, τὸ ἀληθές gathers unconcealment, ἀλήθεια, into a first sounding. But how does this first sounding—this actual history—*resound* within the preliminary, preparatory, and anticipatory "Preview" of *Contributions to Philosophy?* Surprisingly, it resounds as an echo intoning the refusal of be-ing. It is by addressing this refusal that I shall address the last directive Heidegger offers in "Preview."

V

Thinking that seeks to appropriate *Contributions to Philosophy* and wants to understand what transpires as being-historical thinking must remain mindful of the manner in which the unconcealed, τὸ ἀληθές, gathers the unconcealment, ἀλήθεια, into a first sounding. In that case, the unconcealed, τὸ ἀληθές, no longer appears merely as a determination of beingness but as the first sounding of be-ing's swaying that sustains the actual history. But at the end of the 'first beginning,' Plato and Aristotle took the unconcealed, τὸ ἀληθές, only as a determination of beingness and did not project-open the unconcealed, τὸ ἀληθές, into unconcealment, ἀλήθεια. They thus ushered in an epoch in which be-ing's swaying, that is, enowning, primarily appears as refusal—an epoch in which man lacks the strength and is feeble in the face of *Da-sein.* Heidegger addresses this refusal, this lack of strength and feebleness, when he appeals to the theme of enowning and asks, "[I]f enowning is what makes up the essential swaying of be-ing, how close must the danger be that be-ing refuses and must refuse enownment?" His response is that man has become weak and feeble in the face of *Da-sein,* because "the unfettered hold of the frenzy of the gigantic has overwhelmed him under the guise of 'magnitude'" (*Contributions,* 6). The danger that be-ing refuses to grant enownment leaves its mark on the projecting-opening that with Plato and Aristotle shapes the end of the 'first beginning' that the Greeks made. This projecting-opening to which be-ing refuses to grant enownment names the unconcealed, τὸ ἀληθές, without projecting the unconcealed unto unconcealment, ἀλήθεια. Thus the Platonic-Aristotelian projecting-opening is ambiguous. The two and a half millennia of the history of the 'first beginning'—from its end in Plato and Aristotle to its completion in Hegel, Marx, and Nietzsche—demonstrates that philosophical thinking is not at all concerned with the refusal that sustains this projecting and is increasingly oblivious to the ambiguity inhering in the Platonic-Aristotelian projecting-opening. In Heidegger's view, the oblivion to the ambiguity inherent in the first projecting-opening culminates in man's lack of strength, his feebleness in the face of *Da-sein*—a lack that comes from his being overwhelmed by the unfettered frenzy of the gigantic.

The lack of strength, the feebleness of which Heidegger speaks must be carefully considered in the context of be-ing's refusal to grant enownment. When we observe that lack and feebleness in that context, we realize that this refusal does not allow man to become aware of be-ing's turning relation. He lives as though be-ing has no bearing on his thinking. We also realize that this refusal does not allow philosophical thinking to be aware of what sustains the on-going, prevailing Platonic-Aristotelian projecting-opening, namely, the sway of be-ing as dis-enowning. Finally, we realize that this refusal hinders philosophical thinking from understanding that be-ing goes on to unfold, but instead of unfolding as enowning, it unfolds as dis-enowning. The foremost consequence of the ongoing unfolding of dis-enowning is that thinking becomes a dis-enowned thinking, that is, projecting-opening becomes a dis-enowned projecting-opening.

As I mentioned at the beginning of this essay, in "Echo" Heidegger does not use the word dis-enowning. However, on two important occasions he uses the verbal form of the word, and both occasions have a direct bearing on grasping the last directive, namely, the intoning in the first "joining" of be-ing's refusal to grant enownment. The first use of the verbal form occurs in section 57, titled "History of Be-ing and Abandonment of Being." In this section Heidegger tells us that in this epoch "'beings'—what one calls the 'actual' and 'life' and 'values'—are dis-enowned by be-ing [*des Seyns enteignet*]" (*Contributions*, 84). Only when man lacks the strength and is feeble in the face of *Dasein*—only when he is unaware of a projecting-opening to which be-ing refuses to grant enownment—only then does he submit beings to the measures that he calls "actuality," "life," and "values," thereby completing the epoch in the history of be-ing marked by its abandonment. Here Heidegger does not reject "actuality," "life," and "values" offhand. By alluding to them as manmade measures, he draws attention to the central role of a dis-enowned projecting-opening that makes these measures in light of be-ing's refusal to grant enownment.

The second occasion when this verbal form occurs is in section 118, titled "Leap." By referring to the truth of being as awaiting a projecting-opening yet to be enacted, Heidegger here brings more light to man's lack of strength, his feebleness in the face of *Da-sein*. If man would cease to be feeble in the face of *Da-sein*, if he would enact a "leap" and shift into the truth of being, and project-open the enownment that is covered over, then he would become who he is—he would become himself. However, in the present epoch Heidegger finds almost no sign that such a "leap," such a shift and opening takes place: "But how seldom man shifts into this truth; how easily and quickly he is content with a being and thus continues to be dis-enowned of being" (*Contributions*, 164). To be dis-enowned of being means to be delivered over to and be preoccupied with beings—means to have forgotten be-ing and its truth. The ease with which man seems to find contentment with beings is an indication that he has forgotten be-ing.

The two occasions when Heidegger uses the verbal form of the word *dis-enowning* are significant. They show that although dis-enowning is not explicitly mentioned by Heidegger in the text of "Echo," he refers to it when he speaks of abandonment by and forgottenness of be-ing. This occurs for the first time in the verses with which he opens the first "joining," "Echo":

> Echo of the essential swaying of be-ing
> out of the abandonment of being
> through the distressing distress
> of the forgottenness of be-ing.
>
> (*Contributions*, 75)

With these verses he indicates what is central to the entirety of "Echo," namely, abandonment by and forgottenness of be-ing, both of which we must understand if we are to grasp properly what Heidegger conveys with these verses.

Let us begin with what these verses say about the echo: this echo is the echo of the swaying of be-ing, which comes to pass *not* as enowning but as dis-enowning. Coming from dis-enowning this echo echoes the abandonment by and forgottenness of be-ing. To understand this, we must strive to show that dis-enowning has the formal structure of en-owning, has its own attunement, and shapes "Echo," that is, the "joining" in *Contributions to Philosophy* that joins and fits into all the other five "joinings."

Regarding dis-enowning having the formal structure of en-owning, we must first note that the echo of abandonment by and forgottenness of be-ing comes from be-ing's dis-enowning forth-throw and is thus not confined to "Echo." This dis-enowning forth-throw reverberates throughout "Playing-Forth," "Leap," "Grounding," "The Ones to

Come," and "The Last God." Everything that transpires in these "join-ings" attests to a dis-enowned forth-throw, a dis-enowned allotedness. Second, the echo of be-ing's abandonment and forgottenness that comes from be-ing's dis-enowned forth-throw lets be-ing's turning relation to *Dasein* and *Dasein*'s comporting relation to be-ing appear as dis-enowned relations.

As a dis-enowned relation, be-ing's echo that intones abandonment and forgottenness and comes from be-ing's dis-enowned forth-throw is what philosophical thinking needs to project-open. Doing so, philosophical thinking realizes that dis-enowning has the formal structure of en-owning, that is, forth-throw and projecting-opening.

To shed more light on the formal structure of dis-enowning, let us focus on the projecting-opening peculiar to dis-enowning. This project-ing is not one that would shelter be-ing in beings. To go back to our dis-cussion of the unconcealed, we can say that by failing to shelter be-ing in a being, the dis-enowned projecting-opening does away with the ambiguity and question-worthiness of a being, the unconcealed. Not deemed to be worthy of questioning with regard to its ambiguity, the unconcealed now appears in light of the manmade measures called "ac-tuality," "life," and "values," that is, in light of measures that obfuscate be-ing rather than shelter it in a being.

Although "actuality," "life," and "values" obfuscate be-ing rather than shelter it in a being, they do not nullify be-ing, abolish, remove, or eliminate it. "Actuality," "life," and "values" still maintain a relation-ship to be-ing, albeit an obfuscated relationship. It is as this obfuscated relationship that be-ing—its full swaying—resonates and echoes in a being.

Philosophical thinking must take seriously this resonance, this echo, as a refusal. This thinking must go painstakingly through the history of the 'first Greek beginning' and disclose and open up the obfuscating relationship prevailing in this history and marked by dis-enowning. In other words, philosophical thinking must become be-ing-historical and open up this obfuscated dis-enowned relationship—this echo of be-ing's swaying that intones refusal. Only then can philosophical think-ing remember the abandonment by and the forgottenness of be-ing in a being that is dis-enowned by be-ing. We realize how important this re-membering is when we consider that right at the very beginning of "Echo," Heidegger alludes to this remembering by characterizing the task of this "joining" as "[b]ringing this forgottenness forth through a remembering *as* forgottenness in its hidden power—wherein the echo of be-ing resounds" (*Contributions*, 75). If in the midst of beings, humans would remember the relationship to be-ing that is hidden in the forgottenness of be-ing, then this relationship would permit humans to become aware of the incalculable richness peculiar to be-ing's turning relation. Needless to say, this richness has nothing in common with the wealth, plenitude, and riches that belong to beings.

Let us now consider that dis-enowning has its own attunement. Being-historical thinking opens up and discloses the echo that intones refusal and dis-enowning because this thinking is attuned to this echo from the ground up by the grounding-attunement of reservedness, which holds the echo of be-ing in reserve. With the word *Verhaltenheit*, Heidegger stresses not only the element of reservedness but also *Verhalten*, that is, comportment. The latter stands both for the comportment, or *Verhalten*, inherent in be-ing's turning relation as well as for *Dasein*'s comportment to this relation. Reservedness is thus an attunement that holds back and keeps in reserve the echo of be-ing's refusal and be-ing's dis-enowning as well as *Dasein*'s disclosing comportment. This shows that dis-enowning, the echo that intones forgottenness and abandonment by be-ing, has its own attunement.

Finally, we will consider how dis-enowning shapes "Echo." It shapes this "joining" in its entirety because the predominating measures called "actuality," "life," and "values" are measures that reveal a *specific* manner of be-ing's swaying, that is, disenowning. However, since the swaying of be-ing as dis-enowning occurs not only in "Echo" but also in other "joinings," the question becomes how "Echo" relates to and is "present" in other "joinings."

Considering the meaning of the word *Fügung*, "joining," I shall sum up in the following question the central issues involved in the relation between the six "joinings" of *Contributions to Philosophy*: How do we understand and think through the specific manner in which each "joining" joins and fits all the other "joinings"? Does each "joining" join all the others in the manner in which the pieces of a puzzle join and fit one another? Or as we attend to *Contributions to Philosophy* as a whole, can we detect a different kind of joining relationship?

What distinguishes each "joining" is that each says "the same of the same, but in each case from another essential domain of that which enowning names" (*Contributions*, 57). How are we to understand the word *same* in this context? We find the answer in a work of Heidegger's that becomes increasingly more accessible when read in conjunction with *Contributions to Philosophy*, namely, the *Letter on Humanism*. There Heidegger speaks of the determinative "relation of being" (*Bezug des*

Seins) (*GA* 9:313)—determinative because it is paramount for grasping how each "joining" says "the same of the same."

The central issue not only in the *Letter on Humanism* but also in Heidegger's work as a whole is a specific way of thinking that he circumscribes as acting and that accords with the historical-epochal unfolding of be-ing. Heidegger highlights this specific way of thinking by focusing on what it accomplishes. It unfolds what already "is" into the fullness of its ownmost. Since as indicated in the *Letter on Humanism* what already "is" is above all be-ing, accomplishing here means unfolding be-ing into the fullness of its ownmost, which is what thinking does thanks to the already given and prevailing "relation of being" (*GA* 9:313). Not produced, established, or brought about by thinking, this relation is sustained by be-ing's forth-throw. Since thinking as acting unfolds what already "is" into the fullness of its ownmost and since what already "is" is the "relation of being" that comes to thinking as being's forth-throw, and since this forth-throw is the same that sustains each "joining," we understand why Heidegger can say that each "joining" says "the same of the same."

VI

When we look at the "relation of being" in connection with projecting-opening, we must say that the relation of being is proffered to thinking in order to invite thinking into acting, into projecting-opening. Considered in the context of "Echo," the relation of being is a dis-enowning relation that needs to be projected-open, unfolded, and thus led into the fullness of its ownmost. This also means that the dis-enowning relation of being is not proffered to thinking as what is completely and exhaustively thought through. Rather, the dis-enowning relation of being of which the entire "Echo" speaks must be understood in terms of a proffering that is projected-open but not completely and exhaustively thought through. The word that throughout Heidegger's work captures the tension between what is projected-open and what is completely and exhaustively thought through is *questioning*.

In general we can say that questioning in Heidegger is an acting (*Handeln*) that is attuned to an attunement. Consider the Greek questioning that is attuned to the attunement called awe, or the question, how does be-ing sway? which is attuned to the grounding-attunement called reservedness. For Heidegger questioning is an *acting* and as such should be distinguished from what is usually called questioning, and it should be differentiated from "thinking," "remaining silent," "ruminating," and so on. Strictly speaking, questioning in Heidegger's sense means experiencing the tension between what is projected-open and what is completely and exhaustively thought through—the tension that keeps each "joining" of *Contributions to Philosophy* open to further questioning, to further unfolding and disclosing. This tension holds the key for understanding why *Contributions to Philosophy* is inconclusive and why it had to remain so.

For the thinking that seeks to appropriate the first part of this work, "Echo," the tension between what Heidegger projects-open here—dis-enowning, the echo of be-ing, its refusal to grant enownment—and what must be completely and exhaustively thought through is of paramount importance. The preceding account of thinking as acting—as projecting-opening—should make clear that when we focus on the relation of being and thereby attempt to understand Heidegger's projecting-opening of this relation, we have to bear in mind that this projecting is exposed to the tension between projecting-opening and what must be completely and exhaustively thought through. Only by being mindful of this tension can we appropriate the thinking that shapes the first part of *Contributions to Philosophy*.

The significance of the first "joining" of this work, "Echo," consists in revealing the relation of be-ing that comes to the fore as dis-enowning, as be-ing's abandonment and forgottenness and as such is in need of being questioned, projected-open, and thought through. The significance of "Echo" will be missed if it is misconstrued as a body of doctrine that is completely thought through, neatly wrapped up, and presented to us for our intellectual edification and enjoyment. More specifically, the significance of the first "joining" consists in projecting-opening the dis-enowned relation of being—its refusal to grant enownment. Considering what transpires in "Echo" as a whole, we must say that in this "joining" Heidegger projects-open and thus subjects to questioning the abandonment by and the forgottenness of be-ing, that is, dis-enowning and the echo of be-ing's refusal to grant enownment. And by projecting-opening the dis-enowning that comes to pass as this abandonment, this forgottenness, and this refusal, he intimates that they are not exhaustively thought through. To project-open, to think through, and to question dis-enowning that transpires as this abandonment, this forgottenness, and this refusal is the same as inaugurating a historical moment that belongs to a 'beginning' that Heidegger calls the 'other beginning.'

The Place of the Pre-Socratics in "Playing-Forth," the Second Part of *Contributions to Philosophy*

So ist der Mensch; wenn da ist
das Gut, und es sorget mit Gaben
Selber ein Gott für ihn, kennet
und sieht er es nicht.
Tragen muss er, zuvor; nun aber
nennt er sein Liebstes,
Nun, nun müssen dafür Worte, wie
Blumen, entstehen.

Hölderlin

Heidegger's works on the early Greek thinkers that originate from within his being-historical perspective and that have been published or are scheduled to appear in the *Gesamtausgabe* begin with his lecture course text of the summer semester 1932, "Der Anfang der abendländischen Philosophie: Anaximander und Parmenides" (The Beginning of Western Philosophy: Anaximander and Parmenides) and end with the Heraclitus seminar of 1966–67.

Thus, in the span of almost four decades, Heidegger produced an incomparably large body of work devoted to the early Greek thinkers. At the risk of oversimplification, it could be said that in this body of work he accomplishes two closely interrelated goals. First, in his published works on Parmenides (1942–43) and Heraclitus (1944), he totally dismantles the assumption that for almost two millennia had predetermined the understanding of Heraclitus and Parmenides: that Heraclitus is the thinker of change, while Parmenides is the thinker of permanence. Jean Beaufret summarily formulates this long-held assumption when he says: "It is customary to oppose Heraclitus and Parmenides,

like two gladiators, sword in hand, facing each other in the beginning
of thought—a custom which goes back to antiquity, as we find it already well-established in Plato."[27] A significant consequence of undoing this assumption is the need for a new reading of Plato, which Heidegger accomplishes in several works devoted to this philosopher.

Second, with his works on Parmenides and Heraclitus and on other
early Greek thinkers, Heidegger opens up a hitherto concealed and
forgotten domain, that of the alethiological beginning of Western philosophy. This opening is of such unparalleled philosophical magnitude
that at the end of his life and in retrospect of his entire work, Heidegger can say: "In a certain way ἀλήθεια is manifest and always already
experienced."[28]

Whereas in those works that he specifically devotes to early Greek
thinkers, Heidegger tackles the task of undoing and dismantling this
long-held opposition—Heraclitus as the thinker of change and Parmenides as the thinker of permanence—in *Contributions to Philosophy
(From Enowning)* he opens and firmly grounds the domain of the alethiological beginning of Western philosophy. I take seriously the words
"firmly grounds," because although Heidegger's works on the early
Greeks are grounded in *Contributions to Philosophy*, he does not have a
system of thought à la Hegel that beginning with this work assimilates
the whole history of philosophy, including the fragmented writings of
the early Greeks.

Keeping this proviso in mind as we turn to *Contributions to Philosophy*, we find ourselves initially confronted with a surprising omission.
In section 88 of this work, under the title "The 'Historical' Lectures Belong to the Sphere of This Task" (*Contributions*, 123), where Heidegger
programmatically mentions his future lecture courses on the history of
philosophy, he explicitly mentions Leibniz, Kant, Hegel, Schelling, and
Nietzsche but *not* the early Greek thinkers, the so-called pre-Socratics.
How are we to understand this omission?

As I shall demonstrate, this omission points to the place of the
early Greek thinkers in *Contributions to Philosophy*. The first step in this
direction is to grasp the structure of this major work, for through this
structure Heidegger enacts a new thinking of being—so-called being-
historical thinking—and addresses the alethiological beginning of
Western philosophy. This thinking is new because, unlike the
transcendental-horizonal thinking of *Being and Time*, it traverses the
path of the nonhistoriographical history of being (*Geschichte des Seins*),
thereby unfolding the thinking of being as the thinking of enowning.

I

The plan for writing *Contributions to Philosophy* was already laid out as early as 1931 and as late as 1932.[29] Having already traversed the path of transcendental-horizonal perspective and its fundamental ontology, Heidegger in these years realized the need to abandon this perspective in favor of the being-historical perspective. Strictly speaking, this move was guided by the historicity of being itself. In a letter to Elisabeth Blochmann of September 18, 1932, Heidegger alludes to this move. He says: "People already believe and talk about my writing *Being and Time II*. That is all right. But because at one point *Being and Time I* was for me a path that led me somewhere and because I can no longer traverse that path, and it is already overgrown, I can no longer write *Being and Time II*. I am not writing any book at all."[30] The move from the transcendental-horizonal perspective of fundamental ontology *(Being and Time I)* into the being-historical perspective foreshadowed in this letter and alluded to with "*Being and Time II*" is not arbitrary. It is a full and well-rounded response to be-ing's turning relation, which claims Heidegger the moment he engages in the thinking of being. In other words, be-ing's turning relation precedes the move from the transcendental-horizonal perspective and its fundamental ontology to the being-historical perspective. It is not the consequence of the thinking of fundamental ontology having run its course but is precisely the motivating power that sets this thinking in motion.

Heidegger's realization that the thinking of the nonhistoriographical historicality of *Dasein*'s world in *Being and Time* does not reach the dimension of the nonhistoriograpical history of being is rooted in be-ing's turning relation. This realization prompts Heidegger to abandon the path of transcendental-horizonal thinking in favor of the new path of being-historical thinking. His awareness of the philosophical magnitude of this decision gives birth to *Contributions to Philosophy (From Enowning)*.

The move from the earlier transcendental-horizonal perspective to the new being-historical perspective takes along the transformed basic structure of *Dasein* as worked out in *Being and Time,* that is, the structure known as thrown projecting-open, *der geworfene Entwurf.* By taking a look at *Contributions to Philosophy,* I shall address *Dasein*'s transformed basic structure; otherwise it will not be possible to precisely determine the place of the early Greeks in being-historical thinking. One should note, however, that Heidegger's shift to the new being-historical perspective brings along a new language and a new style to _Contribution to Philosophy_. If we are to understand the place of the early Greeks in this work, we must familiarize ourselves with both its language and style.

At the very beginning of _Contributions to Philosophy_, Heidegger alludes to this new language when he addresses the style in which this work is _not_ written. This work calls for a new style because the attempt "to think according to a more originary stance within the question of the truth of be-ing . . . must avoid all false claim to be a 'work' of the style heretofore" (_Contributions_, 3). Avoiding this false claim, _Contributions to Philosophy_ turns out to be a work unlike any other work of Heidegger's. There are at least four reasons for its uniqueness.

Heidegger alludes to the first reason when he characterizes the language of this work as a "saying" of be-ing and differentiates this "saying" from statements _(Aussagen)_ made about be-ing: "This saying does not stand over against what is said. Rather, the saying itself _is_ the 'to be said,' as the essential swaying of be-ing" (_Contributions_, 4). Since according to their structure statements in general are assertions made about something and thus stand over against what they state, we infer from Heidegger's characterization of the language of _Contributions to Philosophy_ as a "saying" of be-ing that this "saying" is _not_ a statement made _about_ be-ing. What is said by the "saying" and the swaying of be-ing are the same. Therefore what is said and the swaying of be-ing do not stand in opposition to each other and do not constitute a vis-à-vis. Thus the first reason that _Contributions to Philosophy_ is unique is the sameness of "what is said" and the "swaying of be-ing," which shapes the language of this work—a language Heidegger differentiates from the language with which one makes statements about things.

The second reason is that this work originates from within an attunement in which what is to be thought is held back and kept in reserve. Heidegger calls it the grounding-attunement of reservedness—grounding because by holding back and keeping in reserve what is to be thought this attunement reveals its unique grounding power. And what this grounding-attunement holds in reserve—what needs to be thought and unfolded—is the swaying of be-ing, that is, enowning.

The third reason is that the being-historical thinking of _Contributions to Philosophy_ unabatedly receives "the further hinting of a hint which comes from what is most question-worthy and remains referred to it" (_Contributions_, 4). This hint, its further hinting, and what is most question-worthy all reverberate in the interplay between the guiding-question of philosophy, namely, what is a being? (τί τὸ ὄν) and the grounding-question, which asks, how does be-ing sway? To understand this reverberation let us consider Kant.

Although in the *Critique of Pure Reason* Kant is concerned with determining the conditions for the possibility of the objects of experience, that is, the beingness of beings—and so follows the terrain of the traditional preoccupation with beings, with ὄν—he does not inquire into the grounding-question, namely, how does be-ing sway? that is, into a swaying occurring at the same time as the manifestness of beings, of ὄν. (Heidegger addresses the simultaneity of be-ing's swaying and manifestness of beings—ὄν—in *Contributions to Philosophy* 10, 155–56.) This shows that Kant does not attend to the hint, its further hinting, and to what is most question-worthy, all of which reverberate in the question concerning the conditions for the possibility of the objects of experience, that is, in the question concerning the beingness of beings.

The fourth reason is that *Contributions to Philosophy* is not divided into chapters, that is, it does not use the device with which an author progressively demonstrates and establishes a preconceived thesis. In Kant's *Critique of Pure Reason,* for example, the three main chapters, "Transcendental Aesthetic," "Transcendental Logic," and "Transcendental Dialectic," progressively demonstrate and establish the thesis according to which the a priori elements inherent in "Sensibility," "Understanding," and "Reason" lay out the conditions for the possibility of the objects of experience. In these three chapters, Kant gradually and progressively establishes the thesis that the ideas of reason—ideas of God, immortality, and freedom—are notions that lack a corresponding object in experience. In contrast, in *Contributions to Philosophy* we find nothing even remotely similar to a gradual, steady progression toward establishing a preconceived thesis. Strictly speaking, with being-historical thinking Heidegger does not demonstrate and establish any thesis at all, which is why he does not hesitate to admit that the question that grounds being-historical thinking is not to be confused with "the purposeful activity of an individual nor . . . the limited calculation of a community" (*Contributions,* 4). This becomes clear as we examine the structure of this work.

Instead of chapters *Contributions to Philosophy* is made up of six "joinings" (*Fügungen*): "Echo," "Playing-Forth," "Leap," "Grounding," "The Ones to Come," and "The Last God." With regard to the word "joining," we should keep in mind that the German word *Fügung* not only means joining but also indicates a predisposition toward joining. By using the word *Fügung,* Heidegger wants to indicate that a given part of *Contributions to Philosophy* "joins" another part because it is predisposed to joining that part. Thus the six "joinings" of this work are parts that are predisposed to conjoining. Although each "joining" perseveres in its own singularity and uniqueness, it simultaneously joins other "joinings" and conjointly says the "same" that is named by the swaying of be-ing, that is, by enowning. Of great importance for properly entering into *Contributions to Philosophy* is the fact that each "joining" perseveres in its own singularity and uniqueness as a fundamental domain that is named by be-ing, that is, by enowning.

Heidegger takes great care to describe the relationships between the six joinings with respect to precisely this fundamental domain: "Each of the six joinings of the jointure stands for itself, but only in order to make the essential onefold more pressing. In each of the six joinings the attempt is made always to say the same of the same, but in each case from within another essential domain of that which enowning names" (*Contributions,* 57). What I call the fundamental domain is the locus where the singularity and uniqueness of each "joining" and what is named as each "joining" come together. Thus each "joining" should be viewed as a fundamental domain in which, within the singularity and uniqueness of each "joining," be-ing comes to articulation as enowning.

To understand the word *essential* in the passage "another essential domain of that which enowning names" according to essence and its connections to *essentia,* ἰδέα, and κοινόν grossly distorts the singularity and uniqueness of each "joining." Rather than taking our orientation from such connections, we should keep in mind that each "joining" manifests be-ing's swaying, that is, enowning in a manner peculiar and specific to that "joining." A case in point is the sixth "joining," "The Last God." The swaying of be-ing, at first a mere echo that in the first "joining," "Echo," intones be-ing's abandonment and forgottenness, fully sways in "The Last God" as the passing of the last god.

It is necessary not only to understand that each "joining" is a region wherein be-ing's swaying unfolds as enowning or as disenowning but also to realize that each "joining" or region involves the transformed basic structure of *Dasein.* To understand this transformed basic structure, we must remember that in thinking being within the transcendental-horizonal perspective, Heidegger determines *Dasein's* basic structure as consisting of "thrownness," "projecting-open," and "being-along-with," all three of which are equally original with discourse, that is, *Rede,* which is the transcendental-horizonal determination of what is ownmost to language.[31] We must also remember that this structure is not rigid and extant, because it is a structure of and for being's disclosure, that is, *Erschlossenheit des Seins.*

To understand the transformation of *Dasein's* basic structure in conjunction with Heidegger abandoning the transcendental-horizonal perspective and his setting out from the historicity of be-ing, we must bear two things in mind. First, in *Contributions to Philosophy* Heidegger often speaks of this structure as an inestimable achievement of *Being and Time.* For example, at the beginning of section 198 of *Contributions to Philosophy,* Heidegger addresses the grounding of *Dasein,* which as en-grounding constitutes a major concern of being-historical thinking. How are we to understand this grounding and en-grounding of *Dasein?* Heidegger responds to this question by directly referring to *Being and Time* and the structure of thrown projecting-open. At the beginning of section 198, he says: "Da-sein never lets itself be demonstrated and described as something extant. It is to be obtained only hermeneutically, i.e., however, according to *Being and Time,* in the thrown projecting-open" (*Contributions,* 226). He calls the grounding of *Dasein* an en-grounding because being-historical thinking achieves this grounding through be-ing. Heidegger characterizes the grounding of *Dasein* as en-grounding, where the prefix *en-* is intended to point to this enabling. The enabled being-historical thinking en-grounds *Dasein* by focusing on its basic structure, which in *Being and Time* is called thrown projecting-open. It is thus clear that without this prior achievement of *Being and Time,* the enabled being-historical thinking had nothing to en-ground. The enabled being-historical thinking en-grounds *Dasein* because this thinking finds lying before itself the basic structure of *Dasein* already worked out in *Being and Time.*

The second thing to bear in mind is that in *Contributions to Philosophy* Heidegger not only acknowledges the achievement of *Being and Time,* that is, the working out of the basic structure of *Dasein*—thrown projecting-open—he also points out that thanks to the "leap" this structure is transformed as soon as it reappears in being-historical thinking. In the following passage, which calls for a careful reading, Heidegger addresses this transformation through the "leap": "[The leap] is the enactment of projecting-open the truth of be-ing in the sense of shifting into the open, such that the thrower of the projecting-open experiences itself as thrown—i.e., as en-owned by be-ing" (*Contributions,* 169). By speaking of the enactment of "projecting-open" as "the leap," Heidegger leaves no doubt that what transpires here cannot be understood without the reappearing of the basic structure of *Dasein* in being-historical thinking. This structure reappears transformed because the passage from the transcendental-horizonal perspective to the being-historical perspective requires that "projecting-open" be enacted as "the leap." Only when this enactment occurs does the "projecting-opening" of the truth of be-ing take place in the sense of shifting into the open. And if we ask how we are to understand that "open" into which the "leap" shifts and projects open the truth of be-ing, Heidegger's response is that the "leap" leaps into "the essential swaying of be-ing itself. We call it *enowning*" (*Contributions*, 6). This is another way of saying that to accomplish the passage from transcendental-horizonal thinking to being-historical thinking requires enacting a projecting-open—enacting a "leap"—that leaps into the truth of be-ing and discloses this truth as the "open," which is none other than the swaying of be-ing itself, the so-called enowning.

But for projecting-open, for the "leap" to be enacted, two things must be open to each other: projecting-open must be open to the swaying of be-ing, the so-called enowning, and be-ing's swaying, that is, enowning must be open to this projecting. To understand precisely what Heidegger means with shifting into the open, we must bear in mind this mutual openness. And this excludes the possibility of conceiving this shift into the open—this projecting which is an acting *(Handeln)*—as initially *closed off* to the openness of the domain of the swaying of be-ing, namely, enowning, and *trapped in a closure*. What is phenomenologically observable is that this projecting shifts into the openness of be-ing's swaying (into enowning) because this projecting-open itself is open and receptive to this openness. In other words, projecting-open is an acting that from the ground up is open to receiving and disclosing the swaying of be-ing, that is, enowning. By receiving and opening this swaying, projecting-open opens the swaying of be-ing and keeps it open. If projecting-open were not fundamentally open to be-ing's swaying, it would amount to the intrusion of a closure into the domain of openness, that is, into the swaying of be-ing, or enowning. If this were the case, projecting-open would designate a juncture where closure to the swaying of be-ing and openness of this swaying would collide. Collision between closure and openness, however, is bereft of phenomenological relevance—it is sheer speculation. If this is the case, then we must reject as irrelevant and misleading the deconstructionist view that there is a closure in Heidegger's thought.

What I have said so far about projecting-open and truth of be-ing as enowning leads us to two directives. The first one, with which we are already familiar, tells us that to properly grasp projecting-open we must not lose sight of its fundamental openness to the swaying of be-ing, that is, to enowning. This directive leads us to the second one, with which we are not yet familiar; it tells us that to properly grasp a projecting that is fundamentally open to be-ing's swaying, we must not lose sight of what the enactment of this projecting reveals about the one who enacts it. One who enacts this projecting "experiences [himself] as thrown into, i.e., as en-owned by be-ing" (*Contributions*, 169). The second directive highlights the simultaneous transformation of projecting-open and thrownness. Projecting-open in the sense of opening up the swaying of be-ing (enowning) cannot be carried out unless the one who projects-open this swaying experiences himself as thrown into and en-owned by be-ing's swaying, by enowning.

Focusing on these two directives, we can now fully grasp the transformation of the basic structure of *Dasein*: Heidegger in *Contributions to Philosophy* sees thrownness no longer as thrownness into the facticity of disclosedness as in *Being and Time* but as thrownness into be-ing's enowning-throw. In the same vein, he sees projecting-open no longer as opening up the facticity of disclosedness but as opening up be-ing's enowning-throw. With this new understanding he realizes that be-ing's enowning-throw needs *Dasein*'s projecting-opening: be-ing's enowning-throw needs to be projected-open and kept open. And this in turn shows that projecting-open is an en-owned projecting.

In summary, we fully grasp *Dasein*'s transformed basic structure when we keep in mind that thrownness indicates thrownness into be-ing's enowning-throw, and projecting-open indicates the acting by which this throw is projected-open and disclosed. This transformed structure upholds and runs throughout the six "joinings," or regions, of *Contributions to Philosophy*. Keeping this transformed basic structure in mind, we now turn to the "joining" called "Playing-Forth" as the region in which early Greek thinking is at home.

II

Early Greek thinking shines forth in the "joining" called "Playing-Forth" without becoming thematic in it in a direct way. Five directives held within the five sentences that make up the opening section of "Playing-Forth" help us see how early Greek thinking is housed in this "joining." To address these directives, we must carefully read both the English translation and the German original of the passage with which Heidegger opens the second "joining" of *Contributions to Philosophy* because the English translation, rather than being a substitute for the German original, instead retains an ongoing reference to it. Given the brevity of the opening passage, this reading can be accomplished fairly quickly:

Coming to grips with the necessity of the *other* beginning from out of the originary positioning of the first beginning. The *guiding-attunement:* delight in alternately surpassing the beginnings in questioning. To this [belongs] everything involved in differentiating the guiding-question and the grounding-question; responding to the guiding-question and actually unfolding it; crossing to the grounding-question *(Being and Time).* All lectures on the "history" of philosophy [belong here]. The decision on every "ontology" [is made here]. (*Contributions*, 119)

Die Auseinandersetzung der Notwendigkeit des *anderen* Anfangs aus der ursprünglichen Setzung des ersten Anfangs. Die *Leitstimmung:* Die Lust der fragenden wechselweisen Übersteigung der Anfänge. Hierzu alles über die Unterscheidung von Leitfrage und Grundfrage; Leitfragenbeantwortung und eigentliche Leitfragenentfaltung; Übergang zur Grundfrage ("Sein und Zeit"). Alle Vorlesungen über "Geschichte" der Philosophie. Die Entscheidung über alle "Ontologie." (*GA* 65:169)

I shall address the five directives in the sequence in which they appear in this opening passage as I draw on its German original.

The first directive for determining the place of the pre-Socratics in "Playing-Forth" acquires the form of an imperative: it is imperative to come to grips with the necessity of the '*other* beginning' by originarily positioning the 'first beginning.' The two words in the German original, *Auseinandersetzung* and *Setzung*, translated here as "coming to grips with," and "positioning," respectively, must be interpreted in light of the necessity of the 'other beginning.' With *Auseinandersetzung* and *Setzung*, Heidegger is not suggesting that thinking should properly position the two beginnings and then initiate a debate between them in order to judge the outcome. Such a suggestion would indicate a mastery of thinking over the two beginnings, which thinking as Heidegger understands it never has. Rather, what he says with these words comes from the necessity that defines the relationship of the two beginnings. This means that the translation and interpretation of *Auseinandersetzung* and *Setzung* as "coming to grips with" and "positioning," respectively, originate from within this necessity. Seen in this light, neither the "coming to grips with" nor the "originary positioning" could be taken as expressing thinking's preference for one beginning over the other. What is decisive here is neither a preference nor a judgment but the necessity that defines the relationship between the two beginnings and calls for coming to grips with them by originarily positioning the 'first beginning.'

We derive the second directive from Heidegger's characterization of the attunement that guides thinking to these beginnings. This attunement is the ineluctable prerequisite for coming to grips with the necessity of the 'other beginning' through the positioning of the 'first beginning.' Since it is an attunement, this prerequisite has nothing to do with an argument. Nonargumentative in nature, this attunement highlights that necessity. Moreover, as an attunement, this prerequisite does not follow the argumentative pattern that in modern philosophy leads to a system. Rather, this attunement precedes thinking, guides and shapes it. Briefly, with the second directive Heidegger makes clear why the first directive has nothing to do with preferring one beginning to the other. Attunement shapes thinking by showing the direction thinking must take; it has to move away from the subjectivity of preference. Considering this attunement, we understand why the imperative to come to grips with the necessity of the 'other beginning' does not originate from within subjectivity. By calling this attunement delight, Heidegger intimates that the second directive does not understand delight in the sense of the pleasant subjective feeling we have when we take possession of something. Unlike such a feeling, delight takes hold of thinking when thinking alternately surpasses the 'first' and the 'other beginning' through questioning.

We encounter the third directive in a differentiation that is of fundamental importance for determining the place of the pre-Socratics in "Playing-Forth" of *Contributions to Philosophy.* This is the differentiation Heidegger makes between the guiding-question, what is a being? and the grounding-question, how does be-ing sway? Based on this differentiation, the third directive distinguishes two ways of dealing with the guiding-question: *responding* to this question, which Heidegger calls *Leitfragenbeantwortung,* and *unfolding* this question, which he calls *Leitfragenentfaltung.* Whereas from Plato to Nietzsche, Western philosophy *responds* to the guiding-question, what is a being?—τί τὸ ὄν? this philosophy does not *unfold* the guiding-question in the direction of the grounding-question by asking, how does be-ing sway? or what is the truth of be-ing's swaying? The distinction between responding to the guiding-question and unfolding this question in the direction of the grounding-question is of paramount importance for determining the place of the alethiological thinking of the pre-Socratics in "Playing-Forth."

The fourth directive comes to the fore when Heidegger notes that all his university lecture courses on the history of philosophy, which include courses on Leibniz, Kant, Hegel, Schelling, and Nietzsche, belong to the domain that opens up when the guiding question, what is a being? unfolds in the direction of the grounding-question, how does be-ing sway? that is, what is the truth of be-ing's swaying?

The fifth and final directive is closely tied to the preceding one. When the unfolding of the guiding-question opens a domain that belongs to the grounding-question—the domain of the truth of be-ing's swaying—then the decision on all ontologies is made. Here we should be aware that the translation of *Entscheidung* as "decision" does not clearly and explicitly reflect that the decision on every ontology is one setting the two beginnings apart. We understand this translation if we bear in mind the connection that the English word *decision* has to the Latin *decidere*, "setting apart." Besides, de-cision in the sense of setting apart reflects more clearly the meaning of the German component *scheiden* in *Entscheidung*. Keeping all this in mind, we can say that decision sets the two beginnings apart and places all ontologies under the necessity that defines the relationship between the two beginnings.

If we take a close look at these directives, we realize that they point to the transformed basic structure of *Dasein*, thrownness and projecting-open. The first directive points to this transformed basic structure by further illuminating the imperative of coming to grips with the necessity of the 'other beginning' from out of the originary positioning of the 'first beginning.' That imperative cannot be accomplished unless *Dasein* is thrown into this necessity. Thus thrown, the basic structure of *Dasein*, thrownness, no longer means thrownness into the facticity of disclosedness. In other words, the transcendental-horizonal determination of thrownness is no longer binding and operating. Now we have a thrownness that should be understood in terms of the necessity that comes from the 'other beginning'—is thrown forth by that beginning.

The first directive points to a transformed projecting-open because this projecting is enabled to open up what the 'other beginning' throws forth. To see more clearly what it is that the 'other beginning' throws forth and *Dasein* projects-open, we draw on the word *Anfang*, "beginning." This word announces the activity of *fangen*, "taking, seizing, holding." The *'other beginning,' der andere Anfang*, seizes *Dasein*. But, in contrast to the seizing that occurs in political and sociological realms, the seizing of the 'other beginning' does not use force. This seizing is reticent, and it comes to pass when the guiding-question is unfolded according to a hint that through the grounding-question intimates the truth of the swaying of be-ing. Given this sense of beginning, or *Anfang*, we can neither interpret nor translate *anfangen* as "making a start" (as suggested by the title of a recent publication, *To Start with Heidegger from the Start*). This interpretation and rendering of *Anfang* and of *anfangen* is misleading. Aside from the mechanical connotation of the word *start* as in "starting the engine," making a start—starting—conveys the impression that, in matters pertaining to the first and the 'other beginning,' thinking on its own can make a start and thus thinking is in charge. But thinking cannot make a start on its own because, as projecting-open, thinking's reference is to that which the 'other beginning' throws forth.

The second directive also points to the transformed basic structure of *Dasein*. No sooner does delight take hold of thinking than this guiding-attunement transforms the basic structure of *Dasein*. The guiding-attunement of delight guides both thrownness and projecting-opening such that, overwhelmed by delight, *Dasein* projects-open what it is thrown into, namely, the 'other beginning's' forth-throw. The guiding-attunement called delight attunes *Dasein* in such a way that it alternately surpasses the first and the 'other beginning' in questioning. Guided by this attunement, the imperative of coming to grips with the necessity of the 'other beginning' becomes accomplishable insofar as delight lets thinking alternately surpass the two beginnings in questioning. This means that coming to grips with this necessity is light and bright, devoid of brooding. Delight guides thinking to the truth of the swaying of be-ing, whose hint hints further at the 'first beginning' as this beginning plays forth unto the 'other beginning,' and as the 'other beginning' plays forth into the 'first beginning.'

The third directive too points to the transformed basic structure of *Dasein*. To unfold the guiding-question, what is a being? in the direction of the grounding-question, how does be-ing sway? that is, what is the truth of be-ing's swaying? requires enacting a projecting-opening that discloses the guiding-question in the direction of the grounding-question. To unfold the guiding-question in the direction of the grounding-question presupposes thrownness into these questions. In short, to open up the guiding-question in the direction of the grounding-question presupposes a transformed thrown projecting-open. With the enactment of this transformed thrown projecting-open, the place of the alethiological thinking of the early Greeks also emerges.

To bring into sharper focus the place of the alethiological thinking of the pre-Socratics, we should keep in mind that it comes to the fore via a thrown projecting-open that is no longer the same as the thrown projecting that belongs to the transcendental-horizonal perspective. The transformed thrown projecting-open, discloses—unconceals—what be-ing throws forth as the 'other beginning.' It enacts this disclosure, this unconcealment, because projecting is not a closure that collides with the openness—with what be-ing throws forth as the 'other beginning.' It is a projecting-open that is always already open to and thus is en-owned by unconcealment, by ἀλήθεια. The enactment of this en-owned projecting brings into view the place of the alethiological thinking of the pre-Socratics.

By enacting this projecting-opening, Heidegger realizes that at the end of the 'first beginning' there is a subtle connection, through ἀλήθεια, between the guiding-question, what is a being? and the grounding-question, how does be-ing sway? that is, a connection between the unconcealed, τὸ ἀληθές, and unconcealment, ἀλήθεια. He explicitly places this interconnection in the foreground when he notes that "Plato and Aristotle . . . always name ἀλήθεια when they name a being: ἀλήθεια καὶ ὄν, the unconcealment, i.e., a being in its beingness" (*GA* 45:121–22).[32] If the primary outcome of this projecting is the real-ization that there is a subtle interconnection between an unconcealed being, τὸ ἀληθές, and unconcealment, ἀλήθεια, then this projecting places in the foreground the unconcealment, ἀλήθεια, as well as the un-concealing of a being, ἀλήθεια καὶ ὄν. In that case the opening distin-guishing the alethiological beginning occurs concomitantly with the opening housing the question, what is a being—τί τὸ ὄν to which at the end of the 'first beginning' Plato and Aristotle refer when they say ἀλήθεια καὶ ὄν—when they speak of the unconcealing of a being. Thus although at the end of the 'first beginning' the guiding-question, what is a being—τί τὸ ὄν is to be carefully differentiated from the grounding-question, how does be-ing sway? that is, from, what is the truth of be-ing's swaying? the guiding- and the grounding-question are related to each other through unconcealment, or ἀλήθεια. While the guiding-question guides thinking to a being, that is, to ὄν, the grounding-question grounds the unconcealing of a being in unconcealment, in ἀλήθεια. This differentiation is important because it sheds light on

Heidegger's fundamental position according to which in the thinking of the pre-Socratics *unconcealment*, ἀλήθεια, *is named but it is not thought*, that is, not projected-open. Thus the alethiological beginning is thoroughly ambiguous.

This ambiguity is that of the guiding- and of the grounding-question. The delight in alternately surpassing the first and the 'other beginning' in questioning not only guides thinking to the generative power hidden in these questions but also to the hint that comes from within this ambiguity and hints at the place the pre-Socratics occupy in the 'other beginning.' In the 'other beginning' a place is assigned to the alethiological thinking of the pre-Socratics insofar as this thinking names the ἀλήθεια (unconcealment) but does not project it open. Thus the alethiological thinking of the pre-Socratics is not identical with the ὄν-oriented thinking of Plato and Aristotle. The alethiological thinking of the pre-Socratics neither *is a response to the guiding-question* nor *does it unfold this question* in the direction of the grounding-question; it is neither *Leitfragenbeantwortung* nor *Leitfragenentfaltung*. This thinking merely names ἀλήθεια.

The fourth directive also points to the transformed basic structure of *Dasein*. For with the emergence of the differentiation between the guiding- and the grounding-question, a projecting-opening occurs that discloses the overwhelming force that for the past two and a half millennia has brought forth a series of responses to the guiding-question. The process of responding to the guiding-question steadfastly hinders its unfolding in the direction of the grounding-question. The fourth directive focuses on the magnitude of these responses by indicating that only the transformed thrown projecting-open can unfold these responses because this thrown projecting is an en-owned thrown projecting. This unfolding happens in all the lecture courses that Heidegger devotes to the history of Western philosophy. In them he focuses on specific responses to the guiding-question and unfolds them to allow what is ownmost to metaphysics come to the fore. He presents an account, unparalleled in its clarity, of these responses and unfolds them in the direction of the grounding-question, of which metaphysics has no inkling. With the fourth directive he shows that only through a transformed thrown projecting-open can these responses be unfolded in the direction of the grounding-question.

The fifth directive again points to the transformed basic structure of *Dasein*. To unfold the guiding-question, what is a being? in the direction of the grounding-question, how does be-ing sway? that is, what is the truth of be-ing's swaying? requires enactment of a projecting-opening as a decision. This decision should not be confused with making a choice since it means a setting apart through which the unfolding of the grounding-question is distinguished from what happens in all ontologies, that is, from the historical responses to the guiding-question. The focus of this decision is a thinking that is not trapped within the 'first beginning' and within this beginning's exclusive concern with the guiding-question.

Thus, when we carefully examine these five directives, we realize that each points to the transformed thrown projecting-open. *Dasein,* understood as transformed thrown projecting-open, discloses the hint that comes from the guiding-question and calls for an originary positioning of the 'first beginning.' In short, we realize that a transformed thrown projecting-open is required for coming to terms with the necessity of the 'other beginning' through an originary positioning of the 'first beginning.'

How does the alethiological thinking of the pre-Socratics relate to this thrown projecting-open? Since the alethiological thinking of the pre-Socratics neither *is a response to the guiding-question* nor *does it unfold the grounding-question,* but merely names the ἀλήθεια, we have to say that this thinking is moving toward the 'other beginning' by crossing the domain of the 'first beginning' toward the domain of the 'other beginning.' But how are we to conceive of this crossing when in fact Heidegger puts forth the originary positioning of the 'first beginning'— which seems to exclude a crossing—as the prerequisite for coming to grips with the necessity of the 'other beginning'? How are the pre-Socratics related to this positioning? Since in section 85 of "Playing-Forth" Heidegger explicitly indicates what he means with this originary positioning, we shall take a close look at this section.

First, let us examine the title of this section, "The Originary Coming-into-Its-Own of the First Beginning Means Gaining a Foothold in the Other Beginning." This title, like all the titles of the 281 sections of *Contributions to Philosophy,* is an integral part of the text itself rather than a heading to be discussed and elucidated in the text that follows. This title implicates the originary positioning of the 'first beginning,' the guiding-question, the grounding-question, the hint from the former to the latter, and the crossing from the one to the 'other beginning.' To grasp this clearly, we shall focus on the original title of section 85, that is, "Die ursprüngliche Zueignung des ersten Anfangs bedeutet das Fußfassen im anderen Anfang," and note that we rendered *Zueignung* as "coming-into-its-own," because the component *Eignung* in this word tells us that it is a member of the family of words in *Contributions to Philosophy* concerning owning. (Indeed, it was with a view toward "owning" that in the first version of this essay I rendered *Zueignung* as "enowning" and thus introduced this word for the first time.) The rendition "coming-into-its-own" facilitates understanding that the originary positioning of the 'first beginning' is not something that thinking accomplishes on its own. This positioning is not an absolute achievement of thinking. What Heidegger says with this title is that only when the 'first beginning' comes into its own and is thus originarily positioned, only then can thinking come to grips with the necessity of the 'other beginning.'

Seen in this light, *Zueignung* in the title of section 85 does not retain its familiar meanings such as "dedication" or "appropriation." Translating *Zueignung* as "appropriation" would be misleading by suggesting that the originary positioning of the 'first beginning' amounts to its being appropriated by thinking. This suggestion does not recognize the significant difference between appropriating the 'first beginning' and letting this beginning come into its own. Rendering *Zueignung* as "appropriation" ignores the fact that the originary positioning of the 'first beginning' cannot be credited solely to thinking. Thinking and its appropriating performance on their own cannot bring about the originary positioning of the 'first beginning.' Because thinking understood as projecting-open is at the service of the 'first beginning'—at the service of its originary positioning—we cannot assume that thinking is the master of this beginning. Not mastering this beginning, thinking cannot be expected to appropriate it. Thus with the title of section 85 Heidegger does not express a concern with appropriating the 'first beginning,' since in his purview what counts is to let the 'first beginning' come into its own.

Having examined the rendering of the title of section 85, let us now read the first paragraph of this section of "Playing-Forth" in order to grasp what Heidegger means when he regards the originary positioning of the 'first beginning' to be the prerequisite for coming to grips with the necessity of the 'other beginning.' The first paragraph reads: "The first beginning's coming originarily into its own (and that means into its history) means gaining a foothold in the other beginning. This is accomplished in crossing from the *guiding-question* (what is a being? the question of beingness, being) to the *grounding-question:* What is the truth of being? (Being and be-ing is the same and yet fundamentally different)" (*Contributions,* 120). If we place the text of section 81 of "Playing-Forth" next to the text of the first paragraph of section 85 and read these two texts together, we notice that in both sections, *Contributions to Philosophy* is engaged in what this work calls *Leitfragenentfaltung,* that is, the unfolding of the guiding-question.

Not to be mistaken for a critical debate with and an assessment of the traditional responses to the guiding-question, the unfolding of this question sheds invaluable light on the grounding-question. This unfolding shows that the question of the truth of the swaying of be-ing is covered over by the tradition of metaphysics in the continuity of its responses to the guiding-question. Moreover, the unfolding of the guiding-question proves to be simultaneously the unfolding of ἀλήθεια (unconcealment) in ἀλήθεια καὶ ὄν (unconcealment of a being), which directly draws on the alethiological thinking of the pre-Socratics. Thus in the ὄν-oriented thinking of the later Greeks (Plato and Aristotle)—in ἀλήθεια καὶ ὄν—ἀλήθεια reverberates, and this reverberation points directly to the alethiological thinking of the pre-Socratics. In other words, the unfolding of the guiding-question demonstrates that the unconcealing taking place in the 'first beginning' (the unconcealing of beings of which ἀλήθεια καὶ ὄν speaks) plays forth into the unconcealment (ἀλήθεια) taking place in the 'other beginning.' This playing-forth holds the key for determining the place of the alethiological thinking of the pre-Socratics in *Contributions to Philosophy.* To bring this playing-forth into a sharper focus, we must say that it is sustained by that hint that hints at the 'other beginning' and guides the crossing to this beginning as a beginning toward which the guiding-question is already underway.

The phrase "coming to grips with" in the text of section 81 of "Playing-Forth" and the compound "coming-into-its-own" in the text of section 85 harbor within themselves the crossing from the guiding-question to the grounding-question. This crossing depends entirely on the unfolding of the guiding-question in accord with the hint that hints at the 'other beginning' and is *the* guide to this beginning. Accordingly, the alethiological thinking of the pre-Socratics has its place in this crossing, that is, in the way the question, what is a being in its being—τί τὸ ὄν? plays forth into the grounding-question, how does be-ing sway? that is, what is the truth of be-ing's swaying? For this reason the alethiological thinking of the pre-Socratics should be viewed as an integral part of the 'other beginning.' And that is why the programmatic outline of Heidegger's lecture courses on Leibniz, Kant, Schelling,

Hegel, and Nietzsche in section 88 of *Contributions to Philosophy* does not include the pre-Socratics. Heidegger in this section does not mention the early Greeks Anaximander, Parmenides, and Heraclitus by name when he indicates the focal points of his future lecture courses on the history of philosophy because the mere thematization of what is entailed in the unfolding of the guiding-question suffices to show the place the pre-Socratics occupy in *Contributions to Philosophy*. There is no need to explicitly mention the pre-Socratics because, insofar as the guiding-question of the 'first beginning' plays forth into the grounding-question of the 'other beginning,' the alethiological thinking of the pre-Socratics takes its place in the interplay of the first and the 'other beginning.'

We must bear in mind that although in "Playing-Forth" Heidegger does not mention the early Greeks by name, after *Contributions to Philosophy* he devotes a considerable number of his university lecture courses and a few treatises to the thoughts of the early Greeks. He thus brings to full fruition something that occupies a significant place in the unfolding of the being-historical thinking of *Contributions to Philosophy*.

III

I would like to conclude this essay with a brief remark on the word *place*, which appears in its title, and offer some reflections on the language used in this discussion. I do so to acknowledge this essay's aims and limits.

Place as it appears in the title of this essay does not have the same meaning as in the parlance of historians of philosophy. In speaking of the "place" of a philosopher, historians of philosophy use this word to indicate the point at which certain philosophical interests and certain philosophical commonalities converge and justify the inclusion of certain philosophers in certain periods. In consideration of such interests and commonalities, historians of philosophy determine, for example, the "place" of Malebranche and Berkeley in the period of modern philosophy and allocate Augustine and Aquinas to the medieval or scholastic period. For historians of philosophy understand the word *place* as the sum total of the conditions set by historians *themselves* that historical figures must meet to qualify for inclusion in certain periods of the history of philosophy. This understanding of the word *place* remains decisive even in those cases in which historians do not agree to which historical period a certain historical figure belongs. A case in point is

Nicholas of Cusa. Historians of philosophy still cannot completely agree whether the bishop of Cusa has his "place" at the end of the medieval period or at the beginning of modern philosophy.

The word *place* in the title of this essay has nothing to do with the periodization common to histories of philosophy, and it does not refer to the conditions that certain philosophers must meet to qualify for inclusion in a period. *Place* simply stands for a juncture in the third part of *Contributions to Philosophy*, "Playing-Forth," in which the alethiological thinking of the pre-Socratics coalesces with the being-historical thinking of this work. By showing how this coalescing puts the alethiological thinking of the pre-Socratics in the crossing toward the 'other beginning,' I allude to the dynamism characteristic of the entirety of "Playing-Forth." Thus the sense in which the word *place* appears in the title of this essay is associated with movement, occurrence, and dynamism and not with that understanding of *place* which historians of philosophy derive deductively by attending to the interests of certain historical figures and to what they may share in common. In other words, in the title of this essay, *place* loses the static meaning it has in the historian's account of the periods of the history of philosophy. As used here it reflects the dynamism peculiar to the showing and manifesting central to hermeneutic phenomenology.

Because the language of this essay deliberately stays close to Heidegger's own language, it may be open to two objections: First, since this essay works with Heidegger's language and in a way repeats this language, it fails to explain what Heidegger says. After all, repeating Heidegger does not achieve anything. Second, by staying close to Heidegger's language, this essay ignores the complexity of reading texts, which always amounts to "reinscribing" them.

But what does staying close to Heidegger's own language mean? It means holding onto an ontological language that ipso facto cannot be replaced by an ontologically neutral language, even if such a language existed. It is my contention that an ontologically neutral language is a chimera, since each and every shaping of language is ontological even when a language is fabricated for the explicit purpose of combating a given ontology.

If Heidegger in *Contributions to Philosophy* brings to language a radically unprecedented thinking of being, then it is naive to assume that an ontologically neutral language stands ready to function as a vehicle for "explaining" this new thinking. The insight into the ontological nature of language, into the relatedness of being and language suggests that there is no such thing as an extant and ontologically neutral language.

Thus an essay such as this one takes seriously the insight into the basically ontological nature of language, a nature operating even in a language with which one wants to "reinscribe" an ontological text on the assumption that one has at one's disposal a language that is free of ontology.

The objection that this essay merely repeats what Heidegger has said does not address what this essay wishes to accomplish. This objection comes from the assumption that beside Heidegger's own language there is an ontologically neutral language that stands ready for explicating Heidegger without repeating him. This assumption ignores this essay's purpose, namely, to look closely at the hidden "features" of Heidegger's thinking of being that call for returning to the forgotten resources of the English language.

As the German language bends and twists to adjust itself to Heidegger's new thinking of being, which gives rise to *Contributions to Philosophy*, so does English in translating this work. English too digs into the treasury of its forgotten words to adjust itself to Heidegger's language. In thinking being, Heidegger took more than two decades to recognize that the fundamental ontology of the transcendental-horizonal perspective must be abandoned and that this perspective is the precursor of the new thinking of being, which originates from within the immanent transformation occurring within the matter that he calls being or be-ing. His thinking requires—needs—a novel language and brings this language to the fore. The epigram to this essay alludes to this requirement. Perhaps better than anyone else, Hölderlin recognized this need and was aware of how strained language may become when it stands at the service of a new thinking of being:

> Nun, nun müssen dafür Worte, wie Blumen, entstehen.

> [Now! Now words must come forth for that like flowers.]

"De-cision" in
Contributions to Philosophy and
the Path to the Interpretation
of Heraclitus Fragment 16

So ist bisweilen das Nichtvollzogene mächtiger und bleibender als
das Gesagte und Verwirklichte.

Heidegger

It is widely known that Heidegger's interpretation of Fragment 16 of
Heraclitus is a small but significant part of a large body of work that he
devoted to the legacy of this philosopher, and that this body of work is
part of Heidegger's extraordinarily large output on the Greeks. Given
the available evidence, we can say that Heidegger's work on the Greeks
has definite and identifiable beginnings that culminate in his *Plato's
Sophist* of 1924–25 and definite endings that come together in the talk he
delivered in Athens in 1976 under the title "Die Herkunft der Kunst
und die Bestimmung des Denkens" (The Provenance of Art and the
Destiny of Thinking). However, what is perhaps not so widely known
is that the being-historical or enowning-historical thinking of *Contributions to Philosophy* casts an invaluable light on Heidegger's entire works
on the early Greeks and thus calls for renewed efforts for hermeneutically coming to terms with these works. In what follows I return to
Heidegger's interpretation of Fragment 16 for the explicit purpose of
reexamining this interpretation in light of Heidegger's discussion of
"de-cision" in "Preview" of his *Contributions to Philosophy*.

Before Heidegger's *Beiträge zur Philosophie* became available in
1989, the main source for interpreting his work on Fragment 16 was
the lecture course text of 1943–44 published as volume 55 of the *Gesamtausgabe* in 1979. Indeed, it was by delving into this lecture course
text that I attempted for the first time to come to terms with

Heidegger's interpretation of Heraclitus Fragment 16.[33] But with the publication of *Contributions to Philosophy* and the light that this work casts on the Heideggerian corpus in general and his extraordinarily large output on the early Greeks in particular, the situation changed drastically. I shall return to Heidegger's interpretation of Fragment 16 to demonstrate that what he says about this fragment in his lecture course text of 1943–44 is grounded in what he addresses in "Preview" of *Contributions to Philosophy* as de-cision *(Ent-scheidung)*. Strictly speaking, with de-cision Heidegger puts in the forefront the hermeneutic precondition for understanding his interpretation of Heraclitus Fragment 16. With an eye toward the exposition of de-cision in "Preview," I will shed new light on Heidegger's interpretation of this fragment.

In this connection three things should be kept in mind. First, according to Heidegger, the Heraclitean fragment, which in the Diels and Kranz edition bears number 16, should bear number 1. Second, although this fragment does not explicitly mention ἀλήθεια, it nevertheless is about ἀλήθεια and nothing else. Third, although Heidegger's interpretation of this fragment in the lecture course text of 1943–44 actually entails the third part of *Contributions to Philosophy,* this interpretation presupposes what Heidegger elucidates in sections 43, 44, 45, and 46 of "Preview" under the title "Decision." In the course of discussing Heidegger's interpretation of Fragment 16 and thus attending to the third point, I shall address the first two points by paying close attention to what he lays out as de-cision in "Preview" and by examining the place this interpretation occupies in "Playing-Forth" of *Contributions to Philosophy.*

But how are we to understand my contention that Heidegger's interpretation of Fragment 16 in his lecture course text of 1943–44 is grounded in "de-cision" and has its place in "Playing-Forth"? Is the word *grounded* to be understood in the sense that all of Heidegger's works on Heraclitus, and not only his interpretation of Fragment 16, are grounded in de-cision as discussed in "Preview"? Does *Contributions to Philosophy* lay the ground for Heidegger's subsequent works on the early Greeks? How are we to understand the grounding character of this work, especially the grounding that emerges in the discussion of de-cision in "Preview"? To respond let us turn to what F.-W. von Herrmann says about the manner in which *Contributions to Philosophy* relates to all of Heidegger's subsequent works and not only to those he devoted to the early Greeks.

According to von Herrmann:

Since the appearance of *Beiträge zur Philosophie* as volume 65 of the *Gesamtausgabe*, anyone who wishes to achieve a hermeneutically adequate understanding of Heidegger's thought must become adept in the perspective and inquiring trajectory of the thinking of enowning. Familiarizing ourselves with this perspective and with this inquiring trajectory as they take shape for the first time in *Contributions to Philosophy,* we obtain from this work a reliable orientation for hermeneutically dealing with Heidegger's writings dating from 1930 onward. An acquaintance with *Contributions to Philosophy* makes us realize the necessity of reading anew Heidegger's writings that appeared prior to the publication of this work.[34]

Here von Herrmann carefully highlights the manner in which *Contributions to Philosophy* relates to Heidegger's works that appeared before 1989. He emphasizes the need for a thorough familiarity with the perspective and inquiring trajectory of the thinking of enowning, since this thinking is *the* reliable guide to a hermeneutically responsible approach to Heidegger's works published prior to 1989. Most importantly, with his characterization of the relation between *Contributions to Philosophy* and the works that appeared before 1989 and with the stress he places on the perspective and inquiring trajectory of the thinking of enowning, von Herrmann alludes to the grounding character of this work.

When I suggest that Heidegger's interpretation of Fragment 16 as laid out in his lecture course text of 1943–44 is grounded in de-cision, I take the word *grounding* in the context of a thorough familiarity with the perspective and inquiring trajectory of the thinking of enowning, not in the sense in which one might use this word in the context of discussing, for instance, the relationship between Hegel's *Phenomenology of Spirit* and his entire system. In my usage the word *grounding* is informed by the perspective and inquiring trajectory of the thinking of enowning, and is thus differentiated from a grounding that supplies a foundation to a system of thought à la Hegel. By using the word *grounding* I am not suggesting that with *Contributions to Philosophy* Heidegger assimilates the entire history of philosophy, including the fragmented writings of the early Greeks, in the same way that Hegel assimilates the entire history of thought in his system of absolute spirit. Here von Herrmann's characterization of the relation between *Contributions to Philosophy* and the work that appeared up to 1989 plays a significant role because with this characterization, von Herrmann attests that Heidegger's thinking is bound to its path. In drawing attention to the path that Heidegger opens with *Contributions to Philosophy*—which articulates the so-called de-cision—von Herrmann indicates that only a thorough familiarity with the perspective and the inquiring trajectory of the thinking of enowning can shed light on all his work. Here the word *grounding* as used in connection with Heidegger's interpretation of Fragment 16 receives its proper meaning. This interpretation is grounded in decision because, as presented in "Preview" of *Contributions to Philosophy,* de-cision opens a path that runs through the perspective and inquiring trajectory of the thinking of enowning.

Having elucidated the sense in which we can say that Heidegger's interpretation of Fragment 16 is grounded in de-cision, let us now take up the details of this interpretation.

I

The preceding elucidations make it clear that my rereading of Heidegger's interpretation of Heraclitus Fragment 16 is prompted by the realization that *Contributions to Philosophy* in general and discussion of de-cision in "Preview" in particular ground his interpretation of this fragment. After reading *Contributions to Philosophy,* we must reread his interpretation of Fragment 16 in the 1943–44 lecture course text, because a hermeneutically responsible account of this interpretation, which also extends to Fragments 123 and 54, presupposes a thoroughgoing familiarity with de-cision.

To explain why Heidegger can say that this fragment should be the first in the numerical order of Heraclitean fragments, and that it is about ἀλήθεια and nothing else, I shall address his interpretation of Fragment 16 in ten points. The first point concerns the wording of this fragment, which to Heidegger suggests a question in which Heraclitus asks: τὸ μὴ δῦνόν ποτε πῶς ἄν τις λάθοι?—how can anyone remain concealed before that which never sets?[35]

The second point of this interpretation concerns Heidegger's analysis of τὸ δῦνόν. He takes these words not only to mean that which sets (goes under) but also setting itself, or going under *(das Untergehen).* Thus he paves the way for substantiating his proposed ranking of this fragment.

The third point of this interpretation concerns "setting," regarding which Heidegger says: "When we think of setting as the Greeks do, we realize that setting receives what is its ownmost from out of an *entering into a sheltering-concealing (Eingehen in eine Verbergung)*" (*GA* 55:49). By italicizing the words *entering into a sheltering-concealing,* he stresses, first, that sheltering-concealing is a focal point of his interpretation and, second, that for the Greek way of thinking setting, τὸ δῦνόν, means entering into sheltering-concealing.

The importance of the fourth point of the interpretation surpasses that of the preceding ones. Reflecting on "μὴ—ποτε" in "τὸ μὴ δῦνόν ποτε," and considering the fact that δῦνόν is placed between μὴ and ποτε, Heidegger concludes that "this simple dividing way of naming δῦνόν renders explicit the verbal meaning of this word and manifests its eventlike foundational character" (*GA* 55:86). Interpreting this verbal meaning as "never setting," Heidegger then suggests that μὴ δῦνόν ποτε, the "never setting," should be taken in the sense of "always rising," and "always rising" should be taken as referring to φύσις: "Always rising in Greek means τὸ ἀεὶ φύον. But instead of τὸ φύον, there could be ἡ φύσις, which literally means rising in the sense of emerging from out of what is closed off, concealed, and enfolded" (*GA* 55:87). On the basis of this explication of τὸ ἀεὶ φύον and φύσις, Heidegger characterizes φύσις as the basic word in the thinking of inceptual early Greek philosophers.

The fifth point of interpretation consists in the connection that Heidegger establishes between "always rising" as φύσις and being and clearing *(Lichtung)*. He notes that φύσις as "always rising" is not an attribute of being. Rather, as always rising φύσις alludes to being and clearing.

The sixth point is the heart of the interpretation. Heidegger's focus on the opposition between "rising" and "setting" represents the crux of his interpretation of Fragment 16. He notes that with this fragment Heraclitus makes a crucial statement on being's sheltering-concealing and unconcealing. He arrives at this statement in his interpretation of Fragment 16 by drawing on and interpreting not only Fragments 8, 30, 32, 35, and 51, but also Fragments 123 (φύσις κρύπτεσθαι φιλεῖ, "rising bestows favor on concealing") and 54 (ἁρμονίη ἀφανὴς φανερῆς κρείττων, "the nonappearing accord is nobler than the accord that comes to appearance"). (See *GA* 55:85–88 and 141–54.)

Heidegger draws on Fragments 123 and 54 because, in his view, it is here that Heraclitus addresses and elucidates "rising" (unconcealing) and "setting" (sheltering-concealing). To demonstrate that this is the case, Heidegger renders φιλεῖ in Fragment 123 as "favor" *(Gunst)*, not as "love," allowing him to capture Heraclitus's elucidation of "rising" (unconcealing) and "setting" (sheltering-concealing) in terms of a friendship between "rising" (unconcealing) and "setting" (sheltering-concealing). This friendship bestows on "rising" and "sheltering-concealing" what is their ownmost, something he elucidates when he says: "The friendship, φιλία, is thus a favor that grants the other what is its ownmost in such a way that with this granting the granted ownmost blossoms unto its own freedom" (*GA* 55:128). It should be noted that here the word *other* refers once to "rising" (unconcealing) and then to "setting" (sheltering-concealing). However, by interpreting the relation between "rising" and "sheltering-concealing" in terms of friendship, φιλία, Heidegger sets the stage for his extended interpretation of this relationship.

I address the seventh point of Heidegger's interpretation of Fragment 16 when I take up the next stage of his interpretation of the relationship between "rising" (unconcealing) and "setting" (sheltering-concealing). In this connection he offers a more detailed interpretation of this relationship when he turns to ἁρμονία in Fragment 54 to demonstrate that by using the word ἁρμονία Heraclitus shows that the relationship between "rising" (unconcealing) and "setting" (sheltering-concealing) preserves what is distinctive to both "rising" and "setting," without bringing the two to a stalemate. The word ἁρμονία, which in the traditional translations of this fragment, appears as "harmony" and thus maintains a connection to sound and music, Heidegger translates as "accord" *(Fügung)*. He thus indicates that the expressive power of this word goes beyond the realm of sound and music: "What is foundational to ἁρμονία is not the realm of ringing and sound but ἁρμός, the joining *(Fuge)*, i.e., that which fits one thing into another, whereby both join in the jointure so that there is accord" (*GA* 55:141). Moreover, when he turns to Fragment 54, Heidegger does not translate ἁρμονίη ἀφανὴς as "invisible harmony," as is done traditionally, but as "nonappearing [*unscheinbar*] accord." He rejects the rendering "invisible harmony" because it misconstrues the accord by subjecting it to the distinction between visibility and invisibility. It is here that one of Heidegger's acute distinctions comes to the fore. He abandons the perspective of visibility-invisibility altogether on the ground that accord should be taken as meaning nonappearing *(unscheinbar)* and not invisible *(unsichtbar)* (see *GA* 55:143). Thus he makes clear that what is at stake in this fragment is the nonappearing, not the invisible.

I disclose the eighth point of Heidegger's interpretation of Fragment 16 in connection with its next decisive stage. The account of the relationship between "rising" (unconcealing) and "setting" (sheltering-concealing) in terms of the accord between the two sets the stage for addressing their "face to face." An opposition between "rising" (unconcealing) and "setting" (sheltering-concealing) announces itself as soon as these two face each other. Heidegger describes what transpires in this "face to face" by saying:

As it rises, rising takes unto itself self-sheltering concealing, because rising can rise as rising only from out of a self-sheltering concealing, that is, rising fastens itself unto self-sheltering concealing. Insofar as rising and self-sheltering concealing grant themselves the favor of what is their ownmost, self-sheltering concealing accords with rising—an accord that at the same time accords rising unto self-sheltering concealing. Rising is the same [*das Selbe*] as self-sheltering concealing, i.e., as setting. (*GA* 55:153)

"Rising" rises by taking unto itself the self-sheltering concealing—by fastening itself unto self-sheltering concealing. And this happens because each grants itself what is its ownmost and thus accords with the other. When "rising" accords with self-sheltering concealing ("setting") and when self-sheltering concealing accords with "rising," they become the same *(das Selbe)*. But same does not mean identical *(das Gleiche)!* Thus the accord between "rising" and self-sheltering concealing (between "rising," and "setting") continues to be an accord in the *sameness,* but not the *identity,* of "rising" and self-sheltering concealing.

I disclose the ninth point of Heidegger's interpretation of Fragment 16 in the conclusion he draws from reading Fragments 123 and 54. This reading complements his interpretation of Fragment 16 that I have already discussed. Succinctly stated, the combined interpretation of Fragments 16, 123, and 54 results in understanding the "face to face" of "rising" (unconcealing) and "setting" (sheltering-concealing) as a "face to face" in which each retains its ownmost by becoming the "same" as the other.

The tenth point of Heidegger's interpretation of Fragment 16 concerns the preeminence *(Vorrang)* of "rising" (unconcealing) over against "setting" (sheltering-concealing).[36] According to Heidegger, Heraclitus has this preeminence in mind when, in contrast to what he says in Fragment 16, in Fragment 123 he speaks of φύσις instead of τὸ δῦνόν. He does not speak in Fragment 123 of "setting" (concealing), τὸ δῦνόν, because he has in mind φύσις, the "rising" that lights all beings. Heidegger makes this point explicit by asking: "Why does he not say τὸ δῦνόν, since self-sheltering concealing, which is ownmost to φύσις, has the same foundational right as rising?" (*GA* 55:154). This is a significant question to which Heidegger responds by alluding to two metaphysical possibilities. Thereafter he goes beyond metaphysics and addresses the relation between φύσις and ἀλήθεια.

To be prepared to understand these two metaphysical possibilities, let us note initially that the question as to why in Fragment 123 Heraclitus speaks of φύσις rather than τὸ δῦνόν is not a question of choice of words. By speaking in this fragment of φύσις instead of τὸ δῦνόν, Heraclitus underscores that what distinguishes φύσις is the preeminence of "rising." But how are we to conceive this preeminence? It is here that we must deal with the two metaphysical possibilities.

We encounter the first when we interpret Fragment 123 as an indicator of Heraclitus's concern with beings and suggest that in this fragment he opts for the word φύσις rather than τὸ δῦνόν because his thinking is oriented to beings as they appear in the clearing that "rising" opens up. Since through "rising" beings light up and are unconcealed, "rising" can claim a preeminence over against beings, whence the stress that Heraclitus places on this preeminence in speaking of φύσις instead of τὸ δῦνόν. However, this metaphysical interpretation cannot be sustained. If Heraclitus were to account for the preeminence of "rising" by focusing on beings, he would be comparing and contrasting "rising" with beings. If he were to compare "rising" with beings, then he would not address the preeminence of "rising" within φύσις in its own right. A thinking given to comparing "rising" with beings equalizes "rising" and beings, refers "rising" to beings and beings to "rising"; this thinking submits to what comparison essentially is, namely, an equalizing: "All comparison, however, is essentially an equalizing, a referral back to a same that as such never even enters knowing awareness but rather makes up what is self-evident in terms of which all explanation and relating receives its clarity" (*Contributions*, 105). To suggest that Heraclitus accounts for the preeminence of "rising" in φύσις by comparing "rising" with beings amounts to saying that he loses sight of "rising" altogether—that he equalizes "rising" with beings and refers "rising" back to beings. In the end this way of understanding Fragment 123 essentially accuses Heraclitus of being concerned only with that which rises and is unconcealed, that is, with a being. But this way of understanding is a misunderstanding because Heraclitus is not concerned with beings; he inquires into "rising" itself. For this reason Heidegger calls the first possibility a metaphysical possibility for dealing with the question concerning the preeminence of "rising" in φύσις.

The second metaphysical possibility for explicating the preeminence of "rising" in φύσις lies in the assumption that "rising" is the same as the pure unconcealing of being that might occur independently of beings. Could we not explicate the preeminence of "rising" in φύσις by appealing to the pure unconcealing of being itself? Heidegger clearly hints at this appeal when he asks: "[C]ould being not hold sway in such a way that there may be the possibility for deciding whether there is a being or not?" (*GA* 55:159). But to explicate the preeminence of "rising" in φύσις by appealing to the pure unconcealing of being itself, that is, by appealing to being's sway regardless of beings, is to forget that rising-unconcealing and sheltering-concealing favor each other, are in accord with each other, and do not occur independently from each other. This possibility for explicating the preeminence of "rising" in φύσις is also a metaphysical possibility, since metaphysics always strives for the sheer unproblematic unconcealing and swaying of being itself.

The preceding analysis and assessment of the two metaphysical possibilities addressed by Heidegger prompts the conclusion that the preeminence of "rising" in φύσις can be explicated neither in view of beings nor in terms of the sheer unproblematic unconcealing swaying of being itself. This preeminence must be explicated nonmetaphysically.

By alluding to the possibility of a nonmetaphysical explication of the preeminence of "rising" in φύσις, the tenth and final point of interpretation of Fragment 16 reaches its apex. How does Heidegger now present his nonmetaphysical explication of the preeminence of rising-unconcealing that distinguishes φύσις?

He begins by addressing a comportment that belongs to those who vis-à-vis φύσις remain fundamentally open, that is, unconcealed. He says: "Only those who do not remain concealed vis-à-vis φύσις do exist [*sind seiend*] in such a way that in their being they correspond to rising" (*GA* 55:173). He further illuminates this comportment by noting that "[t]he comportment corresponding to φύσις must have the basic trait of rising, of self-opening, of not-self-closing, and of not-self-concealing. Not to conceal oneself is to unconceal oneself; is to hold oneself in unconcealing and in sheltering-unconcealment—to express this notion in Greek, it is to hold oneself in ἀλήθεια" (*GA* 55:173). In this passage we have the textual basis for grasping Heidegger's nonmetaphysical explication of the preeminence of rising-unconcealing in φύσις. Central to this explication is a comportment toward φύσις corresponding to φύσις and held within sheltering-unconcealing, that is, within ἀλήθεια. Heidegger's nonmetaphysical explication of rising-unconcealing in φύσις rests entirely on this comportment.

When we look closely at the rising-unconcealing transpiring in and as φύσις, and when we recall that ἀλήθεια "sways out of concealing [*Verbergung*] and in sheltering-concealing [*Bergung*]" (*GA* 55:175) and as such occurs in φύσις, then we realize that the comportment corresponding to φύσις is one held in ἀλήθεια.

With this insight, let us return to Fragment 16 and observe that in this fragment Heraclitus addresses τὸ δῦνόν, which refers to φύσις, which in turn refers to ἀλήθεια, which is "what is ownmost to φύσις" (GA 55:173); and in this fragment Heidegger sees a comportment at work corresponding to φύσις and held in ἀλήθεια—in sheltering unconcealment. Keeping these three points in mind, I refer to the core of Heidegger's nonmetaphysical explication of the preeminence of "rising" in φύσις when I say that this explication is inconceivable without taking into account a comportment that corresponds to φύσις and is held in ἀλήθεια—in sheltering unconcealment. Heidegger has this comportment in mind when he says that in Fragment 16 "ἀλήθεια is thought but not named" (GA 55:173). Here we see the importance of this comportment for an adequate understanding of Heidegger's interpretation of Fragment 16.

It is important to bear in mind that this comportment corresponds to φύσις because it is held in sheltering-unconcealing, that is, held in ἀλήθεια. However, here we face a question central to an adequate understanding of Heidegger's interpretation of Fragment 16 and related to his contention that here through a comportment corresponding to φύσις, ἀλήθεια is thought but not named. What does this comportment corresponding to φύσις and held in sheltering-unconcealment, that is, in ἀλήθεια, presuppose? To ask this question is to inquire closely into the coming to pass of de-cision.

II

Heidegger's discussion in the lecture course text of 1943–44 concerning τὸ δῦνόν, φύσις, and ἀλήθεια reaches its apex when he explicitly states that in Fragment 16 ἀλήθεια is thought but not named. He arrives at this conclusion by addressing and laying out a comportment that sustains his entire interpretation of Heraclitus. As already noted, what distinguishes this comportment is that it corresponds to φύσις and is held in ἀλήθεια. And we have already seen that this corresponding comportment belongs to those who do not remain concealed vis-à-vis φύσις. How are we to understand this corresponding? Is it to be grasped as a *decision* that those to whom this corresponding comportment belongs have to make? What does *decision* here mean? To grasp the significance of this question, we read again the passage in which

Heidegger articulates this comportment: "Only those who do not re-main concealed vis-à-vis φύσις do exist [*sind seiend*] in such a way that in their being they correspond to rising. The comportment correspond-ing to φύσις must have the basic trait of rising, of self-opening, of not-self-closing, and of not-self-concealing. Not to conceal oneself is to unconceal oneself; is to hold oneself in unconcealing and in sheltering-unconcealment—to express this notion in Greek, it is to hold oneself in ἀλήθεια" (*GA* 55:173). Here Heidegger explicitly and straightforwardly points at the most distinctive mark of this corresponding comportment; it corresponds to φύσις, because it *shares* the basic trait of φύσις. And to this we make a significant hermeneutic addendum by suggesting that this comportment corresponds to φύσις and shares its basic traits be-cause it enacts what Heidegger calls de-cision.

Here everything depends on properly understanding what Heideg-ger means by de-cision. To this end I turn to Heidegger's discussion of de-cision in "Preview" of *Contributions to Philosophy,* because this discussion opens the path to his interpretation of Fragment 16. Under-standing this opening of the path is vital to understanding a comport-ment that sustains his interpretation of Fragment 16 and whose en-actment reveals that it *shares* the basic trait of φύσις. However, we must be careful not to confuse this opening of the path—this way-making—with setting up a "principle" upon which Heidegger's interpretation of Fragment 16 may be said to rest. Moreover, the path that the discus-sion of de-cision opens up is not a means by which Heidegger, through his interpretation of Fragment 16 in 1943-44, would render explicit what is implicit in de-cision in *Contributions to Philosophy* of 1936-38. In other words, this opening of the path through the discussion of de-cision in "Preview" is just that, an opening of the way—a way-making. Thus with his discussion of de-cision Heidegger does not advance or stipulate a thesis that would set the stage for his later interpretation of Fragment 16 and support his contention that in this Fragment Hera-clitus thinks but does not name ἀλήθεια. None of these assumptions enable us to grasp that with the discussion of de-cision in "Preview," Heidegger opens the path leading to his later hermeneutic finding ac-cording to which a comportment that corresponds to and shares the basic traits of φύσις holds the key for interpreting and understanding Fragment 16.

To address the discussion of de-cision in "Preview," let us begin by noting that Heidegger opens this discussion by setting off de-cision in its be-ing historical sense against decision in its ordinary sense. He readily admits that it is hardly possible to come close to what is ownmost to decision in its be-ing historical sense without proceeding from men, from us, without thinking of "decision" as choice, as resolve, as preferring one thing and disregarding another, hardly possible in the end not to approach freedom as cause and faculty, hardly possible not to push the question of decision off into the "moral-anthropological" dimension; indeed it is hardly possible not to grasp this dimension anew in the "existentiell" sense. (*Contributions*, 60)

It is indeed difficult to bring into view what is ownmost to de-cision in its be-ing historical sense because as modern human beings we understand decision only in terms of choice, resolve, preference, freedom, cause, and faculty, in short, in terms of the moral-anthropological dimension. However, the anthropological dimension is one in which

we set out from ourselves and, when we think away from ourselves, always only come upon objects. We hasten back and forth to and with this familiar way of re-presenting and explain everything in its context, never pondering whether, underway, this way might not allow a leap-off [*Absprung*] by which we first of all leap into the "space" of be-ing and give rise to de-cision. (*Contributions*, 61)

We must take seriously Heidegger's account here of the working of the anthropological dimension if we are to understand the manner in which in "Preview" he distinguishes de-cision from decision and thus opens the way to his later hermeneutic finding according to which a comportment that corresponds to and shares the basic traits of φύσις holds the key for interpreting and understanding Fragment 16. Equally significant for grasping de-cision as what opens the way to his interpretation of Fragment 16 is Heidegger's suggestion that the anthropological dimension can serve as a "leap-off" for leaping into the "space" of be-ing and for giving rise to de-cision.

Assuming that we see through the anthropological dimension, assuming that we realize that this dimension is determinative for Descartes' *cogito ergo sum*, for Kant's transcendental apperception of the "I," for Hegel's absolute consciousness, and for Nietzsche's overman, we might be able to use this dimension as a "leap-off" for leaping into the "space" of be-ing and for giving rise to de-cision. If we succeed in making this leap, then we realize that "what is called here de-cision shifts into the innermost swaying mid-point of be-ing itself and then has nothing in common with what we call making a choice and the like. Rather, it says: the very going apart, which divides and in parting lets the enownment of precisely this *open* in parting come into play as the clearing for the still un-decided self-sheltering concealing" (*Contributions*,

61). Here we see for the first time that de-cision *de-cides (sets* things *apart)* and allows for shifting into the innermost swaying midpoint of be-ing. Following this shifting an en-owned clearing emerges, which is not only the clearing for the *cogito,* the transcendental "I," the absolute consciousness, the overman, but is also the clearing for the still un-decided self-sheltering concealing. Considering this minute description of de-cision, we can see how de-cision implicates the whole of *Contributions to Philosophy.*

The exposition of de-cision opens the way to Heidegger's later hermeneutic finding of a comportment that according to his 1943–44 interpretation of Fragment 16 corresponds to and shares the basic traits of φύσις. Without this accomplishment, Heidegger would not have been in a position to put forth his later hermeneutic finding of a comportment that corresponds to and shares the basic traits of φύσις, one that as such holds the key for understanding that in Fragment 16 ἀλήθεια is thought but not named.

To understand the central hermeneutic findings of his 1943–44 lecture course on Heraclitus, that is, the contention that in Fragment 16 ἀλήθεια is thought but not named, we must pay close attention to the expositoin of de-cision and the emerging of a clearing as well as everything that transpires within that clearing. When he characterizes clearing as the clearing for the still un-decided self-sheltering concealing, he paves the way for his later hermeneutic finding of a comportment that corresponds to and shares the basic traits of φύσις and is held within sheltering unconcealment, within ἀλήθεια. The pinpointing of a comportment that corresponds to and shares the basic traits of φύσις, central to the interpretation of Fragment 16, would not have been possible without the prior exposition of de-cision and the prior opening of the way to the clearing for the still un-decided self-sheltering concealing. When in interpreting Fragment 16, Heidegger brings to the fore a comportment that not only corresponds to and shares the basic traits of φύσις but also is held within ἀλήθεια, his thinking traverses the path that his exposition of de-cision in "Preview" opens. Because this exposition opens the path to the clearing for the still un-decided self-sheltering concealing, Heidegger can say that in Fragment 16 the rising-unconcealing in φύσις is sheltered within an as yet un-decided self-sheltering concealing that as "ἀλήθεια sways out of concealing and in sheltering-concealing" (*GA* 55:175).

It is imperative that we pay close attention to what Heidegger says in "Preview" about de-cision as that which divides and parts. Without the insight into this dividing and parting, Heidegger would not have been in a position to focus on rising and self-sheltering concealing in Fragments 16 and 123 and to arrive at the significant hermeneutic finding that although rising and self-sheltering concealing are apart and distinct, each favors the other, each is held and fastened unto the other, and each favors what is ownmost to the other. In the following passage, Heidegger, with unsurpassable clarity, outlines what ensues when decision leads to rising in Fragment 16 and sets rising apart from self-sheltering concealing:

As it rises, rising takes unto itself self-sheltering concealing, because rising can rise as rising only from out of a self-sheltering concealing, that is, rising fastens itself unto self-sheltering concealing. Insofar as rising and self-sheltering concealing grant themselves the favor of what is their ownmost, self-sheltering concealing accords with rising—an accord that at the same time accords rising unto self-sheltering concealing. Rising is the same [*das Selbe*] as self-sheltering concealing, i.e., as setting. (*GA* 55:153)

Considering what I have already said about this passage, it should come as no surprise when I say that what Heidegger outlines here comes to him as he steadily and unwaveringly traverses the path that the exposition of de-cision opens and lays out before him. Because he follows this path, he succeeds in not leveling off, in a stalemate, the opposition between rising and self-sheltering concealing in Fragment 16. He avoids this leveling because he remains focused on what the path reveals to him; rising, apart and distinct as it is from self-sheltering concealing, favors self-sheltering concealing, which, apart and distinct as it is from rising, favors rising. He thus preserves and respects the integrity of rising as well as the integrity of self-sheltering concealing.

III

Let us now turn to an issue that is central to this entire undertaking and concerns the precise nature of de-cision. To precisely determine the nature of de-cision requires that we address the nature of the shift as a shift into the innermost swaying midpoint of be-ing itself. How are we to understand this shift? Is it the result of *a decision* that Heidegger makes *in favor of* the innermost swaying midpoint of be-ing? Were this the case, this shift would not be free of choice, preference, and the like. The shift into the innermost swaying midpoint of be-ing itself and the awareness of dividing, parting, rising, and self-sheltering concealing would be the move of a thinking that initially resides outside the innermost swaying midpoint of being, one that is fundamentally extraneous to this swaying but *chooses* to enter into it.

How are we to understand the nature of this shift in Heidegger's sense, that is, in the sense of a shift free of choice, preference, and the like, and that as a shift into the innermost swaying midpoint of be-ing itself becomes aware of dividing, parting, rising, and self-sheltering concealing and attests to the fact that each favors the other in view of what is ownmost to each? We grasp the nature of this shift when we recognize it as enacted by a thinking that thinks being within the being-historical perspective.

It is within this perspective that Heidegger begins his exposition of de-cision in "Preview" and returns to the central concern of his thinking, which is inquiring into be-ing. He formulates this concern in specific terms when he says: "[W]e must inquire into the essential sway of be-ing *as such*. But we cannot then explain be-ing as a supposed addendum. Rather, we must grasp it as the origin that *de-cides* gods to men . . . and *en-owns* one to the other" (*Contributions*, 60). Here Heidegger not only presents his crucial characterization within the being-historical perspective of the thinking that enacts the shift; he also shows how philosophical thinking should enter into the "joining" titled "The Last God." Given what Heidegger says here, we must conclude that this thinking is an en-owned thinking, and we cannot conceive of the shift into the innermost swaying midpoint of be-ing as one enacted by a thinking that is initially extraneous to be-ing's swaying. For if a thinking is extraneous to be-ing's swaying, then it must not be an en-owned thinking. If Heidegger's understanding of this shift is to be our measure, then we must say that thinking that enacts this shift is not extraneous to be-ing's swaying, because this thinking is en-owned by be-ing, that is, by a de-ciding and en-owning origin. The key here is *be-ing, understood as a de-ciding and en-owning origin.*

What does it mean that this shift is enacted by a thinking that is en-owned by be-ing? We must determine what this en-ownedness means. Succinctly put, it characterizes a thinking that as a projecting-opening is en-owned by be-ing. In the context of the interpretation of Fragment 16 this projecting opens up the opposition in this fragment between rising and self-sheltering concealing.

When Heidegger interprets rising in Heraclitus Fragment 16 as one that rises by taking unto itself and fastening itself unto self-sheltering concealing, and when he points out that rising and self-sheltering concealing each grants itself its ownmost and thus favors the other and accords with the other, he offers an interpretation of this fragment which is the direct outcome of projecting-opening the opposition between rising and self-sheltering concealing. He accomplishes this projecting because his thinking is en-owned by be-ing, that is, by an en-owning and de-ciding origin.

Although nowhere in his interpretation of Fragment 16 does Heidegger explicitly maintain that in this fragment "always rising" or "never setting" should be understood in terms of a de-ciding and en-owning origin, given what he says about the opposition between rising ("always rising") and self-sheltering concealing ("setting"), we have to say that he presents an interpretation of this opposition that is persuasive because it ultimately rests on the view that be-ing is a de-ciding and en-owning origin. In other words, thinking that arrives at this interpretation is capable of projecting-open the opposition between rising and self-sheltering concealing because this thinking is en-owned by a de-ciding and en-owning origin called be-ing.

This projecting-opening comes into sharper focus when we realize that the thinking carrying out this projecting is en-owned by be-ing's en-owning forth-throw. What comes to this thinking from be-ing, that is, from a de-ciding and en-owning origin, is an en-owning forth-throw that enables this thinking to project-open the opposition between rising and self-sheltering concealing. Without this en-owned projecting-opening there would be no interpretation of Fragment 16 and no insight into ἀλήθεια as what is thought but not named in this fragment.

IV

Using as a basis the determination of projecting-open as en-owned by be-ing, let us take a retrospective look at Heidegger's interpretation of Fragment 16 in his 1943–44 lecture course text in light of the exposition of de-cision in "Preview" of *Contributions to Philosophy*. Although in 1943–44 he does not characterize his interpretation of Fragment 16 as being-historical, given the preceding account of de-cision, we must recognize this interpretation as one which is thoroughly being-historical. In 1979 I did not realize that this interpretation is being-historical because I had access neither to *Contributions to Philosophy* nor to the exposition of de-cision therein. Rereading Heidegger's interpretation of this fragment in light of his account of de-cision in *Contributions to Philosophy*, I now realize that the accord between "always rising" (unconcealing) and "never setting" (self-sheltering concealing) as well as the comportment that holds itself within ἀλήθεια ultimately become understandable in light of what Heidegger explicates as de-cision. Only *after* he explicates de-cision in "Preview" does he open the way for his interpretation of Fragment 16 and the contention that in this fragment Heraclitus thinks ἀλήθεια without naming it. This interpretation would not have been conceivable without Heidegger traversing the path opened to him by the prior exposition of de-cision in "Preview." Thus understanding the exposition of de-cision in this work is the foremost hermeneutic precondition for grasping Heidegger's interpretation of Fragment 16. And if this interpretation is any indication, then we must consider the understanding of the exposition of de-cision in *Contributions to Philosophy* to be the foremost hermeneutic precondition for grasping Heidegger's overall approach to Heraclitus.[37]

But the path opened by the exposition of de-cision in *Contributions to Philosophy* leads not only to the interpretation of "always rising," "never setting," and ἀλήθεια in Fragment 16 but also to the "joining" in *Contributions to Philosophy* titled "Playing-Forth." Without access to "Playing-Forth" in 1979, I could not realize that this interpretation has its place within this "joining." Accordingly, at the end of this discussion, I will show that Heidegger's interpretation of Fragment 16, made possible by the exposition of de-cision in "Preview" of *Contributions to Philosophy*, has its proper place in the "joining" "Playing-Forth."

Right at the beginning of this "joining," where Heidegger highlights the manner in which the 'first beginning' plays forth into the 'other beginning,' he notes that this "joining" faces the task of "[c]oming to grips with the necessity of the *other* beginning from out of the originary positioning of the first beginning" (*Contributions*, 119). Given this adumbration of the task, we must ask to what extent does the coming to grips with the necessity of the 'other beginning' implicate the interpretation of Fragment 16 and its core contention that in this fragment ἀλήθεια is thought but not named? More specifically, how does the interpretation of Fragment 16 relate to the necessity of coming to grips with the 'other beginning' from out of the originary positioning of the 'first beginning'? Could we say that with the exposition of de-cision in "Preview" of *Contributions to Philosophy* and with the opening of the path to the interpretation of Fragment 16 in 1943–44, Heidegger in 1936–38 already allocates a place to this interpretation in "Playing-Forth"? I must respond positively to these questions, considering Heidegger's account of the relationship of the guiding-question of philosophy to the grounding-question.

At the very beginning of *Contributions to Philosophy,* Heidegger says that questioning "belongs neither to the purposeful activity of an individual nor to the limited calculation of a community. Rather, it is above all the further hinting of a hint which comes from what is most question-worthy and remains referred to it" (*Contributions,* 4). If we juxtapose this account of questioning with what Heidegger calls the guiding-question of philosophy, what is a being? and with what he calls the grounding-question, how does be-ing sway? we see that the connection between "Playing-Forth" and the interpretation of Fragment 16 can be grasped in terms of "the further hinting of a hint which comes from what is most question-worthy."

By extricating questioning from its empirical confinements, that is, from the goal-oriented activity of an individual and from service to a community, Heidegger unravels the historical potentials of questioning. Foremost among these potentials is the functioning of questioning as a hint. Seen in terms of this potential, questioning can be said to function as the further hinting of a hint from the guiding to the grounding-question. Questioning thus precisely reveals the manner in which the guiding-question plays forth into the grounding-question. Grasping the further hinting of a hint in the sense of the interplay of the two questions, we can say that the connection between the "joining" titled "Playing-Forth" and the interpretation of Fragment 16 emerges in the interplay (playing-forth) of the guiding-question and the grounding-question.

To see this as clearly as possible, we must look closely at what transpires in the guiding-question and what distinguishes the grounding-question. What transpires in these two questions, when put concisely, implicates ἀλήθεια, unconcealment *(Unverborgenheit),* insofar as both questions are interrelated through ἀλήθεια. Heidegger alludes to this interrelation in the text of a lecture course that he wrote at the same time as *Contributions to Philosophy.* In this text he points to the connection between the guiding-question, what is a being? and ἀλήθεια when he says that "Plato and Aristotle . . . always name ἀλήθεια when they name a being: ἀλήθεια καὶ ὄν, unconcealment, i.e., a being in its being-ness" (*GA* 45:121–22). He thus indicates that what transpires at the end of 'the first beginning,' namely, the determination of a being, ὄν as unconcealed, τὸ ἀληθές, remains referred to and connected with unconcealment, ἀλήθεια. In short, τὸ ἀληθές, the unconcealed—the response to the question, what is a being?—is a further hinting at, a referral to, and a connection with ἀλήθεια, unconcealment.

With this referral and connection in mind, and in order to determine the extent to which the exposition of de-cision in "Preview" of *Contributions to Philosophy* opens the path for interpreting Fragment 16 as one in which Heraclitus thinks ἀλήθεια but does not name it, let us return to this fragment. Observe first that the question Heraclitus asks, τὸ μὴ δῦνόν ποτε πῶς ἄν τις λάθοι? "How can anyone remain concealed before that which never sets?" reminds us, on the one hand, of the guiding-question and, on the other hand, of the grounding-question. For the segment of this fragment in which Heraclitus asks, "how can anyone remain concealed?" is formulated in view of a being, and the segment in which he says, "before that which never sets—before that which always rises," is formulated in view of a rising held in a self-sheltering concealing. Since rising self-sheltering concealing is the same as sheltering-unconcealment, that is, ἀλήθεια, Fragment 16 in its second segment refers to unconcealment, to ἀλήθεια. If the 'first beginning' is preoccupied with τὸ ἀληθές (the unconcealed, a being) and is thus oblivious to the coming to pass of rising that is held in self-sheltering concealing—is oblivious of sheltering unconcealment, ἀλήθεια—then Fragment 16, in which ἀλήθεια is thought but not named, does not wholly belong to this beginning. If, however, in the 'other beginning' the sheltering unconcealment, ἀλήθεια, is thought as well as named, then Fragment 16 is on the way to the 'other beginning.' This is another way of saying that with the exposition of de-cision in "Preview," Heidegger opens the way for an interpretation of Fragment 16 that shows that Heraclitus's thinking there resides neither wholly in the first nor entirely in the 'other beginning' but takes its place within the interplay of the two beginnings.

I say advisedly that Heraclitus's thinking in Fragment 16 takes its place within the interplay of the two beginnings because in order to come "to grips with the necessity of the *other* beginning from out of the originary positioning of the first beginning" (*Contributions,* 119), we must focus on this interplay. What Heidegger says in his interpretation of Fragment 16 about sheltering unconcealment, ἀλήθεια, and the manner in which this interpretation sheds light on the first as well as the 'other beginning' makes clear why he does not explicitly assign a place to Heraclitus in *Contributions to Philosophy.* Indeed, when at the beginning of "Playing-Forth" Heidegger states unequivocally that all his "lectures on the 'history' of philosophy" (*Contributions,* 119) belong to the sphere of this "joining," he does not mention Heraclitus. More specifically, he does not mention this philosopher by name when he outlines the task that confronts this "joining," which is to make "manifest *Leibniz's* unfathomable manifold shaping of the onset of the question . . . to re-enact *Kant's* main steps . . . to question thoroughly *Schelling's* question of freedom, and to place *Hegel's* system in the commanding view" (*Contributions*, 123). The absence of the name of Heraclitus from Heidegger's outline of his lecture courses on the history of philosophy in "Playing-Forth" does not mean that what his interpretation of Fragment 16 establishes about sheltering unconcealment, ἀλήθεια, is irrelevant to these lecture courses, which are devoted to the play between the 'first' and the 'other beginning.' On the contrary, by not mentioning Heraclitus by name, Heidegger attests to the integral role that this philosopher plays in the interplay of the first and the 'other beginning' insofar as in Fragment 16 he thinks ἀλήθεια, sheltering unconcealment, without naming it. With the exposition of de-cision, Heidegger traverses a path that leads him to his interpretation of Fragment 16, that is, to an interpretation demonstrating that Heraclitus's thinking in this fragment has its proper place in the interplay of the first and the 'other beginning.'

Thus we must follow Heidegger's interpretation of Fragment 16 in order to apprise ourselves of the full expanse of the originary positioning of the 'first beginning.' Insofar as Heidegger demonstrates in the lecture course text of 1943–44 that "always rising" takes self-sheltering concealing unto itself and fastens itself unto self-sheltering concealing, that is, unto sheltering unconcealment, ἀλήθεια—insofar as he interprets Fragment 16 as one in which Heraclitus thinks ἀλήθεια but does not name it—Heidegger shows that de-cision in *Contributions to Philosophy* opens a path running within the interplay of the two beginnings.

It thus becomes clear that a thorough familiarity with the exposition of de-cision is the hermeneutic precondition not only for understanding Heidegger's interpretation of Fragment 16 and its central concern with ἀλήθεια but also for determining the place this interpretation occupies in the interplay of the two beginnings, that is, within sheltering unconcealment, ἀλήθεια.

Keeping in mind the double role that ἀλήθεια plays within the interplay of the two beginnings (ἀλήθεια as unthought in the first but only named therein, and ἀλήθεια as thought as well as named in the 'other beginning'), we glimpse the peculiar power of ἀλήθεια. Returning full circle to what Heidegger says in the epigram of this essay, I must conclude that even though ἀλήθεια, unconcealment, remains in forgottenness, this forgottenness does not diminish its power. For what remains in forgottenness is "more powerful and more enduring than what is said and realized."[38] As Heidegger never tires of demonstrating in his lecture course texts, ἀλήθεια is powerful and enduring because everything that has been said in the history of Western philosophy ultimately becomes fully understandable in light of ἀλήθεια.

On the Last Part of *Contributions to Philosophy*, "Be-ing," Its Liberating Ontology, and the Hints at the Question of God

> And any effort at wanting to force what is said in this beginning
> into a familiar intelligibility is futile and above all against the na-
> ture of such thinking.
>
> Heidegger

If we are to enter the last part of *Contributions to Philosophy (From En-owning)*, titled "Be-ing," and gain access to the liberating ontology that unfolds therein, we must be clear about the following questions.[39] Considering the structure of this work, which precisely reflects its hermeneutic-phenomenological thrust, in what sense can "Be-ing" be said to be the last part of *Contributions to Philosophy*? Do words such as *last* and *part* apply to "Be-ing" without reservation? And more importantly, how are we to grasp Heidegger's characterization of "Be-ing" when he says that it is "an attempt to grasp the whole once again" (*Contributions*, 365)? How does this characterization contribute to our understanding of the relation between "Be-ing" and the "parts" preceding it?

If what being-historical thinking achieves in the six "joinings" (*Fügungen or Fugen*) of *Contributions to Philosophy* ("Echo," "Playing-Forth," "Leap," "Grounding," "The Ones to Come," and "The Last God") is indispensable for entering into "Be-ing," but "Be-ing" is not a summary and conclusion of the six preceding "joinings," then how are we to understand the relation between these "joinings" and "Be-ing," and how are we to enter into this concluding part? If—considering their "contents"—neither "Preview" nor the six "joinings" progressively develop an argument the way introductions and chapters usually do, then the relation between "Be-ing" and the six "joinings" cannot be understood based on the assumption that in *Contributions to Philosophy* Heidegger steadily and gradually develops a central "thesis." If this is the case, then we should seek the guiding clue for grasping how the six "joinings" relate to "Be-ing" and how its liberating ontology unfolds not in such an assumption but in the so-called turning *(die Kehre)*, which is the "happening" that reverberates throughout *Contributions to Philosophy*. Thus enabled, we shall understand what Heidegger means when he intends with "Be-ing" to grasp "the whole once again."

Beginning with a careful discussion of the turning, that is, the "happening" that reverberates in "Be-ing" as well as in the six "joinings" of *Contributions to Philosophy*, we shall see that Heidegger's attempt to grasp with "Be-ing" "the whole once again" should not be misconstrued as the attempt of willful thinking that at the end of the road deems itself to be in control of be-ing and wants to do the impossible, namely, to grasp be-ing as a whole. Rather, by achieving a basic understanding of the turning, we shall see that the last part of *Contributions to Philosophy*, titled "Be-ing," represents the attempt of a thinking that is claimed by be-ing and responds to this claim by coming back, *once again,* to the turning, thereby unfolding a liberating ontology. Why once again? Because turning is not only the "happening" reverberating in the six "joinings" of *Contributions to Philosophy* and its last part, "Be-ing"— thus shaping Heidegger's being-historical thinking—but also one that reverberates throughout the fundamental ontology of transcendental-horizonal perspective. It should then be clear that we must set out from a basic understanding of the so-called turning.[40]

I

When several decades after *Contributions to Philosophy* Heidegger had the opportunity to express himself on the question of turning, he precisely and concisely characterized the turning in three interconnected respects. First, he noted that turning marks "a turning point" *(eine Wendung)* in his own enactment in thinking of the turning; second, he indicated that turning is what occurs within the dynamic *(Sachverhalt)* named "being and time," "time and being"; and finally, he characterized the turning by stressing that this "happening" points directly to be-ing insofar as "the 'happening' of turning . . . 'is' be-ing as such" (Das "Geschehen" der Kehre . . ."ist" das Seyn als solches).[41] Thus, if we want to enter "Be-ing" in a manner that behooves the matter called be-ing, we must first achieve a basic understanding of these three characterizations of the turning.

We shall take our orientation from the last characterization of the turning, because this characterization sheds invaluable light on the entire matter of turning. By characterizing the turning as the "happening which is be-ing as such," Heidegger tells us that this "happening" is nothing other than be-ing's way of holding sway and that it should not be confused with a "move" that his thinking might be said to make. Heidegger makes this point clear when he indicates that turning should be differentiated from what might be instigated by his thinking alone: "Turning is above all not a process in thinking-questioning [*das fragende Denken*]. . . . It is neither invented by me nor does it concern my thinking alone."[42] Accordingly, when we look at the issue called turning in light of this *last* characterization, we realize that it is to be understood as "the happening which is be-ing as such" and should be differentiated from what might be initiated by thinking-questioning and from what would appear to be "invented" by Heidegger and would solely concern his thinking.

Guided by the *last* characterization of the turning, we are in a position to understand its *first* characterization. Precisely because turning is be-ing's way of holding sway—not an event that occurs and thus gets added to be-ing—it cannot be viewed as what is brought about by thinking-questioning. Here there is no "causal" connection between the turning and Heidegger's thinking-questioning. Precisely because turning is be-ing's way of holding sway, it needs to be enacted and projected-open by Heidegger's thinking. When we take *this* projecting into account, then we understand why Heidegger refers to the turning as a "turning point" in his thinking of the turning, that is, in his thinking of being. It is a "turning point" because by projecting-opening the turning, Heidegger's thinking experiences a decisive moment in its own unfolding. That is why Heidegger's first characterization of the turning reads: "The thinking of the turning is a turning point in my thinking" (Das Denken der Kehre ist eine Wendung in meinem Denken).[43] With the first characterization of turning, Heidegger drives the point home that as far as the turning and the thinking of the turning are concerned, he understands thinking in the specific sense of projecting-opening, that is, in the sense of what he calls *Entwurf* and *entwerfen*.[44] The enactment of projecting-opening represents a "turning point"—a decisive moment—in his thinking. Thus as projecting-opening of the turning, and as a "turning point" in his thinking, Heidegger's thinking is held fast within the dynamic of what he calls the turning.

Understood as projecting-opening, this thinking is neither totally autonomous, designing and pursuing its own assignments, nor completely heteronomous, submitting, as it were, to tasks handed down to it. If we insist on taking *Entwurf* in the sense of a static "projection" and if we overlook the dynamism that is the hallmark of *entwerfen* as projecting-opening, then we fail to preserve the distinction between what thinking does totally on its own and what Heidegger's thinking, as enactment of the happening of the turning, does when this thinking projects-open the sway of be-ing, which is precisely this turning.

To understand the second characterization of the turning, namely, the occurrence that pertains to the dynamic of "being and time" and "time and being," we must once again consider the distinction between "the happening of the turning which is be-ing as such" and the enactment in Heidegger's thinking of this happening. The matter belonging to the dynamic called "being and time" and "time and being" is the same "happening of the turning which is be-ing as such"—a matter that in the fundamental ontology of the transcendental-horizonal perspective Heidegger initially projects-open as the horizon of presence for the presencing of beings. What in the fundamental ontology of the transcendental-horizonal perspective Heidegger calls "metontological turning" presupposes that "the happening of the turning which is be-ing as such" is projected-open. This is another way of saying that the metontological turning toward beings is possible only when "the happening of the turning which is be-ing as such" is projected-open as the horizon of presence.[45] (But this is not to suggest that the latter projecting-opening accomplishes the same thing as the projecting-opening that shapes being-historical thinking. For, as we shall see, the projecting-opening that takes place within the transcendental-horizonal perspective undergoes a profound transformation in being-historical thinking.)

What do we learn from these three characterizations of the turning that might serve as a foothold for our entry into the concluding part of *Contributions to Philosophy*, "Be-ing," and for grasping the liberating ontology that unfolds therein? First, a proper understanding of the turning is the prerequisite for placing both the title of the concluding part and this part itself into a proper perspective. Thus a mere orientation toward "Be-ing" as a title—a noun—does not measure up to the task of entry into "Be-ing." Rather than taking this title as a noun—something static—it should be taken as referring to a happening that, as the turning, is be-ing itself. Second, we must be mindful of the intimate connection between thinking and language, because turning and its projecting-opening by Heidegger's thinking determine the language of this part in its entirety. And this means, third, that we cannot divorce the language of "Be-ing" from the thinking that projects-open the turning (be-ing's swaying) and then propose to translate this part into the familiar language of intelligibility. Every basic word of this concluding part becomes understandable against the background Heidegger brings into view when he projects-open the sway of be-ing, that is, the turning. Finally, we learn that to enter "Be-ing" we must heed the enactment of such a projecting-opening, which presents itself as something utterly inseparable from the turning; there is no turning without a concomitant projecting-opening by Heidegger's thinking. This is another way of saying that "turning as the happening which is be-ing as such" is not an occurrence that happens by itself and awaits projecting-opening: *Turning, that is, be-ing's swaying and Heidegger's projecting-opening of the turning happen concomitantly.* Because of this concomitance, understanding Heidegger's projecting-opening of the turning is indispensable for acquiring access to "Be-ing" and for grasping the liberating ontology that unfolds therein. Given the intimate relationship between "Be-ing" and the preceding six "joinings," we can also say that understanding Heidegger's projecting-opening of the turning is also indispensable for grasping what he explicates in these "joinings."

II

The reader standing at the threshold of "Be-ing" must enter this part of *Contributions to Philosophy* by taking his orientation from the matter of the turning. This reader should understand that turning is the sway of be-ing itself, that it is not an "event" brought about by Heidegger's thinking, and that it constitutes a "turning point" in his thinking insofar as his thinking projects-open the turning and thereby unfolds a liberating ontology.

Since it is not enough merely to say that be-ing's sway—the so-called turning—is projected-open by Heidegger's thinking, we must be more specific and explicitly ascertain in what form this turning-sway of be-ing comes to Heidegger's thinking, where it is projected and opened up by his thinking. Can this turning-sway be identified and closely circumscribed when Heidegger's thinking projects it open *as* the echo of be-ing resonating in abandonment by and forgottenness of be-ing ("Echo"); *as* the play between the 'first' and the 'other beginning' ("Playing-Forth"); *as* the leap into the full swaying of be-ing ("Leap")— a leap that is grounding and grounded ("Grounding") by the ones to come ("The Ones to Come"), that is, those who receive the hint of the last god ("The Last God")? Given that be-ing's turning sway is projected and opened up by Heidegger's thinking, can this turning sway be determined in specific terms? What specifically is this turning sway of be-ing that enters the domains of thinking's projecting-opening within language, shapes the text titled "Be-ing," and therein forms the liberating ontology that unfolds not only in "Be-ing" but also throughout the six "joinings" of *Contributions to Philosophy?*

To respond to these questions, we must be clear about what Heidegger achieves on the path of transcendental-horizonal thinking, and we must know how this achievement opens onto the path of being-historical thinking. In this connection we note that there is neither a smooth crossing from the first to the second path nor an abrupt abandoning of the first in favor of the second. Rather, an "immanent transformation" occurs in the matter of be-ing itself that requires Heidegger to use the first path as a "leap-off" for leaping into the path of being-historical thinking.[46]

In contrast to a smooth transition or an abrupt abandoning, the leap into the being-historical path (or perspective) requires that the "leap-off" be carefully prepared. And this "leap-off" is prepared by what Heidegger achieves in the fundamental ontology of the transcendental-horizonal perspective. Specifically, this achievement consists in the discovery, in the course of the fundamental analytic of *Dasein,* that this being is constituted by thrown projecting-open *(geworfener Entwurf).*[47] Furthermore, this achievement consists in the realization in the course of the same fundamental analytic that the thrownness *(Geworfenheit)* of *Dasein* is a thrownness into the facticity of disclosedness, which is the limit beyond which transcendental-horizonal thinking cannot go. Stopping with the facticity of disclosedness, transcendental-horizonal thinking does not inquire into the origin of thrown projecting-open because in the purview of this thinking, thrownness appears as ultimately, intimately, and unsurpassably bound to the facticity of disclosedness.

Heidegger takes the two interrelated discoveries, namely, that of thrown projecting-open and that of facticity, as the occasion for leaping into the being-historical perspective. This leap has far-reaching consequences for the further unfolding of Heidegger's thought. With this leap Heidegger's thinking "experiences itself as thrown—i.e., as en-owned by be-ing" (*Contributions*, 169). I shall call this experience the self-experience of thinking and outline its five consequences.

The first consequence of this self-experience is that for the first time in his philosophical career Heidegger realizes that the turning he knew of and spoke about in the course of his transcendental-horizonal thinking is a turning that en-owns. He calls it turning in enowning (cf. section 255 of *Contribution to Philosophy*, 286).[48]

The second consequence of this self-experience is the realization that turning in enowning en-owns thinking with and through an enowning-throw *(ereignender Zuwurf)*.[49] With this realization we respond to the question raised earlier regarding how to identify and closely circumscribe be-ing's turning sway. We identify it as an enowning-throw.

The third consequence of the self-experience of thinking is that when thinking experiences itself as en-owned by be-ing, Heidegger realizes that turning in enowning is what sustains all the previously held turnings and circles. In retrospect Heidegger finds that turning in enowning ultimately sustains the fundamental-ontological and the met-ontological turnings and circles of which he spoke in the course of his transcendental-horizonal thinking: "The turning that holds sway in enowning is the sheltered ground of the entire series of turnings, circles, and spheres, which are of unclear origin, remain unquestioned, and are easily taken in themselves as the 'last'" (*Contributions*, 286). When Heidegger's thinking experiences itself as en-owned by be-ing, he realizes he must reassess all the previously held turnings, circles, and spheres. This reassessment shows that they are en-owned by be-ing's enowning-throw, that is, ultimately by turning in enowning.

The fourth consequence of the self-experience of thinking is that this thinking realizes it *belongs* to the turning in enowning, belongs to be-ing. To fully understand this consequence, we must properly grasp *this* belonging. Is it correct to say that thinking that reassesses the previously held turnings and circles belongs to be-ing's enowning-throw, or is it the case that be-ing's enowning-throw belongs to that thinking? What kind of belonging is at issue here? Only by clearly grasping and delineating this belonging can we understand how Heidegger's thinking is en-owned by be-ing's enowning-throw and thus shapes the entirety of "Be-ing" and brings into view the contours of a liberating ontology that unfolds in this text.

Let us address this belonging by focusing on turning in enowning, that is, on be-ing's enowning-throw. First, we shall differentiate this belonging from the familiar notion of belonging by recalling that it intrinsically belongs to turning in enowning. Second, we shall ascertain *who* specifically claims this belonging.

These two steps are interrelated, for unlike the turnings that are familiar to us from the domain of the extant (turning a page, turning in a road, etc.)—turnings that *do not intrinsically belong to the one who turns*—turning in enowning intrinsically belongs *to the one who* receives being's enowning-throw, that is, to the *one who is destined* to belong to this throw. Thus belonging as belonging to the turning in enowning is in principle a matter of being fated or destined to belong to this enowning-throw. Therefore the one who projects-open be-ing's enowning-throw is the one who belongs to this throw and is thus fated and destined to project it open.

I put belonging in the foreground when I suggest that it should be differentiated from the ordinary manners of belonging because of the intimacy of this belonging to be-ing's "call," its *Zuruf/Zuwurf*, i.e., to be-ing's enowning-throw.[50] Here belonging refers to the manner in which the being-historical thinker *belongs* to the enowning-throw *as the one who is destined to belong* to and be enowned by this throw. This is to say that the being-historical thinker is not the one who decides to belong to be-ing's enowning-throw but is the one who is called upon to *belong* to this throw. The being-historical thinker is the one who belongs to this throw insofar as this throw comes from turning in enowning. But the being-historical thinker is also the one who is called upon and destined to belong to the enowning-throw insofar as this throw is destined *for* the thinker who, by dint of being *so* called upon and destined, *turns toward* the enowning-throw. Thus enowning-throw and being-historical thinker find themselves in a counter-turning movement which reveals that, strictly speaking, turning in enowning is a counter-turning. Heidegger puts all of this succinctly when he says: "Turning holds sway between the call [*Zuruf/Zuwurf* ("enowning-throw")] (to the one belonging) and the belonging (of the one who is called). Turning is counter-turning [*Widerkehre*]" (*Contributions*, 287, interpolation is mine).

The fifth consequence of the self-experience of thinking is obtaining a self-knowing. Those who are called upon to belong to the turning in enowning have already obtained a self-knowing from this call. Heidegger brings this self-knowing to the forefront when he characterizes the call as "the grand stillness of the most sheltered and concealed self-knowing" (*Contributions*, 287).

This self-knowing holds the key for differentiating the belonging (to turning in enowning) of the one who is destined to belong from the fatalistic predestined belonging. Belonging to the turning in enowning is not fatalistically predestined because as the belonging of the ones who are called upon to belong, it holds within itself a space of freedom that is totally absent from the fatalistic predestined belonging. What distinguishes it from the fatalistic predestined belonging is precisely the fact that belonging to the turning in enowning is the belonging of those who are called upon to belong and as such face the space of freedom.

Heidegger characterizes the self-knowing of the one who is called as sheltered and concealed because in contrast to the self-knowing that is the ideal of *animal rationale* and is motivated by the imperative "know thyself," *nosce te ipsum*, it cannot be obtained through striving, breeding, education, παιδεία, or struggling against the lack of education, ἀπαιδευσία. In short, this self-knowing is sheltered and concealed because it is not the goal that man, understood as *animal rationale,* sets for himself in response to the metaphysical exhortations to know himself. As sheltered and concealed, this self-knowing is not accessible to epistemological reflection or psychological introspection. Inherent in this self-knowing is the stillness of a call that calls upon the thinker to belong to the turning in enowning.

What do we learn from discussing the five consequences of the self-experience of thinking that might enable us to enter into the last part of *Contributions to Philosophy,* "Be-ing"? If we are to enter via understanding be-ing's turning relation, then we achieve this understanding in light of the five consequences of the self-experience of thinking. Heidegger's thinking experiences itself as en-owned by be-ing and becomes aware of the specific sense in which it belongs to be-ing and obtains a self-knowing. And this belonging is not understood properly if we take it to mean that be-ing takes hold of and possesses Heidegger's thinking or that his thinking takes hold of and possesses be-ing. Neither thinking possesses be-ing nor be-ing possesses thinking, because they relate to each other in terms of the counter-turning of the call and belonging. Thus by bearing in mind this counter-turning we can enter "Be-ing," and grasp its liberating ontology.

III

Equipped with the insights we have gained into the turning, the reader standing at the threshold of "Be-ing" should realize that however he or she may conceive of reading—"deconstructively," "linguistic-analytically," "hermeneutically" à la Gadamer—entry into this part of *Contributions to Philosophy* is not merely a matter of reading. More originary and therefore more decisive than reading is what always already transpires before the reading begins, namely, be-ing's enowning-throw—its call—and the belonging to this call in the counter-turning of the call and belonging. In the same vein, we can say that more originary and, therefore, more decisive than reading is the counter-turning of the call and belonging, which, as we shall see, is a temporal-temporalizing and spatial-spatializing counter-turning. This is to say that one enters "Be-ing" through a reading that is aware of itself as occurring within the temporal-temporalizing and spatial-spatializing counter-turning of the call and belonging. Drastically simplified, the reader who stands at the threshold of "Be-ing" should be aware of the "time" (not to be confused with clock time) and the "place" (not to be confused with physical or geographical space) wherein his or her reading of the last part of *Contributions to Philosophy* occurs.

This requires that we observe how time and space emerge as Heidegger projects-open the turning in enowning, that is, the counter-turning of the call and belonging. To do so we must briefly return to the fundamental ontology of the transcendental-horizonal perspective. Temporality and spatiality of *Dasein*, as explicated in that perspective, serve as the "leap-off" for being-historical thinking to leap into and project-open the temporal-temporalizing spatial-spatializing counter-turning of be-ing's call and the belonging to this call. But here the question arises as to where this projecting takes its cue for disclosing the temporal-temporalizing spatial-spatializing counter-turning. It takes its cue from a temporal-temporalizing spatial-spatializing ground.

First, it should be noted that be-ing's enowning-throw, its call, brings to thinking not only its belongingness to this throw but also a ground that is simultaneously *ur-ground*, *ab-ground*, and *un-ground*. As the onefold of an *ur*-ground, an *ab*-ground, and an un-ground, be-ing's enowning-throw brings to thinking a ground that is held unto an ab-ground, that is, a ground that "grounds . . . and yet does not actually ground" because "it is hesitating" (*Contributions,* 265). A ground that grounds and yet does not actually ground is a ground that grounds as an ab-ground, that is, as "the staying away of ground" (265). In *Contributions to Philosophy,* Heidegger captures the process of a hesitating grounding with striking brevity when he says: "*Ab*-ground is ab-*ground*" (265). (See *GA* 65:379, *Ab*-grund ist Ab-*grund*.) By alternately italicizing the prefix *ab-* and the noun *ground*, he presents in a nutshell the process of a hesitating grounding that is impossible to account for in English if Heidegger's word *Ab-grund* is translated as "abyss."[51] Thus he shows that depending on whether we focus on the prefix *ab-* or on the noun *ground*, we might have in mind a ground that *remains* while it *stays away*—a ground whose grounding brings to thinking "the hesitating refusal" *(zögernde Versagung)* *(Contributions*, 265). By bearing in mind the hesitating refusal, we become aware of that which be-ing's enowning-throw brings to thinking: a ground that *remains* by hesitatingly *staying away*.

Since *staying away*, and *remaining* are modes and manners of temporality, we can say that the ground that be-ing's enowning-throw brings to thinking is temporal and temporalizing. This ground temporalizes itself as a hesitating ground that *remains* as it nevertheless *stays away*. But be-ing's enowning-throw also brings to thinking a ground that is spatial and spatializing. This ground spatializes itself as a ground that makes room. This ground *stays* and by staying makes room *as* (not for) what is *coming*. Since *staying* and *making room* point to spatiality, the ground that stays charms into making room, that is, is spatial and spatializing.

To summarize, Heidegger projects-open the counter-turning of the call and belonging by focusing on a ground that is temporal-temporalizing and spatial-spatializing. This ground is held within a temporalizing-spatializing-encircling hold that Heidegger calls "time-space," which "is more originary than" space and time "and their calculatively represented connection" *(Contributions*, 259). By receiving this ground and projecting it open, Heidegger's thinking proves to belong to this ground.[52] All of this is brought to thinking insofar as *all of this* is held in reserve for thinking in the grounding-attunement of reservedness—an attunement that overwhelms thinking as it receives be-ing's enowning-throw.

Accordingly, to enter into "Be-ing," we must be aware of how *we* stand with respect to the grounding of a ground held in a temporalizing-spatializing-encircling hold or "time-space," which is not the same as the calculatively represented connection of time and space. We must be aware of how we stand with respect to a ground reserved in the grounding attunement of reservedness. With this awareness, we can then understand that the happening of the turning—the happening that is be-ing itself—is the happening of a reserved-temporalizing-spatializing counter-turning of be-ing's call and the belonging to this call. This counter-turning brings to the fore be-ing's enowning-throw as well as the belonging to this throw of Heidegger's projecting-opening. This counter-turning, this belonging, this projecting-opening sustains and shapes "Be-ing" as well as each "joining" of *Contributions to Philosophy* and provides access to the liberating ontology that unfolds in the last part of this work.

IV

The foregoing discussion of the turning enables us now to address the question of how to read the text titled "Be-ing." The traditional style of reading requires one to take up each of the twenty-five sections of this last part of *Contributions to Philosophy*, comment on each, and summarize the analysis in a concluding account of "Be-ing." But *Contributions to Philosophy* is not written in a traditional style, and a traditional style of reading does not apply to "Be-ing." Therefore, I propose a reading that takes its orientation from a potential of thinking as projecting-opening, which throughout the preceding discussion I had in mind but deliberately set aside. It is the potential to set thinking free of beings by means of projecting-open. When we understand this potential, we will be able to enter into the liberating ontology that unfolds in the last part of *Contributions to Philosophy*. How do we grasp this potential?

From the preceding analysis of projecting-open, we know that by receiving be-ing's enowning-throw this projecting becomes an enowned projecting-opening *(ereigneter Entwurf)*.[53] This throw en-owns projecting-opening by attuning it to the grounding-attunement of reservedness. (Heidegger calls this attunement a *grounding*-attunement, because it attunes projecting-open to a reserved and preserved ground.) However, equally important as the en-ownedness and attunedness of this projecting is its potential to set thinking free of beings.

Besides being attuned, this en-owned projecting-opening has the potential to set thinking free of beings because it dwells within be-ing's enowning-throw and lingers therein. We must focus on this dwelling and lingering if we want to grasp the potential of the en-owned projecting to set thinking free of beings. How do we grasp the dwelling and lingering of this projecting within be-ing's enowning-throw, and how do we grasp the potential of this projecting to set thinking free of beings?

First, we should keep in mind that this projecting is enabled by be-ing's enowning-throw to disclose a being. *But disclosing a being does not mean disclosing be-ing.* This shows that projecting-opening takes place within the ontological difference while this projecting discloses a being. But how can disclosing a being go hand in hand with a projecting that sets thinking free of a being? To understand the potential of this projecting to set thinking free of beings, we must take a close look at disclosing a being.

It is the destiny of projecting-opening to take place within the ontological difference, to linger within be-ing's enowning-throw in order for this projecting to open up and disclose a being. In so doing, it discloses a being as it (the projecting) simultaneously returns to be-ing's throw, that is, to be-ing, and thus sets thinking free of beings.

Virtually *everything* Heidegger lays out in the entirety of "Be-ing," especially what he says in sections 262 through 269, must be grasped against the background that I allude to when I say that in disclosing a being, projecting-opening moves away from be-ing's enowning-throw, and upon returning to this throw sets thinking free of beings. Whether such a disclosing brings to the fore a being dis-enowned by be-ing, a being that belongs to the epoch of machination and unfolds from within the 'first beginning,' or whether this disclosing puts forth a being that shelters be-ing, puts forth a being that belongs to the 'other beginning,' in either case disclosing a being is concomitant with the projecting that can set thinking free of beings.[54]

We can distinguish in the experience of disclosing a being two nonsequential phases: projecting-opening moves away from be-ing's enowning-throw, and projecting-opening returns to this throw. While lingering within be-ing's enowning-throw, projecting moves away from this throw without severing itself from it and returns to be-ing's enowning-throw to set thinking free of a disclosed being. As projecting-opening moves away from and returns to be-ing's enowning-throw, thinking is set free of beings. To bring this setting free into sharper focus, we must understand why Heidegger characterizes projecting-opening as preparatory.

In section 262 of "Be-ing," Heidegger characterizes projecting-open as preparatory because by returning to be-ing's enowning-throw and by setting thinking free of beings, projecting becomes preparatory to the experience of disclosure as such. He says: "For experiencing a being and for sheltering its truth, 'projecting-open' is only what is preparatory" (*Contributions*, 314). By focusing on projecting-opening as it moves away from and returns to be-ing's enowning-throw, we grasp what

Heidegger means by preparatory. Projecting-opening is preparatory insofar as it prepares for experiencing disclosure as such and via this experience prepares for setting thinking free of beings.

Thus instead of mistaking preparatory to mean a preliminary stage, we must understand it as pointing to the experience of disclosure as such (which is distinct from disclosing beings) and to the experience of setting thinking free of beings. And this is exactly what Heidegger has in mind when he says: "In thinking's knowing awareness, projecting-opening is not something preparatory *for* something else, but rather the most unique and the last and thus the most rare, which holds sway unto itself" (*Contributions,* 314). Heidegger calls projecting-opening the most unique, the last, and thus the most rare because projecting concomitantly experiences disclosure as such and the disclosing of beings.

However, the realization that projecting-opening is pregnant with the possibility of setting thinking free of beings is accompanied by the realization that the one engaged in this projecting is also set free of beings. Focusing on the experience of disclosure as such—the prerequisite for thinking to be set free from beings—in section 263 of "Be-ing," Heidegger identifies the one engaged in projecting-opening—the thrower of this projecting—as the one who "throws himself free of a being unto be-ing, without a being's having already been enopened as such" (*Contributions,* 318). The phrase "without a being's having already been enopened" refers to the experience of disclosure as such.

With the words "throwing-oneself free" *(Sichloswerfen)* and "free-throw" *(Loswurf),* neither of which can be understood in terms of the activities of *animal rationale,* Heidegger also refers to thinking as it experiences disclosure as such and is thus set free from beings. As long as we take our orientation from *animal rationale* and do not realize that *animal rationale* never experiences disclosure as such, we do not grasp the projecting that throws thinking free and thus sets it free from beings. The *animal rationale* does not experience thinking as it throws itself free from beings and does not experience disclosure as such because it cannot experience projecting-opening.

Further, to grasp the experiences of disclosure and of free-throw, we must set aside the familiar concept of man and his properties, for example, reason. The experience of disclosure as such, which is the prerequisite for thinking to be set free from beings that Heidegger also calls free-throw, cannot be achieved by refining and regulating the use of reason, the highest faculty of *animal rationale.* Heidegger warns against assuming that reason can lead to the experiences of disclosure and free-throw when he says: "We must not take man as pre-given in the heretofore familiar properties and now seek the free-throw in him, but rather: throwing-oneself-free must itself first ground for us what is ownmost to man" (*Contributions*, 319). Rather than trying to locate the experiences of disclosure and free-throw within the familiar properties of man, we should take the free-throw as an occasion for grounding what is ownmost to man. And what is ownmost to man is relatedness to be-ing, which must be grounded in the light of the experiences of disclosure and of free-throw.

Considering the preceding account of projecting-opening, we can now say that one must begin reading the text titled "Be-ing" with a clear understanding that projecting-opening is en-owned by and attuned to be-ing; receives be-ing's enowning-throw; opens up the temporalizing-spatializing of this throw; moves away from this throw and returns to it while it (this projecting) discloses a being; and is endowed with the potential to set thinking free from beings. However, in order to enter into the liberating ontology that unfolds in this last part of *Contributions to Philosophy*, it is not enough that the reading of this part sets out from the detail of projecting-opening outlined here. This reading must also take into account what transpires within the full enactment of projecting-opening, to which Heidegger refers with the word returnership *(Rückkehrerschaft)*. Thus such a reading must be aware of a projecting-open that not only occurs as en-owned by be-ing, as attuned to be-ing, as receiving be-ing's temporalizing-spatializing enowning-throw, and as the setting free of beings, but also is aware of the returnership. What is this returnership that holds the key to the liberating ontology of "Be-ing"?

V

Let me first note that although I did not explicitly deal with the theme of returnership in the preceding discussion of projecting-open, it was in my phenomenological purview all along. To focus on this returnership as an explicit theme, we must ask, how can the experiences of the setting free of beings and disclosure "ground for us what is ownmost to man"? (*Contributions*, 319). Heidegger responds to this question by describing what *happens already* with the enactment of projecting-open, that is, with the experiences of disclosure and of throwing oneself free from beings. When projecting-open is enacted, when disclosure and throwing oneself free from beings takes place, projecting occurs as "venturing the open, belonging neither to oneself nor to what is over against and yet to both—not as object and subject but knowing one-self as countering in the open" (*Contributions*, 319–20). With the experiences of disclosure, that is, of the open and of throwing oneself free, projecting-open ventures the open and knows itself as countering in the open. In doing so, projecting-open experiences both the moves *away from* and *the return* to the open that take place within be-ing's enowning-throw. The moves *away from* the open and the *return to* it lead to what *should happen* with the enactment of projecting-open.

Heidegger responds to the question of how the experiences of throwing oneself free from beings and disclosure can "ground for us what is ownmost to man" (*Contributions*, 319) by speaking of the returnership that *should happen* when projecting-open *moves away from* and *returns to* be-ing's enowning-throw. However, the move away from and the return to be-ing's enowning-throw—the experience of returnership—are not one-time occurrences but ongoing. And this ongoing experience of returnership takes a different shape depending on the specific being from which projecting-open sets thinking free and depending on who man is and how he dwells.

Heidegger stresses the significant role that man plays in the experience of returnership when he notes that "[b]y throwing himself free of 'a being' man first becomes man. For only in this way does he return to a being and he *is* the one who has returned" (*Contributions*, 318). Throwing himself free of "a being," man becomes man as he simultaneously returns to "a being." Thus Heidegger leaves no doubt that becoming man cannot be achieved in isolation from "a being" or from beings. He further highlights the role of man by speaking of man's dwelling and of how he dwells and is destined to and gifted for dwelling. Thus he makes clear that, depending on how man throws himself free from beings, how he is gifted for dwelling, and what view of be-ing he *retains as he returns* from a being, the returnership shapes itself differently. In this connection Heidegger says: "One must first know the manner of dwelling and the concomitant gift, as well as the manner in which in the re-turn . . . a being is found . . . as a being—which view of being man as the returner [*Zurückkehrer*] retains" (*Contributions*, 319).

In view of the reading that I propose for "Be-ing," that is, one that fully enacts projecting-opening and uses it as this reading's reliable guide, and because the occurrence of "returnership" outlined here is pivotal for this reading, let us inquire into the returnership as it occurs in the epoch of modernity. By highlighting how "returnership" shapes itself in the epoch of modernity, the reading of "Be-ing" I propose becomes clear and accessible. Let me begin with the dwelling that is peculiar to the epoch of modernity.

This dwelling is marked by an almost total blindness to the experience of returnership. In the present being-historical epoch, this blindness shapes contemporary man's dwelling in such a way that the view of be-ing *he retains as he returns* from beings is forgotten. Forgottenness of the retained view of be-ing is an indication that "man was *not* capable of mastering the returnership [*Rückkehrerschaft*]. This 'not' [is] the ground of his hitherto Western history" (*Contributions*, 319). Thus man was incapable of mastering the returnership by holding on to what be-ing's enowning-throw brings and was incapable of holding on to a ground that remains by staying away and was incapable of holding on to the temporalizing-spatializing that comes with this throw. But since man's relationship to be-ing cannot be severed or eliminated, following this "not mastering" he continues to be exposed to be-ing's enowning-throw, to the ground that remains as it stays away, and to the temporalizing-spatializing that comes with this throw—but with one important difference. The throw of be-ing, which in the wake of that "not mastering" comes to en-own man's thinking as projecting-opening, is a dis-enowned throw and belongs to the "time-space" of machination. The dis-enowned throw held unto the *unground* called machination brings to the fore the forgottenness of be-ing's enowning-throw.

Accordingly, this forgottenness can serve as a measure for understanding "how a colossal disturbance runs through all human progress; how be-ing itself as machination sets itself into what is precisely not its ownmost" (*Contributions*, 319). This forgottenness can serve as a measure for understanding that human progress is interspersed and interpenetrated by a colossal disturbance. This progress is thus neither capable of providing access to what is "most-ownmost-most-remote" to humans nor of rendering superfluous what is "most-ownmost-most-remote" to humans by replacing it.[55]

With the experience of the ongoing returnership, the realization that within this returnership man's throwing himself free from beings occurs, and the insight into the colossal disturbance that runs through all human progress, we have before us the contours of the being-historically liberating ontology that unfolds in "Be-ing." Despite the prevailing effectiveness of dis-enowned beings and the colossal disturbance running through human progress, this ontology is liberating because it shows the way to the ongoing returnership that sets man free from beings and sets him free for be-ing. This ontology rests squarely on the experience of the returnership that occurs along with the enactment of projecting-opening.

To what extent does the reading I propose for "Be-ing" lead to the being-historically liberating ontology that unfolds in this part of *Contributions to Philosophy?* Being guided by the enactment of projecting-opening, this reading uses the insights we have gained into the experience of returnership and realizes that this experience is the key for grasping Heidegger's intention with "Be-ing" to grasp the whole once again. The experience of returnership constitutes the backbone not only of "Be-ing" but also of the six "joinings," "Echo," "Playing-Forth," "Leap," "Grounding," "The Ones to Come," and "The Last God." The returnership constitutes such a backbone because it brings a whole into view that is not the whole *of* what lies "between" disclosing a being and be-ing's enowning-throw but one *that* transpires when thinking *moves away from* and *returns to* be-ing's enowning-throw. The "whole *of*" implies summing up; the "whole *that*" indicates returnership that transpires between be-ing's enwoning-throw and the echo of be-ing; between this throw and the play of the 'first' into the 'other beginning'; between this throw and the leap into being's full swaying; between this throw and the grounding of this throw by the ones to come; between being's enwoning-throw and the last God. With "Be-ing" Heidegger grasps this whole once again because he experiences the returnership. A reading that takes its orientation from a projecting-open that is enowned by be-ing and receives its enowning-throw thus brings into its own purview en-ownedness, attunedness, hesitating grounding, setting free from beings, and returnership. It is this returnership that sustains the liberating ontology of "Be-ing."

VI

With the experience of returnership in mind, we can now address the hints at the question of God that we find in "Be-ing." What distinguishes the being-historical ontology of "Be-ing" as liberating are the hints that this ontology makes toward the question of God. Let me stress that these hints are just that: hints. With them Heidegger does not intend to put forth a new doctrine on the existence of God. To examine this in detail, we must keep in mind the difference between the liberation inherent in the ontology of "Be-ing" and the freedom promised by metaphysical theories. Recalling that by enacting the so-called projecting-opening man can throw himself free from beings, we recognize that at stake in the liberating ontology of "Be-ing" is man's throwing himself free from beings, which is not the same as achieving what is called "freedom from" or accomplishing a detachment that rewards with salvation à la Buddhism. What is liberating in this ontology is the being-historical thinking itself. This liberating thinking should not be confused with doctrines of freedom that are rampant in metaphysics; although these doctrines purport to achieve a freedom from beings, they are unaware that *freedom from beings* is not the same as *throwing-oneself free from beings unto be-ing*. What further distinguishes the liberation inherent in being-historical thinking from the freedom espoused by metaphysics is the fact that being-historical thinking never pretends to free itself from beings even though this thinking throws itself free unto be-ing. Even though this thinking throws itself free unto be-ing, it still retains its relatedness to beings insofar as it can free itself from beings only *by moving away from* a disclosed being and *by returning to* be-ing's enowning-throw—in short, by experiencing the aforementioned returnership.

The experience of returnership upholds everything that Heidegger works out in "Be-ing," and with a significant modification it also renders understandable the hints he makes toward the question of God. This is the modification of this experience as it takes place within the *theological difference* and not within the *ontological difference*. Thus the experience of returnership that upholds the hints at the question of God is shaped differently than the experience of returnership that takes place within the ontological difference. By specifically addressing this question in sections 259 and 279 as the "gods' needfulness of be-ing," he shows how *theologically* fruitful and enlightening the experience of returnership is that takes place within the theological difference. Here we should recall that each and every section of "Be-ing" presupposes the returnership that occurs within the *ontological difference* when thinking as projecting-opening moves away from and returns to be-ing's enowning-throw. However, in the case of "gods' needfulness of be-ing," this returnership occurs within the *theological* and *not* within the *ontological* difference. This is of paramount importance for understanding the hints at the question of God that we find within the being-historically liberating ontology of "Be-ing."

Within this ontology Heidegger addresses the question of God and sets out from the theological difference, thus showing that within this difference the experience of returnership is shaped differently.

Specifically in the case of the "gods' needfulness of be-ing," he shows that he experiences this returnership as it unfolds within the *theological* difference.[56] Accordingly, to complete my account of the experience of returnership as one that is quintessential to the reading of "Be-ing" as well as to the unfolding of the being-historically liberating ontology of "Be-ing," I shall have to highlight this returnership as it takes place within the theological difference. I must elucidate the experience of returnership as it takes place within the theological difference since without this elucidation my account of this returnership is inadequate because it reflects only the returnership as it takes place within the ontological difference.

VII

What is the theological difference, and how does this difference house within itself the returnership we have discussed? Theological difference is the difference between gods and be-ing. To understand how this difference is constituted, we must keep two points in mind. First, in speaking of gods Heidegger does not "set a 'polytheism' as the 'starting point'" (*Contributions,* 308), for what he means by gods is "the undecidability of the being of gods, whether of one single god or of many gods" (ibid.). Second, in speaking of be-ing, we have in mind be-ing's enowning-throw since be-ing itself is nothing other than this throw. Considering these two points, we arrive at a basic understanding of the theological difference, which is the difference between be-ing's enowning-throw and the undecidability of the being of gods. In short, it is the difference between be-ing's enwoning-throw and the being of gods as undecidable.

We further clarify this difference when we leave its two poles intact and observe each. This requires that we refrain from conceiving be-ing's enowning-throw (the one pole) and the undecidability of the being of gods (the other pole) as if that throw and this undecidability were standing over against each other. Thus to observe the two poles of the theological difference intact we must bear in mind that the relationship between be-ing's enowning-throw and the undecidability of the being of gods is not a relationship of opposition. We find *need*, not opposition, in this relationship. There is no opposition between that undecidability and be-ing's enowning-throw since gods need be-ing's enowning-throw. And gods need be-ing's enowning-throw in order to belong to themselves. This means finally that be-ing initially cannot be attributed to gods because it is only by receiving be-ing's enowning-throw that gods belong to themselves.

Heidegger summarizes this when he says: "Not attributing being to 'gods' initially means only that being does not stand 'over' gods and that gods do not stand 'over' being. But gods *do need* be-ing, . . . 'Gods' need be-ing in order through be-ing—which does not belong to gods—nevertheless to belong to themselves" (*Contributions*, 308–9). The clearest indication that in the theological difference be-ing's enowning-throw is needed by gods is that the undecidability of the being of gods makes them need this throw, which eliminates the assumption that be-ing's enowning-throw stands "over" gods and gods stand "over" be-ing's enowning-throw. Furthermore, the undecidability of the being of gods makes them need be-ing's enowning-throw in order for them to belong to themselves through this throw—a throw that as such does not belong to gods.

We recall from the preceding discussion that as projecting-opening takes place within the ontological difference and discloses a being, and as this projecting moves away from and returns to be-ing's enowning-throw, it experiences returnership. But given that the theological difference is the difference not between be-ing and beings but between the undecidability of the being of gods and be-ing's enowning-throw, how can projecting-opening as it is enacted within the theological difference give rise to the experience of returnership? The fact that within the theological difference thinking as projecting does not disclose a being is no reason to assume that in the theological difference projecting-open does not experience returnership. Indeed, within the theological difference such thinking experiences returnership since it throws itself free from the undecidable being of gods unto be-ing *by moving away from the undecidability of the being of gods* and *by returning to be-ing's enowning-throw.* Thus thinking as projecting-opening realizes throughout that be-ing's enowning-throw and the undecidability of the being of gods do not stand over against each other, that this undecidability *needs* that throw, that gods need be-ing's enowning-throw as that which does not belong to gods, and that gods need be-ing's enowning-throw in order to belong to themselves. What in sections 259 and 279 of "Be-ing" Heidegger calls "gods' needfulness of be-ing" now becomes understandable. Equipped with this understanding, we are in a position to shed light on Heidegger's position on traditional doctrines concerning God.

Traditional philosophical doctrines that take shape as monotheism, polytheism, pantheism, and atheism steadfastly deny and reject the undecidability of the being of gods because each takes the being of gods as already decided. Moreover, these doctrines are unaware of the experience that thinking as projecting-opening undergoes when it unfolds within the theological difference, that is, the experience of returning to be-ing's enowning-throw from the undecidability that defines the being of gods. In other words, such philosophical doctrines have no inkling of what transpires when as projecting-opening thinking returns from be-ing's enowning-throw to the undecidability of the being of gods.

I call the ontology that unfolds in "Be-ing" liberating because it demonstrates that thinking as projecting-opening unfolds within the theological difference, experiences returnership, and thus throws itself free—liberates itself—from the undecidable being of the gods of monotheism, polytheism, pantheism, and atheism. However, although this throwing-free is central to the liberating ontology of "Being" and although it is unacceptable to monotheism, polytheism, pantheism, and atheism, the ontology that articulates that throwing-free does not turn Heidegger into an opponent of these doctrines. What matters to him above all is the experience of a returnership that takes place within the theological difference when thinking as projecting moves away from the undecidability of the being of gods of these doctrines and throws itself free unto be-ing. Accordingly, my attempt to illuminate the contours of the being-historically liberating ontology of "Be-ing" and to outline the hints toward the question of God that appear in "Be-ing" is motivated in part by my awareness that monotheism, polytheism, pantheism, and atheism provide fertile ground for philosophical thinking to experience the returnership that takes place within the theological difference when thinking unfolds as projecting-opening.

VIII

In conclusion, let us return to the question raised at the beginning of this essay concerning the entry into "Be-ing" as the last part of *Contributions to Philosophy*. One should bear in mind that this discussion began with the analysis of the turning and ended with an elucidation of returnership because I wanted to show that a proper understanding of the happening of the turning and of the experience of returnership is the prerequisite for entering into and reading "Be-ing." That happening and this experience sustain the entirety of "Be-ing" as well as the six "joinings" of *Contributions to Philosophy*. Since the experience of returnership is irrevocably bound to be-ing's enowning-throw, which enters

the domain of thinking via the happening of the turning, the experience of returnership is integral to an understanding of the happening of
the turning, which, as Heidegger notes, is be-ing itself. By unearthing
the experience of returnership in *Contributions to Philosophy*, Heidegger
brings to *a preliminary completion* his thinking of the turning.

Moreover, since turning is not an "event" that occurs outside language, it has an unmistakable impact on language. The happening of
the turning, which is be-ing itself, is at the same time a turning *within*
language, that is, a turning from the "familiar" language to the "unfamiliar" language of being-historical thinking. This explains why the
present study deliberately retains Heidegger's basic words instead of
abandoning them in search of a more "familiar" and more "intelligible"
language. Precisely because the turning shapes the being-historical language, and precisely because no one else in our time articulates the turning, it is incumbent upon us to retain Heidegger's language. Whether
we understand the turning as that to which the transcendental-
horizonal thinking is a response or as that to which being-historical
thinking is a response, we should retain Heidegger's words because
they emerge from within the turning as the onefold of being and language. Only insofar as these words emerge from within that onefold are
they words "of" the thinking of be-ing and not *ours* to manipulate as we
please.

The notion of a more familiar, more intelligible, and more traditional language is a direct outgrowth of submission to the metaphysical
criteria of comprehensibility and incomprehensibility. These criteria
are held hostage to metaphysics because they divert thinking from
projecting-opening and surreptitiously turn it into a tribunal that in-
evitably operates within metaphysics. The other outgrowth of that
submission is the approach to *enowning*—to *Ereignis*—in terms of the
criteria of comprehensibility and incomprehensibility. This approach
ultimately obfuscates *Ereignis* since by assuming that it "entails that
everything is comprehensible, except the comprehensibility of everything," this approach mistakes *Ereignis* for a means of explaining reality.[57] It thus calculatively distorts *Ereignis*. But as Heidegger shows not
only in "Echo" but throughout *Contributions to Philosophy*, calculative
thinking is held hostage to metaphysics and is thus unaware of the forgottenness of being. Subjecting *Ereignis* as enowning to this approach
and thereby implying that the metaphysical criteria of explainability,
comprehensibility, and incomprehensibility decide what *Ereignis* is
only reveals a fundamental failure to grasp the thrust of hermeneutic

phenomenology that always precedes the criteria of comprehensibility and incomprehensibility. The mere orientation to these metaphysical criteria demonstrates a lack of understanding of both what is ownmost to *Ereignis* and what is ownmost to Heidegger's language that unfolds from within *Ereignis*. Rather than getting bogged down in these metaphysical criteria, we should heed the projecting-opening of the turning that marks a turning point in Heidegger's thinking and shapes *his* words that arise from within *his* enactment in language of the turning in enowning.

II

On the Inception
of Being-Historical Thinking and
Its Active Character, Mindfulness

It seems to require little argument that with the appearance of *Contributions to Philosophy (From Enowning)* and *Mindfulness* Heidegger's thought once again calls for renewed appropriation—once again because with the appearance of Heidegger's lecture course texts that precede *Being and Time* the opportunity for such an appropriation has presented itself once before. Although thus far the availability of these lecture course texts has not led to a renewed appropriation of *Being and Time,* with the appearance of *Contributions to Philosophy* and *Mindfulness* the situation changes considerably.[58] With the availability of these two major works, philosophy today once again is given a unique opportunity for appropriating Heidegger's thought from the ground up. Such an appropriation, should it come to pass, must address the relationship between these two major works and the unfolding of being-historical thinking as mindfulness in both. This task presupposes a familiarity with the transformation of the transcendental-horizonal onset of the thinking of being.

To show that being-historical thinking begins from within the transformation of the transcendental-horizonal onset of the thinking of being and to demonstrate that this inception determines the unfolding of being-historical thinking as mindfulness in both *Contributions to Philosophy* and *Mindfulness* is to fulfill the minimum requirements for a renewed appropriation of Heidegger's thought.

In the following discussion, I take the question of ontological difference, as dealt with in *Contributions to Philosophy,* as an avenue to the inception of being-historical thinking and to its unfolding as mindfulness. This entails examining both Heidegger's reassessment of this difference and his effort to trace it back to enowning by enacting a thinking that unfolds as mindfulness, which in turn requires me to address mindfulness as Heidegger discusses it in *Mindfulness*. We shall see that mindfulness is not an attribute of or an addendum to being-historical thinking but the very enactment of this thinking itself. In this vein, we shall see that being-historical thinking as mindfulness highlights the relationship between *Contributions to Philosophy* and *Mindfulness*.

I

To highlight the transformation of the transcendental-horizonal onset of the thinking of being, and to discuss the unfolding of being-historical thinking as mindfulness, I must address Heidegger's new position on ontological difference as laid out in section 132 of *Contributions to Philosophy*. He presents the gist of this new position in the statement that reads: "Therefore the task is not to surpass beings (transcendence) but rather to leap over this distinction and thus over *transcendence* and to inquire inceptually into be-ing and truth" (*Contributions*, 177). The new stance on the ontological difference requires that the new thinking called being-historical leap over transcendence, that is, over an occurrence that presupposes the difference between being and beings.

In this connection we must ask two questions: who enacts the transcending, and who enacts the leap? The response to both is: *Dasein*, that is, the so-called thrown projecting-open *(der geworfene Entwurf)*. Taking the path of transcendental-horizonal thinking of *Being and Time*, *Dasein* enacts the surpassing or transcending of beings. Staying on the path of being-historical thinking of *Contributions to Philosophy*, *Dasein* enacts the leap. However, there is a significant difference between these enactments. While transcending beings leaves the structure of *Dasein* intact, the leaping over transcendence radically transforms *Dasein*'s structure, that is, thrown projecting-open. Under the impact of the leap, thrownness no longer means thrownness into the facticity of disclosedness and projecting-open no longer indicates projecting-opening the factical disclosedness. Rather, as a consequence of the enactment of the leap, thrownness proves to be en-owned by be-ing and projecting-open proves to be the opening up of this enownment.

This enownment gives rise to being-historical thinking. Heidegger captures this enownment succinctly when he notes: "[The leap] is the enactment of projecting-open the truth of be-ing in the sense of shifting into the open, such that the thrower of the projecting-open experiences itself as thrown, i.e., as en-owned by be-ing" (*Contributions*, 169). Whereas in *Being and Time* Heidegger understands thrownness as thrownness into the facticity of disclosedness and projecting-open as disclosing or opening up of the factical disclosedness, in *Contributions to Philosophy* he understands thrownness as thrownness into be-ing's historical unfolding and projecting-open as disclosing or opening up this historical unfolding. And this happens under the impact of the leap. Under its impact projecting shifts into the open, that is, into be-ing's historical unfolding, and attests to a deciding experience of the thrower (the one who enacts the leap): it (the thrower) now realizes that it is thrown into and en-owned by be-ing's historical unfolding. Because to be thrown means to be thrown into and to be en-owned by be-ing's historical unfolding, thrown projecting-open in *Contributions to Philosophy* clearly no longer means what it does in *Being and Time,* namely, to be thrown into and to open up the factical disclosedness. What counts in *Contributions to Philosophy* is the experience of thrownness as en-ownedness by be-ing which goes hand in hand with the experience of projecting-open as opening up this en-ownedness.

As thrown projecting-open is transformed into an en-owned thrown projecting-open, it marks the inception of being-historical thinking. And with this inception Heidegger's new understanding and assessment of the ontological difference comes to the fore. What is this new understanding and assessment?

II

To see how being-historical thinking begins with leaping over the surpassing, transcending of beings, we must focus on the ontological difference and ascertain why in section 132—notably titled "Be-ing and a Being"—Heidegger characterizes the ontological difference as a discording and disastrous distinction, in what way this difference is involved in the guiding—as well as the grounding—questions of philosophy and via these questions in the 'first' and the 'other beginning,' and in what way the ontological difference opens an avenue into enowning.

To ascertain why Heidegger characterizes the ontological difference as a discording and disastrous distinction, we must carefully read what he says about this difference in section 132 of "Leap." He takes a fresh look at this difference when in the opening paragraph of this section he engages in one of his self-interpretations and self-criticisms, with which the reader of *Contributions to Philosophy* will be familiar. He tells us that although the ontological difference initially was introduced as a distinction for "safeguarding the question of the truth of be-ing from all confusion," it finally proved to be discording *(zwiespältig)* and disastrous *(verhängnisvoll)* *(Contributions,* 176).

On what ground does Heidegger characterize the ontological difference as discording and disastrous? He is critical of the ontological difference as it appeared within the transcendental-horizonal perspective because of what is presupposed by this appearing. As it appears within that perspective, the ontological difference presupposes that a being *is,* that beings *are,* and that consequently be-ing—although acknowledged to be different from a being—can be thought in its own right within the perspective of beings. And this is precisely what happens from Plato to Nietzsche in the 'first beginning.' Thus as the ontological difference appears within the transcendental-horizonal perspective, it shelters within itself the thinking of the 'first beginning.'

The ontological difference is a discording distinction because it introduces discord into the thinking of being by intimating that to think be-ing in its own right it is enough to determine the beingness of beings, which is precisely what happens in the 'first beginning.' Specifically, this distinction does not heed the manner in which a being's shining forth, its manifesting, is inseparable and yet different from the manner in which be-ing as such appears. Had this distinction accounted for the manner in which a being's appearing proves to be inseparable and yet different from be-ing's way of appearing, this distinction would have recognized that when viewed in the light of be-ing, a being *is not*— beings *are not.* However, if we carefully ponder the question whether we can attribute to beings the same "is" that distinguishes be-ing as such and if we carefully ponder whether the "is" peculiar to be-ing is the same "is-ness" peculiar to beings, that is, to what is extant, "exists," and has an essence, then we realize that "be-ing can no longer be thought of in the perspective of beings; it must be enthought from within be-ing itself" *(Contributions,* 5).

Ontological difference is a discording distinction because it fails to take into account the distinction between the "is" peculiar to be-ing and the "is-ness" peculiar to beings. Ontological difference is a discording distinction because it suggests that be-ing can be thought in its own right within the perspective of beings. Insofar as this difference does not lead to awareness of the distinction between the "is-ness" peculiar to beings and the "is" that belongs to be-ing, it introduces a discord into the onefold of be-ing and a being. This onefold, in spite of the discordant ontological difference, *must be thought at all costs.*

Moreover, insofar as ontological difference presupposes that be-ing can be thought in its own right within the perspective of beings, this difference puts forth a presupposition that shows that this difference is unaware that forgottenness of be-ing is endemic to the perspective of beings. In this vein, ontological difference proves to be a disastrous distinction because it consolidates the forgottenness of be-ing. This consolidation has far-reaching consequences; from Plato to Nietzsche it determines the thinking of the 'first beginning' as well as the derivatives of this thinking, that is, nihilism, science, and the global predominance of technology. This forgottenness, in spite of the ontological difference, *must be thought at all costs.*

Heidegger's fresh look at the ontological difference is guided by the insight that it comes into play when in the 'first beginning' the being-ness of beings is determined and thus differentiated from be-ing. When he says, "For this distinction indeed *does* arise from a questioning of beings as such (of being-ness)" (*Contributions*, 177), he alludes to the manner in which the ontological difference comes into play in the determination of the beingness of beings. In the 'first beginning' philosophical thinking determines the beingness of beings and thus forces the ontological difference into the open without going far enough to inquire into the onefold of be-ing and beings. By not inquiring into this onefold, ontological difference bypasses be-ing and consolidates the forgottenness of being. That is why it is a disastrous distinction.

Heidegger characterizes the ontological difference as discording and disastrous not because he wants to reject his transcendental-horizonal stance on this difference and correct it but rather because if left to itself it obfuscates what transpires *in* and *as* the 'first beginning,' namely, thinking's submission to the perspective of beings and to the dominance of the forgottenness of be-ing. Thus instead of taking the designations *discording* and *disastrous* as subjective expressions of Heidegger's dismay about and rejection of his own transcendental-horizonal stance on the ontological difference, we must understand them according to the wording in which ontological difference appears within being-historical perespective, that is, "the leap over the surpassing of beings."

To ascertain in what way the ontological difference is involved in the guiding—as well as the grounding—questions of philosophy, we must consider the implications of this difference for grasping what transpires in the 'first beginning.' Submitting to the ontological difference and thus bypassing the onefold of be-ing and beings, thinking in the 'first beginning' fails to open up the guiding-question, what is a being? and remains oblivious of be-ing. Oblivious of be-ing and failing to open up the guiding-question, the thinking that shapes the 'first beginning' fails to see that the onefold of be-ing and beings is sheltered within the guiding-question. By not subjecting the ontological difference to questioning, the thinking that shapes the 'first beginning' pursues the guiding-question, what is a being? and thus inquires into the being of a being and determines the beingness of beings. By not subjecting the ontological difference to questioning, this thinking remains unaware of the grounding-question of the 'other beginning,' "But how does be-ing sway?" (*Contributions*, 5). This thinking does not go far enough to inquire how exactly be-ing sways. By submitting itself to the ontological difference, by exhausting itself in pursuing the guiding-question, by inquiring into what a being is, and by working out the beingness of beings, thinking in the 'first beginning' consolidates the forgottenness of be-ing.

To ascertain in what way the ontological difference opens an avenue into enowning, we note that in contrast to the thinking of the 'first beginning,' Heidegger looks at the ontological difference while inquiring into the question, "But how does be-ing sway?" This inquiry is an attempt that "brings into dialogue what has first been of be-ing's truth and that which in the truth of be-ing is futural in the extreme" (*Contributions*, 5). Since what has first been of be-ing's truth is the perspective of beings and the forgottenness of be-ing, and because that which in the truth of be-ing is futural in the extreme is enowning, it should be clear that the inquiry into the question, how does be-ing sway? implicates a dialogue between the thinking of enowning and the ontological difference embedded within the perspective of beings. No matter how ontological difference is irrevocably embedded in the perspective of beings, it nevertheless leads philosophical thinking, through enowning, to an "immanent transformation" in the matter of be-ing.[59] To see how the ontological difference leads thinking to this "immanent transformation" and how it is implicated in the question, how does be-ing sway? we must have a basic understanding of this transformation.

The transformation that occurs in the matter of be-ing reveals that be-ing unfolds historically as enowning. This revealing provides the light we need in order to fully appreciate everything for which the ontological difference stands: thinking's submission to the perspective of beings, and thinking's domination by the forgottenness of be-ing.

When we view the ontological difference in light of be-ing's historical unfolding as enowning, we realize that this difference ipso facto opens an avenue to enowning.

The ontological difference opens an avenue to enowning insofar as this difference itself would not occur without the swaying of be-ing. Without this swaying the ontological difference would not appear; it would not reveal what transpires in the 'first beginning,' that is, thinking's submission to the perspective of beings and thinking's domination by the forgottenness of be-ing. The ontological difference opens an avenue to enowning because as *a manner* of be-ing's swaying, this difference itself is thrust forth by enowning. This is the case because enowning is "that self-supplying and self-mediating midpoint into which all essential swaying of the truth of be-ing [and this includes the ontological difference] must be thought back in advance" (*Contributions*, 51, interpolation is mine). Given that the ontological difference presupposes the coming to pass of *a manner* of the swaying of be-ing and that this difference reveals the perspective of beings and the forgottenness of be-ing, it should be clear that the perspective of beings and the forgottenness of be-ing also occur as manners and modes of that swaying and as such are thrust forth by the self-supplying and self-mediating midpoint called enowning. Thus through the perspective of beings and the forgottenness of be-ing, the ontological difference opens an avenue to enowning, which is why this difference must be thought back to enowning.

The expression "thinking back" is fraught with the danger of taking enowning as a metaphysical principle to which the ontological difference must be traced back. However, enowning is not a principle, since it reverberates as a self-supplying and self-mediating midpoint, and thinking this difference back to enowning presupposes that this reverberation enters the phenomenological purview. Therefore, thinking the ontological difference back to enowning is to think this difference back to that reverberating, self-supplying, and self-mediating midpoint that, insofar as it *reverberates*, it shows itself, is manifest and cannot be made *static*—cannot be made into a metaphysical principle.

By taking into account what I have just discussed, we see that Heidegger initiates being-historical thinking when he realizes that the ontological difference must be thought back to enowning since it is prone to strengthening the perspective of beings, consolidating the forgottenness of be-ing, and prolonging the entanglement in the 'first beginning.' At the same time, however, he realizes that since the ontological difference can be thought back to enowning, this thinking back itself reveals the action *(Handeln)* of being-historical thinking. Therefore, to better highlight the action of being-historical thinking, we must refocus on the thinking that thinks the ontological difference back to enowning. What specifically constitutes this thinking back?

III

It will be recalled that manifest in the wording of the ontological difference is the leap over the surpassing or transcending of beings—the leap over transcendence. We must understand the singular constitution of this leap and take it as our guide if we seek to understand, in more specific terms, what it means to think back the ontological difference to enowning through the avenue that this difference opens to enowning.

We find a precise account of the leap's constitution in the opening paragraph of the "joining" titled "Leap." Although presaging and anticipating what unfolds in the entirety of this "joining," the constitution of the leap as outlined in this paragraph shows how this constitution shapes the avenue that the ontological difference opens to enowning and how it makes possible to think back the ontological difference to enowning. To grasp this constitution, we must first read the opening lines of "Leap": "The leap, the most daring move in proceeding from inceptual thinking, abandons and throws aside everything familiar, expecting nothing from beings immediately. Rather, above all else it releases belongingness to be-ing in its full essential swaying as enowning" *(Contributions, 161)*. What this characterization immediately says about the leap's constitution is that it entails abandoning and throwing aside everything familiar, expecting nothing from beings immediately, and releasing the belongingness to be-ing as enowning.

The first constitutive element of the leap is what Heidegger calls abandoning and throwing aside everything familiar. Everything depends on how we understand this abandoning and throwing aside, because as they constitute the leap, abandoning and throwing aside also disclose, in more specific terms, the avenue that ontological difference opens to enowning. Thus to understand this abandoning and throwing aside, we must focus on that which the leap constitutionally abandons and throws aside.

Heidegger eases this task by clearly stating that the leap abandons and throws aside *everything familiar*. The preceding discussion makes clear that "everything familiar" refers to the perspective of beings harboring the guiding-question of philosophy, the determination of the beingness of beings, and the forgottenness of be-ing. If by thus abandoning and throwing aside "everything familiar" we are to bring into view, in more specific terms, the avenue that the ontological difference opens to enowning, we must focus on the perspective of beings, on the guiding-question of philosophy, on the determination of the beingness of beings, and on the forgottenness of be-ing.

Since the leap is constituted in such a way as to unfold by abandoning and throwing aside everything that the ontological difference brings to the fore (the perspective of beings, the guiding-question of philosophy, the determination of beingness of beings, and the forgottenness of be-ing, in short, the 'first beginning'), ultimately what the leap abandons and throws aside is the propensity of the ontological difference to strengthen the perspective of beings and the guiding-question of philosophy; to consolidate the forgottenness of be-ing, and to prolong the entanglement in the 'first beginning.' And the leap abandons and throws aside this propensity of the ontological difference by taking its orientation from enowning, which reverberates within the perspective of beings and, mutatis mutandis, within the guiding-question of philosophy — within the determinations of the beingness of beings and the forgottenness of be-ing. The leap abandons what the ontological difference strengthens and consolidates by taking its orientation from enowning, from that self-supplying and self-mediating midpoint into which all essential swaying of the truth of be-ing must be thought back and which reverberates within this difference. In doing so the leap discloses the avenue that the ontological difference opens into enowning and thereby discloses the action of being-historical thinking that thinks back the ontological difference to enowning.

Heidegger alludes to the second constitutive element of the leap by stating that the leap expects nothing from beings immediately. Everything depends on how we understand this expecting. First, we must not confuse it with the psychological state of awaiting certain events. To say that the leap expects nothing immediately from beings is to say that it expects nothing from the 'first beginning' — from the guiding-question of philosophy, from the determinations of the beingness of beings, and from the forgottenness of be-ing. To expect nothing from beings immediately presupposes that the leap is aware of enowning, of the self-supplying self-mediating midpoint into which all essential swaying of the truth of be-ing must be thought back and which reverberates within the entirety of the 'first beginning.' Since enowning reverberates within the 'first beginning,' expecting nothing immediately from beings means leaving the thinking of beings to the 'first beginning' and instead heeding enowning, which reverberates in this beginning. And since the 'first beginning' harbors the ontological difference, and this difference reveals that enowning reverberates in this beginning, to say that the leap expects nothing immediately from beings is to say that it heeds this reverberating enowning and the avenue to enowning that comes to the fore within this reverberating enowning. Moreover, to say that the leap expects nothing immediately from beings is to say that it aims at the 'first beginning,' heeds the reverberating enowning in this beginning, takes the avenue to enowning, and thus thinks back the ontological difference to enowning. In short, by showing that it expects nothing immediately from beings, the leap ultimately shows that it thinks the ontological difference back to enowning.

Heidegger alludes to the third constitutive element of the leap by speaking of releasing the belongingness to be-ing in its full swaying as enowning. Considering the first two constitutive elements of the leap, we can now see that the first two prepare for the third. However, the third constitutive element, releasing the belongingness to be-ing's full swaying, is not a new accomplishment of the leap, for by abandoning and throwing aside the perspective of the 'first beginning' and everything that is embedded therein, the leap proves to belong to be-ing. Had it not belonged to be-ing, the leap would never have been capable of abandoning and throwing aside the perspective of the 'first beginning' and everything embedded therein. As the leap abandons and throws aside that perspective, it also releases the belongingness to be-ing, the belongingness to enowning.

As soon as the ontological difference opens up the perspective of the 'first beginning' and everything embedded therein, this difference sets the stage for the leap to release the belongingness to be-ing, to enowning. And the leap enacts this releasing by traversing the path that ontological difference opens to enowning. The opening of this path and the leap's releasing the belongingness to be-ing, to enowning amount to the enactment of a thinking that thinks the ontological difference back to enowning. By releasing the belongingness to be-ing, to enowning, the leap de facto thinks the ontological difference back to enowning.

Considering the preceding discussion of the constitutive elements of the leap, we can now summarize the results by saying that the leap thinks the ontological difference back to enowning, abandons and throws aside beings, expects nothing from beings, and releases the belongingness to be-ing, to enowning. By releasing this belongingness, the leap also abandons and throws aside the derivatives of the 'first beginning,' that is, nihilism, modern science, and the global predominance of technology, and expects nothing from them. Moreover, when the leap thinks the ontological difference back to enowning, it *releases* the belongingness of the guiding-question of philosophy to enowning; it *releases* the belongingness of the determinations of beingness of beings to enowning; it *releases* the belongingness of the forgottenness of be-ing to enowning, that is, to the self-supplying, self-mediating midpoint into which all essential swaying of the truth of be-ing must be thought back. Furthermore, by thinking the ontological difference back to enowning, the leap *releases* the belongingness of nihilism, modern science, and the global predominance of technology to enowning, that is, to the self-supplying, self-mediating midpoint into which all essential swaying of the truth of be-ing must be thought back. Concisely put, by thinking the ontological difference back to enowning, the leap *releases* the belongingness of this difference to enowning. The emphasis on the word *release* indicates that this releasing is central to the leap's thinking the ontological difference back to enowning. It is precisely this releasing that lets being-historical thinking begin. Therefore, to understand this beginning of being-historical thinking, we must understand this releasing. What exactly is it?

IV

Generally when we speak of releasing, we mean an action by which something that has been set aside is returned to the normal flow of things. In this sense, we speak of releasing funds, releasing information, releasing prisoners, and the like. What distinguishes this kind of releasing is the power that releasing exercises over that which is released.

The leap's releasing, however, exercises no power at all over what it releases. Without exercising any power, the leap releases the belongingness to be-ing and lets being-historical thinking begin, because the belongingness to be-ing and the inception of being-historical thinking are not set aside and earmarked in advance for releasing. The leap's releasing is totally without power because it happens as mindfulness. Accordingly, the leap's thinking the ontological difference back to enowning and its letting being-historical thinking begin is a releasing that unfolds being-historical thinking as mindfulness. Seen in light of this releasing, mindfulness proves to be the active way in which being-historical thinking unfolds; it is not an attribute of or an addendum to this thinking. With this insight we finally arrive at a juncture where we must address the active character of being-historical thinking, that is, mindfulness.

V

Being-historical thinking leaps over the surpassing of beings—the hallmark of transcendental-horizonal thinking—while remaining mindful of the presence of beings. The mindfulness of this presence is the first indication that being-historical thinking takes shape as mindfulness, and that mindfulness is not an addendum to being-historical thinking but its active way of unfolding.

From the beginning being-historical thinking unfolds as mindfulness not only within "[t]he first full shaping of the jointure (from Echo to The Last God)" (*Contributions*, 42), that is, within the entirety of *Contributions to Philosophy,* but also within the full scope and breadth of the work that Heidegger wrote right after *Contributions to Philosophy, Mindfulness.* By addressing the singular and deciding determination of mindfulness as presented in *Contributions to Philosophy,* by considering the implications of the programmatic pronouncements that Heidegger makes on mindfulness in his "A Retrospective Look at the Pathway" (*Mindfulness,* 363–69), and by analyzing six fundamental determinations of mindfulness, which Heidegger presents at the beginning of *Mindfulness,* I shall demonstrate that from the beginning being-historical thinking unfolds as mindfulness. In what follows I shall take up these three tasks to avoid the misunderstanding that mindfulness is a mode of awareness and also to emphasize that it is not an attribute of or an addendum to being-historical thinking but its active way of unfolding.

(1): It is revealing that the deciding determination of mindfulness in *Contributions to Philosophy* is intimately tied to an equally deciding determination of philosophy. In section 16 of this work we read: "*Philosophy is the immediate, useless, but at the same time masterful knowing from within mindfulness.* Mindfulness is inquiring into the *meaning* (cf. *Being and Time*), i.e., into the truth of be-ing" (*Contributions,* 31). By alluding, on the one hand, to the intricate connection between *Sinn* and *Be-sinn-ung* (which is lost in rendering *Sinn* as "meaning" and *Besinnung* as "mindfulness") and, on the other hand, to the intricate connection between mindfulness and philosophy, Heidegger here makes clear what mindfulness is. It sustains philosophy as a mode of inquiry into the meaning of being *(der Sinn des Seins)* or into what *Contributions to Philosophy* calls the truth of be-ing.

Understood as the inquiry into the meaning or the truth of be-ing, philosophy emerges from within mindfulness as a useless but masterful knowing. Heidegger thus indicates that philosophy's emergence from within mindfulness depends on the meaning or the truth of be-ing, that is, on what be-ing of its own accord offers to questioning-thinking. Thus the inquiry called philosophy is not entirely at the discretion of the inquirer since it is also determined and shaped by the meaning or the truth of be-ing.

Accordingly, to properly grasp the emerging of philosophy as mindfulness, we must above all take into account the intimate relationship between being-historical thinking and what be-ing offers of its own accord to this thinking. Given be-ing's offerings to this thinking, this relationship is not a hegemonic relationship of subjugation and control but one of service, which implies freedom. Philosophy as being-historical thinking emerges as mindfulness of what be-ing offers of its own accord to this thinking, because this thinking is free to be at the service of be-ing. It is at the service of be-ing insofar as this thinking projects-open be-ing's enowning-throw, that is, what be-ing of its own accord offers to this thinking, namely, be-ing's meaning or truth. Accordingly, philosophy's emerging as being-historical thinking from within mindfulness takes shape as an inquiry into the meaning or the truth of be-ing's enowning-throw. In this vein, strictly speaking, "[t]he first full shaping of the jointure (from Echo to The Last God)" (*Contributions*, 42) presents an inquiry that is mindful of be-ing's enowning-throw.

But being mindful of be-ing's enowning-throw is not the same as being consciously aware of this throw. Conscious awareness or its opposite, an unconscious mind, have nothing to do with this throw because it is inexhaustible and as such it cannot become the limited object of consciousness or of the unconscious mind. Moreover, being mindful of be-ing's enowning-throw helps us understand why the "first full shaping of the jointure," that is, *Contributions to Philosophy (From Enowning)* as a whole, is inconclusive. It is inconclusive because be-ing's enowning-throw is inexhaustible.

Two consequences follow from acknowledging this inexhaustibility. First, we realize that the inexhaustibility of be-ing's enowning-throw and the inconclusiveness of *Contributions to Philosophy* go hand in hand. With this realization comes the recognition that the projecting-opening of being's enowning-throw does not deliver a conclusive and exhaustive account of this throw. Second, we realize that the inexhaustibility of be-ing's enowning-throw is reflected in being-historical inquiry because this inquiry is mindful of this inexhaustibility. This mindfulness distinguishes the unfolding of being-historical thinking and should not be misconstrued as a mode of awareness that is subsequently added to this thinking.

In connection with the first consequence, it should be noted that once we properly grasp the inexhaustibility of be-ing's enowning-throw, we also understand why *Contributions to Philosophy* must remain inconclusive. Only when the legitimacy and unavoidability of this inconclusiveness is overlooked can one come to the absurd conclusion that this work is a compilation of Heidegger's working notes, fragmented pieces, and the like. Even the incompleteness of certain sentences in this work does not justify such an assumption; rather this incompleteness is another indication of the inconclusiveness of *Contributions to Philosophy*. Once we realize that this inconclusiveness is a direct consequence of the inexhaustibility of be-ing's enowning-throw, we also realize that the inconclusiveness of this work does not deprive it of its status as Heidegger's second major work after *Being and Time*.

It should be pointed out that Richardson misconstrues this characterization of *Contributions to Philosophy*, which I take over from von Herrmann.[60] When Richardson says that with this characterization, I "touted" *Contributions to Philosophy* as Heidegger's "second major work after *Being and Time*," he fails to distinguish between a whimsical and prejudicial characterization and one that is not.[61] My characterization is based on the insight into the inexhaustibility of be-ing's enowning-throw, on the inconclusiveness of Heidegger's projecting that opens up this throw, and finally on a precise understanding of this projecting as one that unfolds from within the thrown projecting-open, that is, from within the structure whose discovery is one of the important achievements of Heidegger's first major work, *Being and Time*. Since this insight rests entirely on projecting-opening as achieved in *Being and Time*, the characterization of *Contributions to Philosophy* as Heidegger's second major work is based solely on this achievement and thus has nothing to do with "touting" or attributing an unwarranted importance to this work.

Regarding the second consequence, we should note that since being-historical thinking is mindful of the inexhaustibility of being's enowning-throw and of the inconclusiveness of its projecting-opening, mindfulness is not an attribute of or an addendum to being-historical thinking but its very unfolding.

(2): No sooner does Heidegger complete the writing of *Contributions to Philosophy* than he finds it necessary to explicitly point out that this work is inconclusive. By projecting-open be-ing's inexhaustible enowning-throw, Heidegger enacts being-historical thinking as a projecting-opening, which, considering this inexhaustibility, must remain inconclusive. It is in view of the inexhaustibility of be-ing's enowning-throw that Heidegger characterizes as inconclusive the entirety of *Contributions to Philosophy*, that is, the so-called "first full shaping of the jointure (from Echo to The Last God)" (*Contributions*, 42). We find this characterization in the appendix to *Mindfulness* (361–78). There Heidegger refers to the inconclusiveness of *Contributions to Philosophy* by taking a retrospective look at seven inexhaustible major realms that are closely related to the six "joinings" of being-historical thinking, "Echo," "Playing-Forth," "Leap," "Grounding," "The Ones to Come," and "The Last God."

To fully appreciate the thrust of this retrospective look, we must remember that the first full shaping of being-historical thinking, titled *Contributions to Philosophy (From Enowning)*, "cannot avoid the danger of being read and acknowledged as a vast 'system'" (*Contributions*, 42). However, to avoid this danger one must take into account the difference between a detailed unfolding of what being-historical thinking projects-open and the sheer unpredictable range of the question of being. Heidegger is mindful of this difference when in the appendix he says: "In its new approach this *Contributions to Philosophy* should render manifest the range of the question of being. A detailed unfolding here is not necessary because this all too easily narrows down the actual horizon and misses the thrust of questioning" (*Mindfulness*, 377). By foregoing a detailed unfolding, being-historical thinking *perseveres* within the manifest range of the question of being and thus *preserves* the thrust of questioning. That is why Heidegger considers a detailed unfolding to be unnecessary.

Thus persevering, being-historical thinking becomes mindful of seven distinct but inexhaustible major realms within the range of the question of being: the realms of "the differentiation between beings and be-ing," of "Da-sein," of "the truth and time-space," of "the modalities," of "the attunement," of "the language," and finally, of "questioning as the *ur-action* of Da-sein" (*Mindfulness*, 375–76).

We must not take these seven realms as extraneous to the six "join-ings" of *Contributions to Philosophy,* since in various degrees these realms are present in all six "joinings." Although throughout *Contribu-tions to Philosophy* these realms are already projected-open by being-historical thinking in fundamental respects, their inexhaustibility limits that projecting to a mere enacting of being-historical thinking as mind-fulness of these realms. Already projected-open by being-historical thinking throughout *Contributions to Philosophy* yet needing further un-folding, these major realms are opened up by being-historical thinking, which is mindful of the *Sinn*/meaning or the truth inherent in them. Considering these major realms, we understand why for Heidegger what counts above all is to be mindful of these realms instead of trying to unfold them in detail. Thus mindfulness of these realms amounts to the very unfolding of being-historical thinking. And as such an unfold-ing, mindfulness shows that it is not an addendum to this thinking.

(3): The inexhaustibility of the seven major realms is reflected in six foundational determinations of mindfulness that Heidegger presents at the beginning of *Mindfulness.* Before attending in some detail to these six determinations of mindfulness, I should note that each entails a *retrospective* look at the seven inexhaustible realms—all present in vari-ous degrees in all six "joinings" of *Contributions to Philosophy*—and a *prospective* look at what still remains to be accomplished. While Heideg-ger enacts the retrospective look throughout *Contributions to Philosophy,* he enacts the prospective one in *Mindfulness.* What are the six closely interrelated foundational determinations of mindfulness that Heideg-ger offers at the beginning of *Mindfulness?*

The first determination circumscribes mindfulness as philosophy's mindfulness of what is of today, that is, philosophy's mindfulness of modernity. However, this mindfulness never culminates in taking ac-tion against modernity to alter a particular historical situation since it is mindfulness of what sways within modernity and hints beyond moder-nity. In Heidegger's words, "[p]hilosophy's mindfulness of itself must know what is of today, not for purposes of practical enhancement and alteration of the status of a 'historical situation,' but by taking what is of today as fundamental hints at that which being-historically sways in the epoch of modernity" (*Mindfulness,* 38–39). Philosophy's mindful-ness of what is of today is mindfulness of the fundamental hints at what historically sways in the epoch of modernity. Correlated to these hints, this mindfulness is not the same as the much discussed and widely practiced reflection on modernity for the purpose of practically altering and controlling it. This mindfulness already takes place in the first "joining" of *Contributions to Philosophy*, "Echo." In this "joining" being-historical thinking projects-open what sways in the epoch of modernity, that is, the echo of be-ing that intones the abandonment by be-ing, and is mindful of the fundamental hints at what sways in the epoch of modernity, that is, the abandonment by be-ing. Thus to understand how philosophy becomes mindful of itself by becoming mindful of its time requires a thorough familiarity with the entirety of "Echo," that is, with the fundamental hints at the abandonment by be-ing.

However, given the fact that *Contributions to Philosophy* is a "jointure," the first determination of mindfulness, that is, mindfulness of the echo of be-ing is not only present in "Echo" but also in the other five "joinings." More specifically, the first determination of mindfulness is reflected not only in the fundamental hints at the resonance of be-ing's abandonment ("Echo") but also in the play between the 'first' and the 'other beginning' ("Playing-Forth") and in the leap into the full sway of be-ing ("Leap")—a leap that is grounding and grounded ("Grounding") by the ones to come ("The Ones to Come"), that is, by those who receive the hint of the passing of the last god ("The Last God"). In short, for philosophy to become mindful of itself in the epoch of modernity—the first determination of mindfulness—philosophy must become mindful of itself as the being-historical thinking enacted in all six "joinings."

In each of the six "joinings," philosophy as being-historical thinking is mindful of the fundamental hints at what sways in the epoch of modernity, that is, is mindful of the echo of be-ing's abandonment that comes to thinking as be-ing's enowning-throw. By minding the inexhaustibility of be-ing's enowning-throw, being-historical projecting-opening remains unavoidably inconclusive. Thus philosophy's mindfulness of itself in the epoch of modernity is also mindfulness of this unavoidable inconclusiveness. In short, philosophy's mindfulness of itself is mindfulness of being-historical thinking as an inconclusive thinking and is thus not an addendum to this thinking.

The second determination of mindfulness centers entirely on the venturing that is endemic to philosophy: "Through mindfulness philosophy ventures unto the mandate of what is set ahead of philosophy— a venturing unto what is to be en-thought and to be grounded in Da-sein by virtue of this thinking, so that the mystery of man's being will be *saved* rather than abolished" (*Mindfulness*, 39). The mandate of what is set ahead of philosophy is the mandate of be-ing's inexhaustible enowning-throw. By venturing unto this inexhaustible mandate, philosophy is enacted as being-historical thinking which is grounding in and as *Dasein*. This thinking saves and preserves rather than abolishes the mystery of man's being. The immediate outcome of mindfulness of this inexhaustible mandate is that philosophy relinquishes all aspirations either to render transparent man's being (rationalism) or to do away with its mystery (irrationalism). Being mindful of this mandate, philosophy knows that it is not in charge of be-ing's enowning-throw.

Philosophy's mindfulness of itself is mindfulness of the mandate set ahead of it by be-ing's enowning-throw; it is mindfulness of the inexhaustibility of this throw. Since philosophy is enacted as being-historical thinking of this inexhaustible throw that is set ahead of philosophy, its mindfulness of itself as being-historical thinking is mindfulness of this inexhaustibility and is thus not an addendum to this thinking.

With the third determination of mindfulness, Heidegger characterizes it as mindfulness of the truth of be-ing: "Through mindfulness—inquiring-musing—man enters the truth of be-ing and thus takes man 'himself' unto the fundamental transformation that arises out of this truth: the expectancy of Da-sein" (*Mindfulness*, 40). Inquiring-musing, man enters the truth of be-ing; thus he enters into the fundamental transformation that arises out of this truth, that is, the expectancy of *Da-sein*. This expectancy comes to man by be-ing's inexhaustible enowning-throw. Being mindful of this expectancy, man is mindful of that inexhaustible throw. The third determination makes clear that *Dasein* is not simply identical with man but becomes accessible to him through be-ing's enowning-throw, which brings to man the expectancy of *Dasein*, that is, the transforming experience ensuing from the truth of be-ing.

Stressing the expectancy of *Da-sein*, Heidegger with this third determination of mindfulness shows how removed *Da-sein* is from being the essence of man, for the closest man comes to *Da-sein* is by way of being admitted into the expectancy of *Da-sein*. With this determination, Heidegger makes clear that *Da-sein* cannot be thought of as a "self-evident possession . . . never as a general determination . . . but as what is rare, noble and sustaining."[62] Thus philosophy's mindfulness of itself as mindfulness of being-historical thinking of itself takes place within man's expectancy—his prospect—of *Da-sein*, which distinguishes *Da-sein* from a possession of man. Mindfulness of this prospect is constitutive of being-historical thinking, which shows that mindfulness is not an addendum to this thinking.

With the fourth determination of mindfulness, Heidegger indicates that philosophy becomes mindful of itself as the "overcoming [of] 'reason,' be it as mere receiving of what is pre-given (νοῦς), be it as calculating and explaining *(ratio)*, or be it as planning and securing" (*Mindfulness*, 40). Philosophy becomes mindful of itself as the overcoming of reason, of that which with the 'first beginning' of philosophy dominates philosophy first as νοῦς and then as the calculating, explaining *ratio*, and securing. Here again we see that insofar as being-historical thinking as philosophy is mindful of the overcoming of reason, of νοῦς, of *ratio*, mindfulness is constitutive of this thinking and not an attribute of or an addendum to this thinking.

The fifth determination of mindfulness emerges when Heidegger observes that mindfulness and attunement are always together: "Mindfulness is attuning of the grounding-attunement of man insofar as this attunement attunes him unto be-ing, and unto the groundership of the truth of be-ing" (*Mindfulness*, 40). Heidegger thus distinguishes mindfulness from the attunement-bereft reflection in epistemology. Mindfulness *as* attuning of the grounding-attunement means that philosophy becomes mindful of itself when it completely evolves under the disclosing power of attunement. The grounding-attunement of being-historical thinking, reservedness *(Verhaltenheit)*, attunes philosophy's mindfulness of itself from the ground up. Without the disclosing power of this attunement, being-historical thinking cannot become mindful of itself. Seen in light of this attunement, being-historical thinking unfolds as mindfulness and *is* the mindfulness of this attunement. Considering this attunement, we realize that mindfulness is constitutive of being-historical thinking and is not an attribute of or an addendum to this thinking.

Finally, the sixth determination of mindfulness emerges when Heidegger recognizes language and word as the domain of mindfulness. The connection to mindfulness here is philosophy: "*Philosophy:* this sole struggle for the imageless word 'of' be-ing in an epoch of asthenia and lack of enthusiasm for the swaying word" (*Mindfulness*, 40). With the last determination, Heidegger relegates mindfulness to the imageless word "of" be-ing. Philosophy's mindfulness of itself is the mindfulness of the struggle within philosophy for the imageless word "of" be-ing. Since mindfulness is philosophy's mindfulness of itself as being-historical thinking, and since this thinking struggles for the imageless word "of" be-ing, we can see that mindfulness of this struggle is constitutive of being-historical thinking. This shows once again that mindfulness is not an addendum to this thinking.

Considering this understanding of the deciding determination of philosophy as a useless but masterful knowing, of the inconclusiveness of *Contributions to Philosophy,* and of the six foundational determinations of mindfulness—mentioned above as three tasks—we must conclude that mindfulness is the active character of being-historical thinking: its unfolding.

Since mindfulness is not an addendum to being-historical thinking, with *Mindfulness* Heidegger neither revises *Contributions to Philosophy* nor offers a commentary on this work. To take *Mindfulness* as Heidegger's commentary on *Contributions to Philosophy* is to assume that mindfulness is something other than the active character of being-historical thinking—something other than its unfolding within this work. Considering the unfolding of being-historical thinking in *Contributions to Philosophy* and taking into account the six foundational determinations of mindfulness, we must reject this assumption as unfounded. Thus the relationship between *Mindfulness* and *Contributions to Philosophy* is already determined by the unfolding of being-historical thinking as mindfulness within the latter work. Instead of getting mired in the chronology of 1936–38 and 1938–39 (the dates of the writing of *Contributions to Philosophy* and *Mindfulness,* respectively) and instead of assuming that *Mindfulness* is a commentary on *Contributions to Philosophy*—thus unquestioningly succumbing to the hegemony of chronological order—we must understand the relation of these two works in light of their temporally equal originality, which dislodges that hegemony.

VI

By explicating the ties between ontological difference and enowning and by demonstrating that being-historical thinking unfolds as mindfulness, I allude to what seem to be the minimum requirements that philosophy should meet if it is to recognize the need for a renewed appropriation of Heidegger's thought. Rather than obstinately and unquestioningly holding on to the entrenched assumptions that have determined the appropriation of Heidegger's work up to now, philosophy should address the issue of the ontological difference as that which emerges from within the 'first beginning' and determines the entire course of this beginning from Plato to Nietzsche. Relinquishing that entrenched assumption requires abandoning the periodization of Heidegger's thought into a Heidegger I and a Heidegger II, for the inception of being-historical thinking from within a transformed thrownness—from within a thrownness en-owned by be-ing—demonstrates how misleading it is to assume a "break" in Heidegger's thought and attempt to divide his work accordingly. Moreover, the inception of being-historical thinking from within a transformed and historically en-owned thrownness renders totally irrelevant all the assumptions claiming that *Ereignis,* enowning, already occurs in Heidegger's early thinking.

If being-historical thinking has its inception in the transformation of the transcendental-horizonal onset of the thinking of being, that is, in the transformed thrown-projecting-open, then the path of thinking that Heidegger traverses with and after *Being and Time* is that of a transformed but continuing unfolding of the thinking of being. It is a transformed thinking of being because the thinking of being as thinking of enowning cannot be found in the works of Heidegger prior to and including *Being and Time.* Yet this thinking represents a continuing unfolding because being-historical thinking has its inception within a transformed thrown projecting-opening. One important consequence of such an understanding of Heidegger's path of thinking is recognizing as irrelevant the point that H.-G. Gadamer has made in talking about a "turning before turning," that is, placing the turning in Heidegger's thought before *Being and Time.*[63]

Finally, with the realization that mindfulness is not an attribute of or an addendum to being-historical thinking but is its unfolding, our relationship to Heidegger's language of the thinking of being appears in a new light. Since this language is shaped from within a "saying" that is itself the swaying of be-ing, we must regard as irrelevant and counterproductive any attempt to take this language out of that "saying" in order to force it into another language presumed to be more "intelligible" than Heidegger's. The key to entering into the being-historical thinking of *Contributions to Philosophy* and *Mindfulness* lies not in "transferring" Heidegger's language of the thinking of being into another more "intelligible" language but precisely in dwelling within Heidegger's language of the thinking of being.

Mastery of Be-ing and Coercive Force of Machination in Heidegger's *Contributions to Philosophy* and *Mindfulness* and the Opening to His Nietzsche Interpretation

Two major works of Heidegger's, *Contributions to Philosophy (From Enowning)* and *Mindfulness*, the German originals of which appeared in 1989 and 1997, respectively, present a thinking as "revolutionary" as did *Being and Time* when it appeared in 1927. Generally speaking, these works entail directives for thinking that come from and lead to be-ing's self-showing and manifesting. But whereas in *Being and Time* these directives come from and lead to a transcendental-horizonal disclosure of being, those in *Contributions to Philosophy* and *Mindfulness* come from and lead to the disclosure of be-ing's historically self-transforming self-showing and manifesting. The circle these directives traverse in coming from and leading to those disclosures is bequeathed only to thinking-mindfulness.

One of the decisive yields of be-ing's historically self-transforming showing in both *Contributions to Philosophy* and *Mindfulness* is the insight into the mastery of be-ing and the coercive force of machination. This essay seeks to carry this insight further to elucidate Heidegger's understanding of the mastery of be-ing and the coercive force of machination and show how this understanding provides access to his interpretation of Nietzsche. First, however, I must highlight the background against which we will observe be-ing's historically self-transforming showing and manifesting.

We find this background in the domain of hermeneutic phenomenology as it unfolds in *Being and Time, Contributions to Philosophy,* and *Mindfulness.* Focusing on this domain, we also find that the measure for assessing the achievements of these three works lies not outside this domain but in the onefold of "interpretation" (*Auslegung, ἑρμηνεύειν*) and "what-shows-itself-in-itself, the manifest" *(Phänomen "das Sich-an-ihm-selbst-zeigende, das Offenbare")* (*GA* 2:38–50). More specifically, the measure for assessing Heidegger's achievement in these three works lies in the λόγος of this phenomenology, that is, in the onefold of "interpretation" and "the manifest." And it is precisely in this λόγος, in this onefold that we find at work Heidegger's insight into the mastery of be-ing and the coercive force of machination. Therefore, before embarking on a discussion of this mastery, let us take a brief look at the earlier and later shapings of this onefold within hermeneutic phenomenology.

In *Being and Time* Heidegger presents a transcendental-horizonal onefold of "interpretation" and "being as it shows-itself—in-itself." But in *Contributions to Philosophy* and *Mindfulness,* he puts forth the onefold of "interpretation" and "be-ing's historically self-transforming self-showing and manifesting." Thus, in moving from *Being and Time* to *Contributions to Philosophy* and *Mindfulness,* we see that a transformation in being's self-showing as "the manifest" occurs, which has profound implications for understanding Heidegger's insight into the mastery of be-ing and the coercive force of machination.

This transformation is best characterized with the words of F.-W. von Herrmann as an "immanent transformation."[64] What distinguishes *Being and Time, Contributions to Philosophy,* and *Mindfulness* is that while in *Being and Time* Heidegger's thinking projects-open the transcendental-horizonal disclosure of be-ing's self-showing, in *Contributions to Philosophy* and in *Mindfulness* his thinking projects-open be-ing's *historically self-transforming* showing and manifesting. By bearing in mind be-ing's *historically self-transforming* showing, we can elucidate Heidegger's insight into the mastery of be-ing and the coercive force of machination. Heidegger's thinking projects-open machination—this manner of be-ing's historically self-transforming showing—because his thinking is *en-*owned *(er-eignet)* by be-ing. (It will be recalled that the prefix *en-* in English conveys the sense of "enabling" or "bringing into the condition of." With *en-* and *own* coming together in *en-owned,* we have in English the closest approximation to *er-eignet.*) It is be-ing itself that enables Heidegger's thinking to address the unfolding of machination, that is, the unfolding of a specific manner of be-ing's historically self-transforming showing. Thus Heidegger's thinking does not stand vis-à-vis be-ing (if that were possible)—does not objectify be-ing—since his thinking is from the ground up en-owned and thus enabled by be-ing.

It is of paramount importance for understanding this enowning, enabling power of be-ing to keep in mind that be-ing's historically self-transforming showing is not something that happens *to be-ing* as if this showing were something other than be-ing itself; be-ing comes to pass *as this self-showing*. The enabling power that en-owns Heidegger's thinking and enables it to gain insight into the mastery of be-ing and the coercive force of machination operates at the very core of the thinking that unfolds in *Contributions to Philosophy* and in *Mindfulness*. This enabling power also highlights the background against which the mastery of be-ing and the coercive force of machination are to be understood.

In order to bring this enabling power of be-ing more clearly into view, we must take into account a perspective *(Blickbahn)* that comes from and leads to be-ing's historically self-transforming showing.[65] As he adopts this perspective, Heidegger relinquishes the transcendental-horizonal path and begins to traverse that of being-historical thinking. What is the perspective of be-ing's historically self-transforming showing, and how does it prompt Heidegger to abandon the perspective of being's transcendental-horizonal disclosure?

I

To understand the range and scope of the enabling power that comes from be-ing, we must address the question, how does thinking that traverses the transcendental-horizonal path become a thinking that is mindful of being's historically self-transforming showing? F.-W. von Herrmann calls the transcendental-horizonal path of Heidegger's thinking "the first path for working out the question of being," thereby alluding to a perspective (he uses the word *Blickbahn*) within which Heidegger opens the second path for working out this question.[66] This second *Blickbahn*, this second perspective as it belongs to and is en-owned and enabled by be-ing, allows Heidegger's thinking to become mindful of being's historically self-transforming showing.

It is important to understand this perspective as one in which a *Blick* (regard, glance) and a *Bahn* (path, track) come together. Both this track and that regard, in short this perspective, lie within the domain of be-ing's historically self-transforming showing, which Heidegger calls enowning. With regard to the insight into the mastery of be-ing and the coercive force of machination, this insight too is held within this perspective, which shelters the power that enables Heidegger's thinking to gain this insight. I call it the perspective of enowning and note that out of this perspective Heidegger speaks of the mastery of be-ing. Because of this central role of enowning, we must first ask, what shape does it take in *Contributions to Philosophy?*

We must respond to this question carefully because an adequate understanding of what Heidegger means by mastery of be-ing largely depends on this response. Accordingly, it should be noted that throughout the six "joinings" of *Contributions to Philosophy* and in a nonlinear, gradual, cohesive, systematic, and closely interrelated manner, Heidegger unfolds a thinking that as being-historical-thinking is en-owned by enowning. In each of the six "joinings," the primary and decisive character of this thinking consists in its saying the same of the same from within another foundational domain of enowning: "Each of the six joinings of the jointure stands for itself, but only in order to make the essential onefold more pressing. In each of the six joinings the attempt is made always to say the same of the same, but in each case from within another essential domain of that which enowning names" (*Contributions, 57*). Focusing on what Heidegger here calls "saying the same of the same," we realize that whether we deal with "Echo" or with any one of the other five "joinings" ("Playing Forth," "Leap," "Grounding," "The Ones to Come," "The Last God"), each "joining" says "the same of the same" from within another foundational domain that enowning names, for instance, in "Echo" and "Leap," where "Echo" names the resonance of be-ing's abandonment (one domain), and "Leap" names the leap into be-ing's full swaying (another domain).

When we consider the decisive character of being-historical thinking, that is, its saying "the same of the same" in the context of the perspective of enowning, we realize that this perspective leads thinking not only to each "joining" as each is conferred and en-owned by be-ing as enowning but also to enowning itself. (If this were not the case, Heidegger could not say in each of the "joinings" of *Contributions to Philosophy* "the same of the same" of that which enowning names.) Thus as enabled and en-owned by be-ing, that is, by enowning, this perspective is not constituted by thinking; it is *conferred upon* thinking by be-ing. Having been *conferred* by be-ing and *coming from* be-ing, this perspective is be-ing's enowning forth-throw (*der ereignende Zuwurf*).[67] Thus, whether in *Contributions to Philosophy* we consider the echo of be-ing or the manner in which the 'first beginning' plays forth into the 'other beginning,' or the leap into the swaying of be-ing or the grounding of this swaying by the ones to come, that is, by those who receive the hints of the passing of the last god, it is always this perspective that enables Heidegger's thinking to unfold the sixfold "joinings" of enowning.

However, because I am concerned mainly with the insight into the mastery of be-ing and the coercive force of machination, I must turn to the first "joining" of *Contributions to Philosophy*, where, within a perspective enabled and en-owned by be-ing, Heidegger unfolds the echo of be-ing and names it machination. But to what extent does the mastery of be-ing echo or reverberate within this perspective *along with* the coercive force of machination? The response to this question comes from *Mindfulness*, in which Heidegger determines the ownmost of machination after he returns, in a manner most worthy of our attention, to machination's initial self-showing as articulated in *Contributions to Philosophy*. To grasp the response to the question concerning the reverberation within this perspective of the mastery of be-ing *along with* the coercive force of machination, we must understand how in *Mindfulness* Heidegger determines what is ownmost to machination. And this requires that we first become acquainted with machination, which Heidegger lays out in the first "joining" of *Contributions to Philosophy*.

II

The perspective that leads to be-ing's historically self-transforming showing yields five directives in the first "joining" of *Contributions to Philosophy* for grasping the specific manner of this showing, which Heidegger calls machination. Heidegger presents these five directives in the following passage:

In the context of the being-question this word [machination] does not name a human comportment but a manner of the essential swaying of being. Even the disparaging tone should be kept at a distance, even though machination fosters what is *not* ownmost to being. And even what is *not* ownmost to being should never be depreciated, because it is essential to what is ownmost to being. Rather, the name should immediately point to *making* (ποίησις, τέχνη). . . . Machination as the essential swaying of beingness yields a faint hint of the truth of be-ing itself. (*Contributions*, 88, interpolation is mine)

The first directive states that machination does not name a human comportment. The second directive indicates that machination is a manner of the swaying of be-ing. The third directive announces that machination points to making in the sense of ποίησις and τέχνη. The fourth directive guides us to beingness as residing in machination. The fifth directive refers to the elusive connection between machination and the truth of be-ing. By leading to be-ing's historically self-transforming showing, the first directive mainly fulfills a prohibitive function: machination should not be confused with a human comportment. With the second directive Heidegger indicates that machination is to be thought in terms of the swaying of be-ing. With the third directive he indicates that machination is at work in the thinking of the Greeks. With the fourth directive he recognizes the connection between machination and the beingness of beings. With the fifth directive he notes the hidden relationship between machination and unconcealment, that is, ἀλήθεια, and the possibility of grounding this relationship. Let us take a brief look at each of the five directives.

With the prohibitive function of the first directive, Heidegger safeguards machination from being misunderstood according to ordinary meanings of the word; in *Contributions to Philosophy, machination* does not mean plotting, conniving, and the like. With the second directive he proceeds from this prohibitive function to a precise characterization of machination; it is *a manner* of the full swaying of be-ing. Although machination as a manner of the full swaying of be-ing is not what is ownmost to be-ing, it is not unrelated to what is ownmost to be-ing. We shall see later that precisely *this manner* of the full swaying of be-ing allows for a phenomenological viewing of the mastery of be-ing.

With the third directive Heidegger highlights the domain of "making" and "makability," ποίησις and τέχνη, in the 'first beginning' as a domain already shaped by machination. He also implies that in Plato and Aristotle "making" and "makability"—manners and modes of machination—bring the 'first beginning' to its end and push φύσις aside.[68]

With the fourth directive Heidegger indicates that the ever-first-inceptual grasping of the beingness of beings as "makable" is shaped in light of machination. This directive leads us to the inceptual possibility of recasting this beingness. With the preponderance of "making" and "makability"—modes of machination—in the 'first beginning,' the beingness of beings is grasped in light of what is not ownmost to be-ing, that is, machination. Along with "making," and "makability" (ποίησις and τέχνη), ἰδέα and οὐσία in Plato and Aristotle emerge and dislodge φύσις.

The fifth directive derives from the knowing awareness of a hidden relationship between machination and the ever-first-inceptual occurrence called unconcealment, ἀλήθεια. Accordingly, this directive is the most important of the five and extends to all the ramifications of machination.

With regard to the mastery of be-ing and the coercive force of machination, what do we learn from discussing these five directives? We learn that be-ing's full swaying comes to pass simultaneously along with *a manner* of this swaying. We also learn that machination as a manner of the full swaying of be-ing fosters and discloses—reveals—disenownment by be-ing. Thus when beings are unconcealed in light of machination as makable, be-ing's disenowning forth-throw *(enteig-nender Zuwurf)* emerges in the foreground.[69] But to come to terms with each of these points, we must keep in mind that machination, disenownment by be-ing, and be-ing's disenowning forth-throw are all reserved and preserved within the grounding-attunement that Heidegger names reservedness. Accordingly, we must discuss the range and scope of the grounding-attunement called reservedness.

III

We find the ultimate justification for the persuasiveness marking hermeneutic phenomenology in Heidegger's discussion of the grounding-attunement that he calls reservedness. This attunement shapes his thinking but is not its preexisting condition. If Heidegger's thinking interprets "the manifest" (machination) as "*a manner* of the essential swaying of be-ing," it (thinking) does so not because it is unfree and conditioned by a preexisting hegemonic power but because it is *attuned* to "the manifest" from the ground up.

In the context of the question of being and in the course of the unfolding of hermeneutic phenomenology, Heidegger often remarks concerning the attuned character of thinking. He first notes that a thinking bereft of attunement has no access to the domain of hermeneutic phenomenology and is not exposed to the question of being. Specifically, a thinking barred from the grounding-attunement does not receive and project-open the "manifest"; such a thinking is engaged in a game with empty words: "If the grounding-attunement stays away, then everything is a forced rattling of concepts and empty words" (*Contributions*, 15–16). Only the thinking that through grounding-attunement is attuned to "what-shows-itself-in-itself, the manifest," has access to the domain of hermeneutic phenomenology. Thus attuned, such a thinking names *a manner* of the full swaying of be-ing, machination. A thinking bereft of attunement has nothing to say about hermeneutic phenomenology and the full swaying of be-ing. No wonder then that, as attunement-bereft, epistemology, Anglo-American analytic philosophy, and French deconstruction have no access to hermeneutic phenomenology.

Realizing the important role played by the grounding-attunement called reservedness in thinking the "manifest," that is, "machination," "*a manner* of the essential swaying of being," one may want to prepare for such attunement by naively expecting to bring it about through analysis and definition of the grounding-attunement. But a preparation for and evocation of grounding-attunement by way of an analysis or definition are pointless: "Everything would be misinterpreted and would fail if we wanted to prepare the grounding-attunement with the help of an analysis, or even a 'definition'" (*Contributions*, 15). Thus no definition and no analysis of the grounding-attunement can evoke it and prepare for it, since by themselves definitions and analyses do not bring about the "manifest," that is, machination. Rather than trying to evoke this attunement, one would do well to recall that the grounding-attunement is an unexpected and unintended happening that unexpectedly attunes thinking. Instead of being content with pondering a definition of this attunement and analyzing it, one should be mindful of its unexpected and unintended way of "breaking-in." In Heidegger's words, "[e]very mindfulness of this grounding-attunement is always only a gentle preparation for the attuning breaking-in [*Einfall*] of the grounding-attunement, which must remain fundamentally an unintended happening [*Zufall*]" (*Contributions*, 16–17). With these remarks Heidegger touches on the profound manner in which the transforming experience of mindfulness of the grounding-attunement shapes his thinking. He thereby alerts us that if we want to understand this thinking, we too must take our orientation from thinking's total dependence on the grounding-attunement. Being mindful of this attunement, we realize that it "breaks-in" of its own accord and is thus completely beyond our control. This shows how central, crucial, and fruitful mindfulness of this grounding-attunement is for the thinking of being. Unlike reflection, which depends wholly on objectifying thinking and thus has no access to "the manifest," that is, to machination, mindfulness of the grounding-attunement is not an objectifying reflective thinking; it comes upon thinking as a transforming experience. Being mindful of the grounding-attunement called reservedness reveals that thinking is transformed from the ground up and is thus prepared for receiving and interpreting the "manifest," the machination as it breaks-in.

Heidegger calls this thinking essential thinking *(wesentliches Den-ken)* and describes how its pronouncements emerge from within the grounding-attunement when he says: "All essential thinking requires that its thoughts and sentences be mined, like ore, every time anew out of the grounding-attunement" *(Contributions, 15)*, that is, mined from within the grounding-attunement he calls reservedness. Thus he makes clear that words and phrases such as *machination* and *essential swaying of be-ing* are also "mined" from within this grounding-attunement.

In view of the preceding discussion of the grounding-attunement, we should understand machination as a being-historical word in which come together the "manifest," that is, be-ing's full swaying, and *a man-ner* of this swaying that is not ownmost to be-ing. More importantly, we should keep in mind that this word is reserved and preserved in the grounding-attunement called reservedness. Besides this word, the three concealments of the abandonment of being in machination, that is, "acceleration" *(Schnelligkeit)*, "calculation" *(Berechnung)*, and the "claim of massiveness" *(Anspruch des Massenhaften)*, are also reserved and preserved in this grounding-attunement.[70] (These three conceal-ments mark the completion of the epoch of modernity as one domi-nated by the acceleration of things, by the calculation of things, and by the massive formation of things.)

IV

The further unfolding of machination in the direction of what consti-tutes its ownmost, however, takes place in *Mindfulness*. This further un-folding provides the basis for understanding the insight into the mas-tery of be-ing and the coercive force of machination. To ascertain what such an unfolding entails, I must briefly discuss Heidegger's character-ization of the task of *Contributions to Philosophy* and his assessment of this work because a deeper understanding of everything discussed thus far—the en-owned character of the being-historical perspective, its residing within the full swaying of be-ing as enowning, and its leading to machination—depends on understanding this characterization and assessment.

According to Heidegger, the task of *Contributions to Philosophy* is to project-open "the grounding enopening of the free-play of the time-space of the truth of being" *(Contributions, 4)*. The projecting-opening to which Heidegger alludes here is specific since it grounds the enopening of the free play of the time-space of the truth of being. In other words, at stake in this projecting is the task of *grounding* this free play. Thus the thinking that shapes *Contributions to Philosophy* not only projects-open the free play of the time-space of the truth of be-ing but also must ground this free play. As such, this projecting shapes the "joinings" called "Echo," "Playing-Forth," "Leap," "Grounding," "The Ones to Come," and "The Last God."

However, this task of projecting-opening is not conclusively carried out in *Contributions to Philosophy* and is extended further into *Mindfulness,* because Heidegger characterizes *Contributions to Philosophy* as a work that is bent on maintaining the thrust of questioning and thus stops short of unfolding in detail the free play of the time-space of the truth of be-ing. As Heidegger observes: "In its new approach this *Contributions to Philosophy* should render manifest the range of the question of being. A detailed unfolding here is not necessary because this all too easily narrows down the actual horizon and misses the thrust of questioning" (*Mindfulness,* 377). Looking at the preceding discussion of machination in light of this characterization of *Contributions to Philosophy* and taking into account what Heidegger accomplishes in *Mindfulness,* I suggest that with *Mindfulness* he presents a further and detailed unfolding of the free play of the time-space of the truth of be-ing. To cite only one text in support of this suggestion, I should mention the first main part of this work, titled "Leaping Ahead unto the Uniqueness of Be-ing" (*Mindfulness,* 9). Precisely in this part of *Mindfulness* Heidegger returns to the first "joining" of *Contributions to Philosophy,* that is, to "Echo."[71]

How are we to understand Heidegger's returning in the first main part of *Mindfulness* to the first "joining" of *Contributions to Philosophy?* What is entailed in this returning? Because the full unfolding of machination cannot be divorced from Heidegger's returning in this part of *Mindfulness* to the first "joining" of *Contributions to Philosophy,* because this returning presents a detailed unfolding of machination, and because through this unfolding we can distinguish the mastery of be-ing from the coercive force of machination, I must carefully delineate what this returning entails.

V

In the first main part of *Mindfulness,* Heidegger returns to the first "joining" of *Contributions to Philosophy* and further unfolds machination.

However, this returning should not be construed as coming back to a "thesis" that had earlier been insufficiently expressed and now needs further elaboration. We fail to grasp what actually transpires in this returning if we take it as Heidegger's "subjective" decision to return to a "thesis" that he left inadequately expressed in the first "joining" of *Contributions to Philosophy*. Rather, Heidegger returns to machination because its further unfolding is preserved in a perspective *(Blickbahn)* that we discussed earlier and that is reserved in the grounding-attunement called reservedness. Everything that results from this returning is already preserved in that reserved perspective. In the final analysis, Heidegger's returning in the first part of *Mindfulness* to machination as it is presented in *Contributions to Philosophy* is a returning to "the manifest" that together with "interpretation" constitutes the onefold of hermeneutic phenomenology. In this onefold the "manifest" and "interpretation" are distinct, and this distinctness differentiates that onefold from a "thesis" and its "adequate expression." Thus machination as it is presented in *Contributions to Philosophy* and called *a manner* of the full swaying of be-ing is not a "thesis" that needs a more adequate "expression."

Heidegger returns in the first main part of *Mindfulness* to machination in order to actualize the perspective that, like machination, is reserved in the grounding-attunement of reservedness. By actualizing this perspective and further unfolding machination, Heidegger does not "add" anything "new" to it because what results from this actualization is already reserved and preserved as the ownmost of machination in the grounding-attunement of reservedness. And what is ownmost to machination is an annihilating and coercive force. We glean this from Heidegger's remarks: "Already constantly annihilating in the very threat of annihilation, machination expands its sway as coercive force" (*Mindfulness*, 12). The very threat of annihilation reveals the annihilating coercive force as what is ownmost to machination. How are we to understand this force?

It should be noted that this annihilating coercive force does not come upon an already unconcealed being because machination, whose ownmost this annihilating coercive force is, is *a manner* of the full swaying of be-ing and as such is *a manner* of unconcealing beings. What makes a being annihilable and coercible is not that it can be exposed to an extant physical force *but rather the manner in which such a being is unconcealed.* Thus the annihilating coercive force, that is, the ownmost of machination, is not a force that affects a being *after* that being is unconcealed. As the ownmost of machination, the annihilating coercive force itself is an unconcealing force. Heidegger directs us to the unconcealing annihilating coercive force by disclosing the configuration of machination and annihilation: "But then machination adjoins beings as such to the space of a play that continually plays into machination as an ongoing *annihilation*"(*Mindfulness*, 12). Therefore, a continual annihilation gives machination a range and scope within which beings are unconcealed and thus attain specificity. Moreover, this annihilating coercive force is subordinated to power and because of this subordination is fundamentally unfit to ground mastery. In Heidegger's words, "[t]he coercive force that is released within the sway of machination is always subordinated only to power and never grounds mastery, because machination reaches ahead of everything makable, blocks and finally undermines all decision" (*Mindfulness*, 12). A coercive force that is subordinated to power is released within machination (within *a manner* of the full swaying of be-ing, that is, within *a manner* of unconcealing). The releasing of this force, its unconcealing, shows that although machination blocks all decision, it is nevertheless *a clearing within which beings are unconcealed as annihilable and coercible.*

As *a manner* of the full swaying of be-ing within which an unconcealing annihilating power is released, machination occurs in a way that reminds us of the mastery of be-ing itself. This reminder comes from the unconcealing that *is* machination; machination prevails *as unconcealing* because it is *a manner* of the full swaying of be-ing. The unconcealing that occurs as machination, however, prevails as the annihilating coercive power that *cannot at all block the prevailing mastery of be-ing.* However driven and guided by power this prevailing unconcealing of machination may be, it nonetheless lacks mastery and cannot block the mastery of be-ing because machination is *a manner* of the full swaying of being and not *the manner* of this swaying. What is retained and reserved in *a* manner of the full swaying of be-ing is *the mastery of be-ing.* Considering this mastery, we can say that the prevailing unconcealing machination cannot continue to *be* without the swaying mastery of be-ing. Without that mastery, machination ceases to be what it is, namely, a clearing for a certain manner of unconcealing. Herein lies a significant difference between machination—the prevailing clearing—and the mastery of be-ing.

Whether beings belong to the sphere of praxis (art, technicity) or to a private, public, scientific, or religious sphere, in the clearing called machination they are all unconcealed as annihilable and coercible. However, the prevailing machination, wherein an annihilating coercive

force is released, owes its unconcealing prowess to be-ing, since machination is *a manner* of the full swaying of be-ing. Thus the mastery of *the
full swaying of be-ing* (not to be confused with *a manner* of this swaying)
echoes in machination's power as a prevailing clearing. Therefore, the
full swaying of be-ing and machination as *a manner* of this swaying are
simultaneous. This simultaneity is that of the full swaying of be-ing and
the clearing called machination; it is the simultaneity of the mastery of
be-ing and the coercive force released within machination. In essence
this simultaneity holds the key for grasping the difference between the
mastery of be-ing and the coercive force of machination. One way of
approaching this difference is to discuss the role of "decision."

Heidegger casts new light on machination when he says that machination, the prevailing clearing, "reaches ahead of everything makable,
blocks and finally undermines all decision" (*Mindfulness,* 12). But does
not "making" require decision? How can Heidegger say that because
machination precedes whatever is makable, it blocks and undermines
decision?

We must bear in mind that the clearing that prevails as machination
(wherein an annihilating coercive force unfolds) is the ground for
projecting-opening and unconcealing beings as annihilable and coercible. Because machination houses such a projecting-opening, this clearing precedes whatever is deemed to be projected-open as makable. We
must recall that since the full swaying of be-ing is a ground that is simultaneously abground (*Abgrund*), unground (*Ungrund*), and urground
(*Urgrund*), machination, *a manner* of this full swaying, is an unground
that simulates an abground. Accordingly, to project-open and unconceal
a being—be it a pair of shoes or Nietzsche's new god—in keeping with
this unground, thinking takes its orientation from the making inherent
in this unground, that is, in machination.[72] In this vein thinking unconceals every conceivable being as makable. By unconcealing a being as
makable, such thinking takes its bearings from machination and aborts,
blocks, and undermines a "decision" in favor of an unconcealing—a
projecting-opening—that does not rest on that unground but on a
ground that stays away and while staying away somehow *is.* Let us see
how this "other" unconcealing or projecting-opening occurs.

First, we note that blocking and undermining all decision is the consequence of a thinking that projects-open a being, that is, unconceals
a being—any being—solely as makable, annihilable, and coercible. In
this respect such a thinking unconceals a being in complete accord
with *a manner* (not *the* manner) of the full swaying of be-ing, that is,

in complete accord with machination. To fully elucidate such a thinking would require a detailed analysis of what Heidegger says about projecting-open in sections 122, 182, 183, 203, 262, and especially 263 of *Contributions to Philosophy*. Instead, at the risk of oversimplifying one of the most illuminating achievements of this work, I offer the gist of what Heidegger discusses in these sections and suggest (a) that thinking is fundamentally a thrown-projecting-open; (b) that as such a projecting-open, thinking moves unto the utmost manifestness of "the manifest," which as *a manner* of the full swaying of be-ing is none other than machination; (c) that after thus moving unto *this* manner of the full swaying of be-ing, machination, thinking then returns to *the full swaying of be-ing*; (d) that thinking thus proves to be a "returner" *(Zurückkehrer)*; and (e) that accordingly, thinking testifies to the ever-present possibility of experiencing and thus being transformed by this returnership *(Rückkehrerschaft)*. Because I can presuppose a basic familiarity with that to which I allude under (a) and (b), I shall put both aside and briefly examine what I mention under (c) (d), and (e), because moving unto and returning from machination and experiencing the transforming returnership comprise the necessary condition for elucidating the difference between the mastery of be-ing and the coercive force of machination.

What is the difference between the thinking that experiences the transforming returnership and the thinking that unconceals a being in light of the prevailing clearing called machination? The difference consists in the failure of the thinking that unfolds within the prevailing clearing to recognize its own deeper character as a thinking that is enowned by be-ing. The thinking that is under the sway of the prevailing clearing called machination and projects-open annihilable and coercible beings is a thinking dis-enowned *(ent-eignet)* by be-ing. This thinking is dis-enowned because only as such can it operate within machination, that is, within the clearing for the unconcealing of annihilable and coercible beings. Such a thinking has no awareness that it has moved *unto* and returned *from* machination and has experienced the transforming returnership. However, we must be careful not to confuse this awareness with the awareness that is consciousness, for that which this awareness is aware of is not something already given to reflective consciousness. Strictly speaking, consciousness does not provide access to the move unto and the return from machination and to the returnership since each of these presupposes the enownment of thinking, that is, the enownment of projecting-open (not of consciousness) by enowning, and each of these requires the most thorough grounding.

Heidegger elucidates the "move unto," the "returning," and the "returnership" when, with a view toward the history of metaphysics as the history of the projecting-opening of be-ing's forth-throw, he draws on the *differentiation* of a being and be-ing (ontological difference) and says explicitly that this history would not have been possible without "[m]an up to now . . . being able to experience this differentiation and even to ground it" (*Contributions*, 318–19). He further notes that to initiate such a grounding, "[o]ne must first know the manner of dwelling and the concomitant gift, as well as the manner in which . . . what . . . is initially met with as . . . a being . . . is found as a being—[one must first know] which view of being man as the returner [*Zurückkehrer*] retains" (*Contributions*, 319, interpolation is mine). And this means that to proceed with the grounding, one must know "how this return . . . is *forgotten* and how everything becomes an extant, orderable, and producible possession . . . ; how *in this way* then everything is destroyed; how a colossal disturbance runs through all human progress; how be-ing itself as machination sets itself into what is precisely not its ownmost" (*Contributions*, 319).

Thus a thinking that experiences the differentiation of beings and being (the ontological difference) but does *not* ground this differentiation; a thinking that does *not* know that the unconcealing of annihilable, coercible beings as makable is the result of the concomitant gift of being thrown into the clearing called machination; a thinking that does *not* return from this unconcealing and does *not* experience the returnership is one that is *dis-enowned* by be-ing and one whose projecting-opening of be-ing's forth-throw is also a *dis-enowned* projecting-opening. Since such a thinking unfolds within the prevailing clearing called machination, it blocks and undermines the decision that could lead to the experience of returnership. But what is more important is that by failing to experience the returnership, such a thinking has no awareness of the mastery of be-ing. On the contrary, it is totally ensnared by and sucked into the coercive power dominating the clearing that occurs as machination.

But there is another side to blocking and undermining all "decision," one implicating not only *a manner* of the full swaying of be-ing named machination but also *the* full swaying of be-ing. Since the full swaying of be-ing is needed for beings to be unconcealed as annihilable and coercible, and since the full swaying of be-ing is what Heidegger calls unconcealment or ἀλήθεια, the blocking and the undermining of "decision" indicate a blocking and an undermining of an unconcealing through which beings are exclusively unconcealed not as annihilable and coercible but as sheltered in unconcealment, in ἀλήθεια. Thus rather than an unconcealing that unconceals annihilable and coercible beings, an unconcealing emerges that unconceals beings sheltered in unconcealment itself, in ἀλήθεια. In *Contributions to Philosophy*, Heidegger refers to such an unconcealing with the word *Bergung*, "sheltering."[73] Such a sheltering hints at the reticent sway of the mastery of be-ing.

However, for this sheltering to occur, not only must be-ing's full swaying, its truth, happen unimpeded, but this truth must also be grounded. By actualizing the perspective within which machination is reserved, thinking succeeds in putting forth "decision" in favor of such actualization without pretending to be able to bring about the grounding. This "decision" merely puts the grounding in the purview of thinking. However removed from thinking the grounding of the truth of be-ing may be, this grounding is nevertheless within the purview of thinking. Thus the blocking and undermining of all decision involves both the unimpeded sway of the truth of be-ing as well as the grounding of this truth by thinking. And this means that *decision is not at all to be made solely by thinking; rather, it implicates be-ing and points to its mastery.*

By understanding machination as a clearing for unconcealing annihilable and coercible beings and by alluding to "decision" as what inheres in this clearing and points to the mastery of be-ing, we understand why, on the one hand, the talk of an annihilating coercive force brings to mind familiar historical and sociological realities of the turbulent twentieth century and why, on the other hand, the clearing within which this force unfolds is withdrawn from those realities. Discussion of an annihilating coercive force reminds us of those realities because the destruction and devastation referred to presuppose an unconcealing of coercible and annihilable beings within the clearing called machination, that is, within a clearing that reveals coercive force. At the same time, this clearing is withdrawn from historical and sociological realities of destruction and devastation that are the hallmarks of the twentieth century. Thus taken by *themselves* these realities do not reveal the mastery of be-ing and do not lead to a "decision" presupposing the unimpeded and full sway of be-ing's truth and its grounding.

To understand what in *Contributions to Philosophy* is called the "move unto" machination, the "returning therefrom," and the transforming experience of "returnership," we must bear in mind that what transpires in this "returnership" is sheltered in unconcealment, in ἀλήθεια. Keeping this sheltering in mind as we examine Heidegger's interpretation of Nietzsche, we realize that the "move unto" *a manner* of the full

swaying of be-ing, machination, the "return therefrom" to this swaying, and the transforming experience of "returnership" open the way
for Heidegger to interpret Nietzsche's philosophy of the will to power.
Given this opening of the way, with the availability of *Contributions to
Philosophy* and *Mindfulness* we must reexamine Heidegger's interpretation of Nietzsche.

VI

Heidegger began his extensive interpretation of Nietzsche in the years
in which he wrote *Contributions to Philosophy* and *Mindfulness*. A significant element of this interpretation takes shape in *Mindfulness* when
Heidegger says of machination that "[u]nder all kinds of disguises of
manifold coercive forces [it] fosters in advance the completely survey-
able calculability of the subjugating empowering of beings to an accessible arrangement" (*Mindfulness*, 12). With this statement Heidegger
outlines a crucial ground upon which his entire interpretation of Nietzsche rests, for, as we know from his lectures on Nietzsche, he interprets
the will to power as a will that empowers itself to overpowering and
is instantly releasable, transformable, and without discretion. Reading
Heidegger's lectures on Nietzsche after *Contributions to Philosophy* and
Mindfulness, one cannot help but recognize these lecture course texts as
Heidegger's steady effort to show that Nietzsche's thinking "moves
unto" machination—*a manner* of the full swaying of be-ing—or the
clearing for a prevailing, annihilating, and coercive power, but that
Nietzsche's thinking does not "return therefrom" to the full swaying of
be-ing and consequently does not undergo the transforming experience
of "returnership." *Nietzsche's thinking thus remains unaware of the mastery
of be-ing.* To see this we must take a brief look at that juncture in Heidegger's lectures on Nietzsche where he deals with the will to power and
the eternal return of the same and shows that Nietzsche is stuck within
the confines of a thinking that determines the beingness of beings in
terms of *essentia* and *existentia*.

At the juncture that I have in mind, Heidegger suggests that Nietzsche develops the doctrine of the will to power in response to the question, what is the essence *(essentia)* of a being? and he formulates the
doctrine of the eternal return of the same in response to the question,
how does a being exist (how does one determine its *existentia*)? Since
these questions are inherent in the guiding-question of philosophy,
Heidegger concludes that Nietzsche develops the doctrines of the will

to power and the eternal return of the same in response to the guiding-question of philosophy, what is a being?

Heidegger sums this up when he says: "The designation 'will to power' is a response to the question concerning a being *with respect to its constitution;* the designation 'eternal return of the same' is a response to the question concerning a being *with respect to its mode of existing.* However, constitution and mode of existing belong together as determinations of the beingness of a being."[74] He thus makes clear that in his view Nietzsche's doctrines of the will to power and the eternal return reveal that his thinking takes its orientation from the traditional determinations of the beingness of beings in terms of *essentia* and *existentia.*

However sophisticated and subtle the relationship may be that connects the doctrines of the will to power and the eternal return to the determinations of beingness of beings in terms of *essentia* and *existentia,* we cannot overlook the fact that in order to bring power into his philosophical purview, Nietzsche's thinking must "move unto" the clearing that, as machination, houses, nurtures, and unfolds power. Here the question is whether subsequent to "moving unto" machination, Nietzsche returns from this clearing to the full swaying of be-ing.

Nietzsche's orientation to the questions, what is the essence of a being? and how is its existence to be determined? indicate that his thinking "moves unto" a domain wherein a being is unconcealed in the light of the clearing that, as *a manner* of the full swaying of be-ing, Heidegger calls machination. But Nietzsche's thinking does not go far enough to prompt him to return from machination to *the* full swaying of be-ing. Thus Nietzsche does not undergo the transforming experience of "returnership."

It is a moot point to say that Nietzsche would never explicitly admit that he deals with the question concerning the beingness of a being. Because he advances the thesis that each and every being is nothing but a quantum of the will to power that eternally returns as the same, Nietzsche shows that the doctrines of the will to power and the eternal return are his responses to such a question. Moreover, when Nietzsche describes his philosophy of the will as a "theory about a will to power that is in play in every happening" *(Theorie eines in allem Geschehen sich abspielenden Macht-Willen),* he leaves no doubt that his thinking is immersed in the unconcealing-process in and through which beings are unconcealed as quanta of the will to power.[75]

However, my contention that Nietzsche does not return from machination, unto which he moves, to the full swaying of be-ing is not intended as a negative judgment of him. Precisely the "move unto" machination—*a manner* of the full swaying of be-ing—without "return-ing from" *this manner* to *the* full swaying of be-ing make clear why Hei-degger honors Nietzsche by calling him "a crossing," that is, "the high-est that can be said of a thinker" (*GA* 43:278).

For Heidegger, Nietzsche is a crossing—*ein Übergang*—because his "moving unto" *a manner* of the full swaying of be-ing and his "not re-turning" therefrom, taken by themselves, are hints *at* the full swaying of be-ing. These hints are also at work in Nietzsche's doctrine of educa-tion. By appealing in this doctrine to the Apollonian constraints and Dionysian excesses and by putting forth the notion of rank, Nietzsche proves to have an inkling of the hint of the full swaying of be-ing, which sustains those that Heidegger in *Contributions to Philosophy* calls "the few and the rare."

Heidegger and Christianity
A Look at His Correspondence
with Bernhard Welte

From the very beginning of his philosophical career, Heidegger maintains a complex relationship to Christianity—complex because, for one
thing, this relationship is not one of rejection or acceptance of the
dogma and articles of faith of this religion and, for another, this relationship points directly to the very core of Heidegger's being-historical
approach to the question of God. Although its claim is only of minor
importance for the task of understanding this complex relationship, the
recently published volume *Briefe und Begegnungen / Martin Heidegger,
Bernhard Welte* (Correspondence and Encounters / Martin Heidegger,
Bernhard Welte) is noteworthy in many respects. It not only presents
the thirty-three letters that Heidegger and Welte exchanged from 1945
to 1976 but also includes several essays that Bernhard Welte, a Catholic
theologian and priest, devoted to Heidegger's thought. What prompts
the reader to approach this volume with great expectation is the fact
that Welte was not only the priest with whom Heidegger discussed the
matter of his Christian burial and whom he requested to deliver the fu-
neral oration but also a thinker whose intellectual importance Heidegger had recognized.

Heidegger's complex relationship to Christianity is reflected in certain facts of his life. These include: Heidegger had a Catholic upbring-
ing and a predominantly Catholic education but abandoned Catholi-
cism without formally joining the Protestant church, spent extensive
time in the Benedictine abbey of Beuron near his birthplace, Meßkirch,
where he wrote some of his important works, and requested and re-
ceived a Christian burial.[76] His friendships with the Protestant theologian Rudolph Bultmann—whose seminars he attended in Marburg—
and his ties to the Catholic theologian Bernhard Welte as well as his

association with another Catholic theologian, Karl Rahner, are well known and reflect his close relationship to and interest in Christianity.[77]

Setting aside the minor importance that *Briefe und Begegnungen* undoubtedly has for the biography of Heidegger still to be written, in what follows I shall examine this volume with two questions in mind: How did Heidegger himself perceive his relationship to Christianity? and How did Welte understand Heidegger's thought? By emphasizing these two questions, I do not intend to present Heidegger's own perception of his relationship to Christianity as a "principle" against which Welte's understanding of Heidegger's thought should be measured, for they are two different matters. I address Heidegger's perception of this relationship because his confrontation with Christianity and Welte's commitment to this religion constitute two fundamentally different issues: Heidegger's intention in confronting Christianity is shaped by the being-historical insight into the "flight of gods," while Welte's commitment to this religion shapes his theology. The reader of *Briefe und Begegnungen* would do well to keep this difference in mind if he or she wants to go beyond a mere biographical understanding of this correspondence.

After addressing the two questions, I conclude with a brief look at the quality of the editorial work on the volume.

I

As I have indicated, Heidegger's perception of his relationship to Christianity is closely tied to his being-historical insight into the "flight of gods." This emerges perhaps nowhere more clearly than in a text he wrote in 1937 and 1938. Available now as an appendix to his second major being-historical treatise, *Mindfulness*, Heidegger in that text reflects on his life's path, surveys his published and unpublished works, talks about his Catholic past, and, most importantly, places his relationship to Christianity in the being-historical context of the "flight of gods."[78] He says:

And who would not want to recognize that a confrontation with Christianity reticently accompanied my entire path hitherto, a confrontation that was not and is not a "problem" that one "takes up" to address but a preservation of, and *at the same time* a painful separation from one's ownmost provenance: the parental home, homeland, and youth. . . . It is not proper to speak of these most inward confrontations since they do not revolve around issues that concern the dogma of Christianity and articles of faith, but rather only around the sole question: whether god is fleeing from us or not and whether we, as creating ones, still experience this flight genuinely. (*Mindfulness*, 368)

By explicitly characterizing his relationship to Christianity as a confrontation *(Auseinandersetzung)*, Heidegger makes one thing clear: anyone interested in understanding this relationship should have no illusion that although it is confrontational it is not hostile; it is not an encounter with the dogma and articles of faith of Christianity but is motivated and shaped solely by the being-historical insight into the "flight of gods."

The ramifications of this insight are many. In the section of *Mindfulness* titled "Gods," Heidegger addresses each of these ramifications in detail and with unsurpassable precision, all the while distancing himself from theism, monotheism, polytheism, and pantheism *as well as* atheism. He then speaks of "godlessness," of which atheism, among other things, is a manifestation: "Only when man learns to have an inkling that it is not for him to decide on godlessness but that godlessness is the highest loss for gods themselves, only then does he enter the path of mindfulness which shows him how godding as retroattainment [*Rückfindung*] of godhood enowns itself solely out of be-ing" (*Mindfulness*, 211).[79] In speaking of his relationship to Christianity, Heidegger explicitly mentions the "flight of gods," which should sufficiently indicate that this "flight" accounts for "godlessness as the highest loss of gods themselves." Moreover, by referring to this "flight" as he speaks of his relationship to Christianity, Heidegger offers a perspective that we should adopt to grasp this complex relationship. Finally, if we grasp the implications of what he says about "godlessness"—which is connected to the "flight of gods" and his relationship to Christianity—then we will not preconceive this relationship as the kind of atheism we find in Bertrand Russell's *Why I Am Not a Christian*, for example.

Thus what counts is not to lose sight of the insight into the "flight of gods." Emerging out of hermeneutic phenomenology, depending on its method and its presuppositions, this insight is one of the many gifts of being-historical-enowning thinking that unfold in *Contributions to Philosophy* and *Mindfulness*.[80] As intrinsically hermeneutic-phenomenological, the insight into the "flight of gods" precedes the experiences to which Heidegger alludes when he speaks of "a preservation of, and *at the same time* a painful separation from [his] ownmost provenance" (*Mindfulness*, 368).

If we want to gain access to the nonbiographical dimension of

Heidegger's complex relationship to Christianity, that is, if we want to access this relationship as a hermeneutic-phenomenological issue, we must keep in mind the being-historical-enowning insight into the flight of gods and its implications. As indicated earlier, such access has no bearing on our assessment of the understanding of Heidegger's thought that Welte displays in this correspondence. With this proviso in mind, I will now address the question of how Welte understood Heidegger's thought by focusing on Welte's reaction to one pivotal issue in Heidegger's thought: the "end" and "completion" of philosophy in Hegel.

II

Throughout his correspondence with Heidegger and in the essays he wrote about his thought, Welte often speaks from a proximity to Heidegger's thought that is hermeneutically *note-* and *question-worthy.* Properly assessed, this proximity may shed light on the hermeneutic situation out of which Welte approaches the philosopher's work. A significant instance in which Welte articulates this proximity occurs in a letter he wrote to Heidegger, thanking him for the offprint of the essay "Hegel und die Griechen" (Hegel and the Greeks). Acknowledging how much he has learned from this essay, Welte observes:

It seems to me that everything supports the view that after Hegel's interpretation of Christianity, there will no longer be a theology in the sense hitherto, and that the future gestalt of theology cannot be achieved without going through Hegel and overcoming him as well as everything that coalesces in him. This thought, which has been at work in me since long ago, has become more clear to me through you. And now when I wanted to address Hegel's theological thinking this thought became radiantly clear to me by reading the offprint of "Hegel und die Griechen."[81]

In the absence of an analysis by Welte of "Hegel und die Griechen"—an analysis that might better articulate his purported proximity to Heidegger's thought as suggested by Welte's insistence that after reading this essay, Hegel's theological thought became radiantly clear to him—it becomes clear that we can justifiably view this text as the key for assessing that hermeneutically note- and question-worthy proximity. What do we find in "Hegel und die Griechen" that might attest that proximity? To respond, we must consider what Heidegger actually accomplishes in this essay.

A detailed analysis of "Hegel und die Griechen," which requires at least a cursory look at Heidegger's exposition in the "joining" of *Contributions to Philosophy* titled "Playing-Forth" (119–57), is beyond the scope of this essay. At the risk of oversimplifying one of the most revealing texts of being-historical thinking, I shall instead limit my discussion to what is minimally essential and begin with what Heidegger says at the beginning of this text. There he points out that the word *Greeks* stands for "the beginning of philosophy" and the word *Hegel* for "its completion."[82] He then determines the relationship between this "beginning" and its "completion" by focusing on Hegel's treatment of the four basic words of Greek philosophy: ἕν, λόγος, ἰδέα, and ἐνέργεια.

Addressing Hegel's interpretation of each of these words, Heidegger shows that Hegel takes Parmenides' view on ἕν, Heraclitus's view on λόγος, Plato's view on ἰδέα, and Aristotle's view on ἐνέργεια as the necessary outcome and, in this sense, as the "by-product" of the "productive" process of the dialectical thinking in and through which "subjectivity" returns unto itself and becomes absolute. In his lectures on the history of philosophy, Hegel alludes to this dialectical process of returning by saying that "in the Greek world man had not yet returned unto himself [*noch nicht in sich zurückgekehrt*] as in our time, he was indeed a subject but had not yet posited himself as the subject" (*GA* 9:433).

According to Heidegger, the "returning of man unto himself" as the posited subject is the key for grasping Hegel's dialectical determinations of the four basic words of Greek philosophy—words that belong to the "beginning" (*Anfang*) and are inceptual (*anfänglich*). Hegel relegates the "beginning" of Greek philosophy, and along with this "beginning" its four basic and inceptual words, to the stage of "not yet mediated" in the dialectical movement, because Greek thinking has "not yet" returned unto itself and has "not yet" become absolute. For Hegel the thinking devoted to ἕν, λόγος, ἰδέα, and ἐνέργεια is on the way to returning unto itself and becoming absolute subjectivity. Because for Hegel Greek philosophy is in the stage of "not yet mediated," this philosophy does not reach the stage of "consciousness," that is, the stage that Descartes obtains in modern philosophy. Since the Greek "beginning" has "not yet" attained the stage of the "productive" thinking of absolute subjectivity, the basic words of this "beginning" belong to the dialectical stage of "not yet determined" and "not yet mediated." Once absolute subjectivity returns unto itself, these basic words cease to be

undetermined and unmediated, for the dialectical movement of absolute subjectivity, which enables it to return unto itself, renders these
four basic words determined and mediated. By interpreting each of
these words as dialectically determined and mediated, that is, by viewing them in light of absolute subjectivity's return unto itself, Hegel
brings the "beginning" of Greek philosophy to a "completion."

But for Heidegger these four basic words entail a different matter
altogether since each speaks "the language of the guiding word *being*
[*Sein*], that is, εἶναι (ἐόν)" (*GA* 9:434). Thus Heidegger can sum up
Hegel's interpretation of these basic words by saying that

> Hegel understands ἔν, λόγος, ἰδέα, and ἐνέργεια in the horizon of "being" that
> he grasps as the abstract universal. What is represented in the word *being* and
> thus in these basic words is *not yet* determined and *not yet* mediated in and
> through the dialectical movement of the absolute subjectivity. The philosophy
> of the Greeks occupies the stage of the "not yet." The philosophy of the Greeks
> is "not yet" the completion, and nevertheless and exclusively it is grasped from
> out of this completion—a completion that has determined itself as the system of
> speculative idealism. (*GA* 9:438)

Hegel's views on the Greek "beginning" and what he represents in the
word *being*, that is, the abstract universal, require him to allocate
these four basic and inceptual words to the stage of the dialectical
movement that he calls "not yet determined" and "not yet mediated."

However, the driving force behind Hegel's elevation of the subject to
absolute subjectivity and his subsequent relegation of the four basic
and inceptual words of the Greeks to the dialectical movement that
brings to "completion" the Greek "beginning" lie, according to Heidegger, in Hegel's understanding of another basic and inceptual word,
ἀλήθεια. By understanding ἀλήθεια as truth and truth as "the absolute
certainty of the self-knowing absolute subject" (*GA* 9:439), Hegel subjects ἀλήθεια to the process of the unfolding of the absolute subjectivity.
In other words, Hegel does not *let* ἀλήθεια *be*. In this way Hegel recon-
ceives the Platonic-Aristotelian ἀλήθεια in light of the absolute certainty of absolute subjectivity. Understood by Hegel in the sense of the
absolute certainty of absolute subjectivity, ἀλήθεια loses its inceptuality
and, as the truth of absolute subjectivity, becomes the distinguishing
mark of the "completion" of the Greek "beginning."

Although brief, the preceding account of "Hegel und die Griechen"
should suffice for highlighting the proximity that is hermeneutically
note- and question-worthy and that marks the approach Welte takes to

Heidegger. To articulate that proximity with the radicalness that philosophy requires, we must ask whether anything in Heidegger's account of Hegel's dialectical "completion" of the Greek "beginning" might be unreservedly extended to Christian theology. This question is central to understanding Welte's admission that after he read "Hegel und die Griechen," Hegel's theological thought became radiantly clear to him. Is there anything in Heidegger's analyses in this essay that might be unreservedly extended to Hegel's theological thought and by extension to Christian theology? Given the textual evidence presented here, I must say no, for Parmenides' view on ἕν, Heraclitus's view on λόγος, Plato's view on ἰδέα, and Aristotle's view on ἐνέργεια grow out of the soil of Greek philosophy, not of Christian theology. To understand this fully, we must delineate the background sustaining our observations thus far.

Since Heidegger's account of Hegel's treatment of the four basic and inceptual words is inseparable from the being-historical, inceptual inquiries in *Contributions to Philosophy* and *Mindfulness,* this account, should we do it justice, must be considered in the hermeneutic-phenomenological context defined by the following four inceptual questions: "What is a being, τί τὸ ὄν?" "How does being [*Sein*] sway [*west*] in the Greek beginning?" "How does a being sway in the other beginning?" and finally "How does be-ing [*Seyn*] sway?"[83] Considering what Heidegger's being-historical thinking achieves in *Contributions to Philosophy* as well as in *Mindfulness,* we can glean his responses to the first two questions: the Greek "beginning" determines the being of a being in the horizon of being, which this "beginning" conceives as "beingness" *(Seiendheit).* We can also glean his responses to the last two questions: in the other "beginning" a being is restored to its being insofar as in this beginning be-ing sways as enowning.[84] Accordingly, when Heidegger deals with Hegel's treatment of ἕν, λόγος, ἰδέα and ἐνέργεια, he implicitly bases it on the ground that sustains the aforementioned four inceptual questions. In short, those four inceptual questions constitute the background against which "Hegel und die Griechen" should be read and interpreted.

Keeping this background in mind, let us return to Welte's contention that after reading "Hegel und die Griechen," Hegel's theological thinking and by extension the end of Christian theology became radiantly clear to him, a statement articulating what I consider to be Welte's hermeneutically note- and question-worthy proximity to Heidegger's thought. And here the question is whether after reading this essay,

Welte achieved these insights on the ground that sustains the essay and to which I alluded with the preceding four inceptual being-historical questions. An affirmative response to this question is possible only if we assume that Christian theology also raises those four questions. But we cannot make this assumption because the questions "τί τὸ ὄν?" as well as the other three inceptual questions outlined here grow, in the strict sense of the word, out of the soil of Greek philosophy, not of Christian theology.

III

To further elucidate the point I have made about the four being-historical questions that grow out of the soil of Greek philosophy, let us focus on the way in which the first inceptual question, what is a being? comes into play in an essay that Welte wrote about Heidegger, "Rückblick auf die Metaphysik" (In Retrospect of Metaphysics). Heidegger made a number of critical comments about this essay that directly reflect his thinking of being.

To understand Heidegger's comments on this essay better, we should note that after Welte sent "Rückblick auf die Metaphysik" to Heidegger, he changed its title to "Thomas von Aquin und Heideggers Gedanke von der Seinsgeschichte" (Thomas Aquinas and Heidegger's Thought on the History of Being). This change of the title is important since it makes clear that the focus of the essay is on Aquinas as seen from within the purview of Heidegger's thought on the history of being. Welte refers explicitly to this purview when he says that his main objective in this essay is to extend and transmit—in his words, *herangelangen zu lassen*—an inquiry into the metaphysics of Aquinas shaped by Heidegger's thought on the history of being (79–80). Here we encounter once again Welte's purported and hermeneutically note- and question-worthy proximity to Heidegger's thought as evidenced, for example, in Welte's revised title.

In this essay Welte inquires into Aquinas's views on *ens* (a being) and *esse* (being) and characterizes his ontological thinking as "a thinking of beings in their beingness" *(ein Denken des Seienden in seiner Seiendheit)* (81). He then notes that for this thinking, *esse* appears in several ways. First, *esse* "appears in all things or in all beings. *Ipsum esse est actualitas omnium rerum* [Being itself is the actuality of all things]. Thus *esse* is the beingness of each and every being" (82). Welte further observes that, second, "*esse* appears in the domain that Aquinas calls *ratio* or *intellectus*, that is, in human thinking. . . . Man can think the beingness of each and every being, and he can do this in such a way that he does not have to think through every individual being or every individual kind of being. In this case then he thinks of the beingness that is common to all beings, that is, of *esse commune*" (82–83). Welte finally indicates that "what is called *esse* appears as *ipsum esse subsistens*. Here *esse* proves to be neither the being of 'beings in a whole' [*das Seiende im Ganzen*] nor being as the general concept in thought. Rather, *esse* is in itself and sustains itself. . . . As pure being . . . *esse* is what everyone calls God" (83).[85] However, for Heidegger this last manner of the appearing of being as *ipsum esse subsistens*, or God, entails a contradiction that Welte does not address. When Welte takes up the manifold ways of the appearing of being, or *esse*, in Aquinas, he does not see this contradiction. Instead, he merely stresses two theses, namely, "God is the self-subsisting being itself" *(Deus est ipsum esse subsistens)* (29 and 83), and "God does not reside in another genus" *(Deus non sit in aliquo genere)* (29 and 84). (Here Welte translates *genere* as *Art*, "kind," and not as *Gattung*, "genus"—a rendering to which Heidegger, as we shall see, objects.)

However, these two theses contradict each other because by saying that God subsists in God's own genus and that God is the self-subsisting being, Aquinas uses the word *subsists* without taking into account that this word belongs to *genus* and is inapplicable to *being*. The reason for this inapplicability lies in the difference between the generality of the genus and the generality of being. If the generality of being is taken into account, then one cannot say that God is being itself and that God *subsists* in God's own genus. As Heidegger remarks to Welte in his letter of February 29, 1968, "*subsistentia* is the first γένος of the *genera*" and as such stands in the light of the generality of the genus, which is to be strictly distinguished from the generality specific to being. In short, the word *subsists* remains within the generality specific to genus and cannot be extended to the generality of being with which Aquinas identifies God. Specifically, Heidegger says:

Of course, I cannot reconcile the two theses, *Deus est ipsum esse subsistens* and *Deus non sit in aliquo genere*. Even if this reconciliation is set aside, the contradiction in Aquinas [between the two theses] must be worked out. For *subsistentia* is the first γένος of the *genera*. Why do you translate this word on page 753 with *kinds* [*Arten*]? Here the problem goes back to Aristotle's *Metaphysics* B 3, 998 b 22, οὔτε τὸ ὂν γένος. See *Sein und Zeit*, page 3. (29)

The theses that God subsists in God's own genus and that God is thus the self-subsisting being itself contradict each other. These theses do not take into account the difference between the generality of the genus and the generality of being. Given this difference, being cannot be conceived as a genus. Appealing to his analyses at the beginning of *Being and Time*—analyses that worked out the achievements as well as the limitations of the Aristotelian views on the generality of being and the generality of the *genus*—Heidegger here draws Welte's attention to the fact that *subsistentia* belongs to the generality of genus and thus cannot be used to establish that God is God's own genus and hence God is being itself.[86] Instead of addressing this contradiction, Welte once again purports to have a proximity to Heidegger's thought that is hermeneutically question-worthy and jumps to the conclusion that "insofar as the divine is *ipsum esse,* and *non est in genere,* it falls outside the . . . domain that Heidegger calls metaphysics" (85). What besides this proximity emerges when Welte ascertains that the divine as conceived by Aquinas falls outside the domain that Heidegger calls metaphysics?

Since Aquinas does not take into account the difference between the generality of the genus and the generality of being, his two theses cannot be reconciled. Aquinas's understanding of the divine falls within metaphysics even though the inceptual question, "what is a being?" reverberates in his thinking. The rootedness of this first inceptual question in the soil of Greek philosophy requires that this difference be taken into account, even though, as Heidegger demonstrates in *Being and Time* and beyond, ultimately the notion of the generality of being must be abandoned.

IV

Let me conclude these observations by taking a brief look at the work of editing that has gone into *Briefe und Begegnungen*. The fact that the letters of Heidegger's published in this volume will be republished in volume 92 or 93 of the *Gesamtausgabe*, to be titled "Ausgewählte Briefe" (Selected Letters), and will thus be subjected to more rigorous editorial scrutiny, does not diminish the importance that should be attached to the editing of the present volume.[87] Have the editors of this volume met their editorial responsibilities by preparing a flawless text? I am not in a position to assess the reliability and accuracy of their work as far as their reading and transcribing of the original texts of these letters are concerned because I do not have access to these originals. However, if we consider their failure to distinguish between the German *sie* and *Sie*—see, for example, pages 26 and 31—then we must question the quality of their work. I cannot help wondering why the editors of *Briefe und Begegnungen* did not submit their work prior to publication to the scrutiny of someone who commands German grammar and orthography in order to purge from the text such easily avoidable errors.

Questioning Richardson's "Heidegger I, Heidegger II" Distinction and His Response in Light of *Contributions to Philosophy*

—Aber Lebendige machen alle den Fehler,
daß sie zu stark unterscheiden.

Rilke

One of the indisputably significant aspects of Richardson's *Heidegger: Through Phenomenology to Thought* is the preface to this work, which Heidegger consented to write after reading the German version of a résumé of Richardson's research and findings.[88] Two points here should not go unnoticed. First, because the text of the résumé does not have the form of a dialogue, with two exceptions, it is unclear what questions Richardson put to Heidegger in the course of their "long and wide-ranging discussion."[89] Second, Heidegger's preface to Richardson's book was not originally written as a preface but rather as a response to a letter that Richardson wrote to him on March 1, 1962.

The difference between Richardson's letter and his résumé is significant because Heidegger clearly states his intention at the very opening of his response: "It is with some hesitation that I attempt to answer the two principal questions you posed in your letter of March 1, 1962." The two principal questions are "How are we properly to understand your first experience of the Being-question in Brentano?" and "Granted *that* a 'reversal' has come-to-pass in your thinking, *how* has it come-to-pass? In other words, how are [we] to think this coming-to-pass itself?"[90]

It is presumably in conjunction with this second question that Richardson introduces his celebrated distinction between a "Heidegger I" and a "Heidegger II." We glean this from Heidegger's comments on and reactions to this distinction: "The distinction you make between Heidegger I and Heidegger II is justified only on the condition that this is kept constantly in mind: only by way of what Heidegger I has thought does one gain access to what is to-be-thought by Heidegger II. But [the thought of] Heidegger I becomes possible only if it is contained in Heidegger II."[91] How are we to understand the proviso under which Heidegger places Richardson's distinction between "Heidegger I" and "Heidegger II"? It states clearly that the thought of Heidegger I becomes possible only if it is contained in Heidegger II. But when we turn to Richardson's résumé for some clue to understanding this proviso, we find almost nothing.

Richardson's summary of his findings as presented to Heidegger consists of five points. The first point ascertains a transformation of phenomenology necessitating "the transfer of focus from There-being [*Da-sein*] to Being." The second point presents an interpretation of *die Kehre* as a *shift* of focus "imposed by the dynamism of Heidegger's original experience of Being." (In his own translation of the preface as well as throughout *Heidegger: Through Phenomenology to Thought*, Richardson renders *die Kehre* as "reversal.") The third point explains why *Sein und Zeit II* never came to be written. Here Richardson alludes to the inadequacies of the language of metaphysics—inadequacies that Heidegger II gets rid of by "making in his own way a re-trieve of Heidegger I." The fourth point explains the forgottenness of being in terms of the finitude of being, and finally the fifth point considers how Heidegger's dialogues with the philosophers of the past ensue from a method of re-trieve, that is, "a manner of articulating his own experience of Being."[92]

Whether we consider these points individually or together, we do not find a satisfying interpretation of *die Kehre* that would make Heidegger's proviso fully understandable. This is especially true if we consider the second and third points together; if "Heidegger II" shows a "shift" in which Heidegger "makes in his own way a re-trieve of Heidegger I," this re-trieval still does not account for how the thought of Heidegger I becomes possible only if it is contained in Heidegger II. Clearly we must approach this matter in a way that is different from Richardson's résumé. If we draw from volumes of Heidegger's *Gesamtausgabe*, especially *Contributions to Philosophy (From Enowning)*—none of which was accessible to Richardson in 1962—we find fertile ground for determining the roots that give rise to Heidegger's proviso according to which the thought of Heidegger I becomes possible as contained in Heidegger II.

To briefly mention a point I shall discuss later at some length, let me say that Heidegger's proviso becomes understandable if we reconsider the theme of *die Kehre*, the turning, and, along with this, we address the way in which the basic structure of *Dasein* is retained as Heidegger abandons the fundamental ontology of the transcendental-horizonal perspective. The retaining of the basic structure of *Dasein* and the abandoning of the fundamental ontology of the transcendental-horizonal perspective are called for by the claim of *die Kehre*, the turning, which in *Contributions to Philosophy* Heidegger circumscribes as *der kehrige Bezug des Seyns*, "the turning relation of be-ing" (*Contributions*, 6). We shall understand Heidegger's proviso according to which the thought of Heidegger I becomes possible as contained in Heidegger II as one that unmistakably points to this turning.

I

Initially, Heidegger in thinking being takes the path of the fundamental ontology of the transcendental-horizonal perspective. This thinking is laid out in *Being and Time*, in its sequel *The Basic Problems of Phenomenology* (*Die Grundprobleme der Phänomenologie*, 1927), in *The Metaphysical Foundations of Logic* (*Metaphysische Anfangsgründe der Logik im Ausgang vom Leibniz*, 1928), and in *The Fundamental Concepts of Metaphysics: World, Finitude, Solitude* (*Die Grundbegriffe der Metaphysik: Welt, Endlichkeit, Einsamkeit*, 1929–30).

Closely interrelated, these works unfold the thinking of being as transcendental-horizonal thinking that sets out from the unprecedented philosophical determination of humans as *Dasein*, that is, as beings that understand being. Following *Being and Time*, the central locus of this understanding is called "existence" *(Existenz)*. Understanding of being occurs as "existence" insofar as in and through "existence" *Dasein* enacts the disclosure of being as transcendence. This enactment is accessible to phenomenological observation and demonstration in *Dasein*'s intentional comportments toward beings and takes place within the horizonal disclosure of being as *praesens*. Thus the thinking that enacts fundamental ontology is called the transcendental-horizonal thinking of being. Among other things, this thinking discloses the ontological difference and, along with it, the turning from fundamental ontology to metontology, which as the turning from the temporality of being to beings in a whole *(das Seiende im Ganzen)* should not be confused with the "turning relation of be-ing."[93]

However, it should be kept in mind that the fundamental ontology of transcendental-horizonal thinking presents an analysis of *Dasein* through which its ontological-existential structure is disclosed as a structure of and for being's disclosure *(Erschlossenheit des Seins)*. This structure is well known: it consists of "thrownness" *(Geworfenheit)*, "projecting-open" *(Entwurf)*, and "being-along-with" *(Sein-bei)*. All three are inseparably bound to *Rede*, "discourse," understood as the deepest unfolding of language.[94] This structure is not rigid and extant— it is not *vorhanden*—because it belongs to and is for being's disclosure. When with *Contributions to Philosophy* Heidegger abandons the transcendental-horizonal perspective and embarks on the path of being-historical thinking, this structure reemerges as a transformed structure. However, this does not happen overnight.

Soon after Heidegger works out the fundamental ontology of the transcendental-horizonal perspective, a deep dissatisfaction upsets the whole matter of the thinking of being. Heidegger expresses this dissatisfaction in a letter to Elisabeth Blochmann.[95] He also alludes to it in his lecture course on Schelling.[96] In another letter to Blochmann, he writes: "People already believe and talk about my writing *Being and Time II*. That is all right. But because at one point *Being and Time I* was for me a path that led me somewhere and because I can no longer traverse that path and it is already overgrown, I can no longer write *Being and Time II*. I am not writing a book at all."[97] This letter, written in September 1932, shows that the dissatisfaction with the transcendental-horizonal perspective occurs in that year. Interestingly enough, in the spring of the same year the plan for the writing of *Contributions to Philosophy* took shape.[98]

Heidegger's dissatisfaction with the transcendental-horizonal perspective should be understood in light of the "immanent transformation" that occurs within the matter to which his thinking is devoted and that he calls sometimes being *(Sein)* and sometimes be-ing *(Seyn)*.[99] Despite the indisputable achievements of transcendental-horizonal thinking, it does not escape Heidegger that this thinking does not fully recognize be-ing's turning relation to thinking and the implicated non-historiographical but historical *(geschichtlich)* appearing and unfolding of be-ing. In sum, this thinking does not fully recognize what this turning relation yields, namely, the insight that be-ing displays a non-historiographical but historical unfolding.

Having already spoken in 1936–38 in *Contributions to Philosophy* about the turning relation of be-ing, Heidegger refers to it in his *Letter on Humanism* (1947) merely as *die Kehre,* "the turning." Although many commentators on the *Letter on Humanism* have taken up the issue of the turning, they have done little to ease the task of understanding it, perhaps because they did not have access to *Contributions to Philosophy.* Also the style in which the *Letter on Humanism* is written does not allow Heidegger to make clear that what he calls turning in this letter is precisely the same as what he presents in *Contributions to Philosophy* as the turning relation of be-ing. In other words, to grasp clearly the turning that Heidegger speaks of in the *Letter on Humanism,* one must understand it as an abbreviated form of what in *Contributions to Philosophy* he calls be-ing's turning relation. Since this turning relation occurs as a turning *unto* Heidegger's thinking, his thinking becomes aware of being's historical *(geschichtlich* and not *historisch)* appearing and unfolding. With the occurrence of this turning, which heralds an immanent transformation within the matter to which Heidegger's thought is devoted, he realizes that he must abandon the transcendental-horizonal perspective in favor of an unprecedented thinking of being, which he calls being-historical thinking.

What have the abandonment of the transcendental-horizonal perspective and the initiation of being-historical thinking to do with a proper understanding of the proviso under which Heidegger places Richardson's "Heidegger I, Heidegger II" distinction? The answer lies in the role that thinking plays in be-ing's turning relation.

Heidegger has this role in mind when in the *Letter on Humanism* he states: "Thinking enacts the relation of being to what is ownmost to man. Thinking does not make or effect this relation."[100] He thus leaves no doubt that in his view thinking enacts the relation of being to what is ownmost to man, since as he points out in *Contributions to Philosophy,* be-ing's *turning relation* is a turning *unto* thinking. In other words, being's turning relation requires an enactment by thinking since this relation is a relation to what is ownmost to man.

Everything depends on how we understand turning as a *turning unto* thinking. This turning turns unto thinking because it needs thinking to sustain it. And for thinking to respond to this need and thus to sustain be-ing's turning relation, it must act—must occur as acting *(Handeln).* (The importance of this acting of and by thinking is evidenced in what Heidegger says in the opening sentence of the *Letter on Humanism:* "We are still far from decisively enough considering what is ownmost to acting.")[101] Be-ing's turning relation turns *unto* thinking so that by acting thinking sustains this turning relation and opens it. Thus thinking does not make or effect be-ing's turning relation.

It is against this background that we must understand Heidegger's response to Richardson's question concerning *die Kehre,* the turning, which Richardson understands and translates as "reversal." Only when we understand be-ing's turning relation in the sense of *turning unto* thinking, and only when we understand that by acting thinking sustains and opens up this turning do we grasp the proviso under which Heidegger places Richardson's Heidegger I, Heidegger II distinction. When Heidegger notes, "The turning [relation of be-ing] is above all not a procedure adopted by the thinking [that] questions (being) . . . I did not invent it, nor does it concern merely my thinking," he makes clear that only when we understand be-ing's turning relation in the sense of turning *unto* thinking do we grasp that neither is turning a procedure adopted and invented by Heidegger's thinking nor does be-ing's turning relation concern Heidegger's thinking alone.[102]

Clearly, by acting thinking proves to be engaged in be-ing's turning relation. Because the transcendental-horizonal thinking of being faces be-ing's turning relation but does not fully respond to this turning and because it is unaware of the "historical" unfolding of being, Heidegger abandons the transcendental-horizonal perspective. In light of an acting by which Heidegger's thinking sustains and opens up be-ing's turning relation, he realizes that he must abandon the transcendental-horizonal perspective even as he must retain the basic structure of *Dasein.* It is not difficult to understand that he must abandon this perspective, but why must he retain the basic structure of *Dasein?* To anticipate the answer, which shall occupy us in some detail later, we can say that Heidegger must retain this structure because one of its components, namely, "projecting-open" *(Entwurf),* entails the acting by which thinking is engaged in be-ing's turning-relation.

While the transcendental-horizonal thinking of being is fully aware of the nonhistoriographical historicality *(Geschichtlichkeit)* of *Dasein* as being-in-the-world, transcendental-horizonal thinking is not aware of be-ing's historicality. Thus if Heidegger is to become cognizant of be-ing's historicality, he must take seriously the insight into be-ing's turning relation that reveals be-ing's historical appearing and unfolding, and consequently he must abandon the transcendental-horizonal perspective. The turning relation of be-ing confronts Heidegger with the new task of disclosing, that is, projecting-opening, the dynamic,

nonhistoriographical but historical unfolding of be-ing itself. To accomplish this task, Heidegger abandons the transcendental-horizonal
perspective in favor of a thinking that is engaged in and opens up
being's historical appearing and unfolding and is called being-
historical thinking.

But although this abandonment becomes clearly necessary, it
does not extend to what Heidegger's thinking achieves in the fundamental ontology of transcendental-horizonal perspective, namely, the
basic structure of *Dasein*. Not abandoning this structure requires Heidegger to carry over all the questions and issues of the transcendental-
horizonal perspective into the newly opened being-historical perspective. He abandons the transcendental-horizonal perspective, while in
being-historical perspective he retains the transformed basic structure
of *Dasein*.

Heidegger retains the basic structure of *Dasein* because it is engaged in the acting by which thinking sustains and opens up be-ing's
turning relation. Throughout this engagement *Dasein*'s basic structure, "thrownness," "projecting-open," and "being-along with," operates as transformed, which shows that abandoning the transcendental-
horizonal perspective is not the same as abandoning the basic structure
of *Dasein*. On the contrary, as he makes a new beginning with being-
historical thinking, Heidegger retains this basic structure.

On the one hand, be-ing's turning relation must be sustained and enacted; on the other hand, the sustaining and enacting of this turning is
possible only when the basic structure of *Dasein* is transformed. Against
the background of this enactment and transformation, Heidegger says
in the preface that "only by way of what Heidegger I has thought does
one gain access to what is to-be-thought by Heidegger II."[103] This is the
case because the fundamental ontology of transcendental-horizonal
thinking (Heidegger I) does indeed provide significant access to the
thought of Heidegger II insofar as the basic structure of *Dasein* as un-
covered by the thinking of Heidegger I reappears in the thinking of
Heidegger II. Although Heidegger abandons the fundamental ontology of the transcendental-horizonal perspective, he does not relinquish
the basic structure of *Dasein*. Indeed, he thinks through this structure
and illuminates it according to what he receives from be-ing's turning
relation. Throughout *Contributions to Philosophy* the basic structure of
Dasein—albeit transformed in accord with be-ing's turning relation—
operates at various levels of being-historical thinking. This is particu-
larly true of the "parts" of this work titled "Leap" and "Grounding."

What is significant about these "parts" of *Contributions to Philosophy* is that the transformed basic structure of *Dasein* becomes apparent and manifest in them. To understand this transformation, we must examine the way in which it is manifest in "Leap" and "Grounding." Properly understood, this transformation shows that the thought of Heidegger I is contained in the thought of Heidegger II. By considering "Leap" and "Grounding" in *Contributions to Philosophy*, however, we shall also understand why Heidegger can say that the thought of Heidegger II becomes possible as contained in the thinking of Heidegger I.

II

When we approach "Leap" and "Grounding," however, we find that we cannot address the transformation of the basic structure of *Dasein* straight away, because in these "parts" of *Contributions to Philosophy* Heidegger does not address this transformation as a specific topic. We must thus be prepared to understand this transformation by dealing with the following three issues: the manner in which the transformation of the basic structure of *Dasein* relates to Heidegger's dissatisfaction with the transcendental-horizonal perspective; the question of the appropriateness of the word *part* in reference to "Leap" and "Grounding," where that transformation emerges; and finally the role of the English renderings of the key German words with which Heidegger circumscribes the range and scope of "Leap" and "Grounding" and their impact on our understanding of that transformation.

Regarding the first issue, from the brief remarks I have made so far about the emergence of the basic structure of *Dasein* in the being-historical perspective, it should be clear that this emergence has to do with Heidegger's dissatisfaction with the transcendental-horizonal perspective. The key to understanding the nature of this dissatisfaction lies in the active engagement of Heidegger's thinking in be-ing's turning relation. If we take this dissatisfaction as something "personal" and "subjective" rather than as deriving from such an engagement, this dissatisfaction and the ensuing abandonment of the transcendental perspective remain inexplicable and mysterious. They are, however, perfectly understandable in light of be-ing's turning relation. Since Heidegger's thinking is actively engaged in be-ing's turning relation, he becomes dissatisfied with the transcendental-horizonal perspective and consequently becomes aware of the new shape that the basic structure of *Dasein* takes in light of be-ing's turning relation. This new shape is what I have called the transformed appearing of the basic structure of *Dasein*. However, the basic structure of *Dasein* appears transformed not because the fundamental ontological thinking runs its course but because this transformed appearing is already foreshadowed in the engagement of Heidegger's thinking in be-ing's turning relation.

Regarding the second issue, to draw upon "Leap" and "Grounding" to elucidate the transformed basic structure of *Dasein*, we are referred to sections 122, 132, 133, and 182 of these "parts" of *Contributions to Philosophy*. To grasp this transformation as it appears there and thus to understand how this structure becomes pivotal for being-historical thinking, we must first gain some clarity about the word *part* because it alludes to the context in which that transformation is manifest.

Can we apply the word *part* without reservation to *Contributions to Philosophy?* Strictly speaking, to use *part* in connection with this work is misleading. This work does not focus on a whole that could become accessible through its parts. The relation between "parts" and "whole" is no longer relevant to this work. Rather than taking our orientation from the word *part* in order to gain access to the context in which the transformation of the basic structure of *Dasein* is manifest, we must set out from what Heidegger in contradistinction to "part" terminologically calls "joining" *(Fügung)*. Instead of combining various "parts," *Contributions to Philosophy* brings together six "joinings" *(Fügungen)* whose conjoining, coming together, makes up the "jointure" called *Ereignis*, enowning. In other words, be-ing's turning relation unfolds in each of the six "joinings" as they come together in the one "jointure" called enowning. This "coming together" has significant implications for revealing the context in which the transformation of the basic structure of *Dasein* is manifest in "Leap" and "Grounding."

To further underscore the inappropriateness of the word *part* in relation to *Contributions to Philosophy*, let us consider what the word *preview* indicates in "Preview" of this work. If the word *part* proves to be inapplicable to *Contributions to Philosophy*, then "Preview" cannot be regarded as the first "part" of this work, which under other circumstances would have to be designated an introduction. Thus with the word *preview*, Heidegger does not have an introduction in mind. If "Preview" is not an introduction, then what is it? An introduction progressively acquaints the reader with a preconceived thesis and is thus at the service of that thesis. But what "Preview" does for *Contributions to Philosophy* is remarkably different from what an introduction does for a thesis. Strictly speaking, "Preview" does not introduce the reader to a thesis called enowning, since "Preview" is nothing but enowning *in pre-view (im Vor-blick)*.

Heidegger highlights the "coming together" of the six "joinings" by addressing enowning from within the purview of "Preview." In this vein he notes that "[e]nowning is that self-supplying and self-mediating midpoint into which all essential swaying of the truth of be-ing must be thought back in advance" (*Contributions*, 51). As a self-supplying and self-mediating midpoint, enowning endows each "joining" with a distinct identity that the "joining" relinquishes as it conjoins other "joinings." Thus each "joining" becomes a "part" but instantly ceases to be one, since it is destined to join other "joinings." Conjoining other "joinings," each "joining" relinquishes its initially obtained identity. In "Preview" Heidegger addresses the initially obtained but thereafter relinquished identity of each "joining" with these words: "Each of the six joinings of the jointure stands for itself, but only in order to make the essential onefold more pressing. In each of the six joinings the attempt is made to say the same of the same, but in each case from within another essential domain of that which enowning names" (*Contributions*, 57). In this passage Heidegger makes two points that are of paramount importance for understanding why *Contributions to Philosophy* has no "parts." First, each "joining" has its own identity insofar as each stands for itself. But each "joining" stands for itself and has its own identity insofar as each "joining" makes more pressing the essential onefold of all "joinings." Second, each "joining" says the same of the same but from within *another* essential domain of that which enowning names.

Considering these two points together, we realize that to properly grasp the context in which the transformed basic structure of *Dasein* appears in "Leap" and "Grounding," we must be clear about the "identity" of each of these "joinings"—their temporary appearance as "parts"—and about the sense in which each joining is "another essential domain of that which enowning names." The crux of the matter lies in the words *identity* and *another essential domain*. How are we to understand these words? With this question in mind we must address the English renderings of Heidegger's key words *wesentliche Einheit* and *Wesensbereich* as "essential onefold" and "essential domain," respectively, because of the impact these renderings have on our understanding the context in which the transformed basic structure of *Dasein* appears in "Leap" and "Grounding." And this brings us to the third issue.

It is important to keep in mind that in addressing the "joinings" of *Contributions to Philosophy* Heidegger says not that "each 'joining' says the same of the same from within enowning" but that "each 'joining' says the same of the same from within *another essential domain* of that which enowning *names.*" The distinction is an important one. Heidegger does not say "from within enowning" because he knows that enowning is not a basis or a foundation. If enowning were a basis, it would have to be thought as an "underlying addendum," what the Greeks called ὑποκείμενον. But enowning does not have the function of an underlying addendum, a foundation, or a basis for what Heidegger lays out in all the "joinings" of *Contributions to Philosophy.*

In the "joinings" called "Leap" and "Grounding," enowning occurs in such a way that each of these "joinings" turns out to be *"another essential domain* of that which enowning names." At stake in these "joinings" is "the essential onefold" called "Leap" and the "essential onefold" called "Grounding" as "the essential domains" of that which enowning names. Insofar as enowning is a self-supplying and self-mediating midpoint, that which enowning names an essential onefold and another essential domain—in this case "Leap" or "Grounding"—is also self-supplied and self-mediated. Thus naming "Leap" and "Grounding" each an essential onefold and another essential domain is a self-supplying and self-mediating naming. Therefore the words *essential onefold* and *essential domain* with which these "joinings" are named should be understood as a self-supplying and self-mediating naming. Does such naming take place when in English we say "essential onefold" for Heidegger's *wesentliche Einheit* and "essential domain" for his *Wesensbereich?*

One must acknowledge that these renderings are precarious. If we understand the word *essential* exclusively in terms of its etymological connection to *essence* and *essentia,* we obfuscate the self-supplying and self-mediating naming that reverberates in Heidegger's *wesentliche Einheit* and *Wesensbereich.* He characterizes the onefold of the six "joinings" and their domains as *wesentlich,* that is, essential, not because he wants to suggest that that onefold and these six domains have a *Wesen* in the sense of *essence* and *essentia.* Heidegger uses the words *wesentlich* and *Wesensbereich* precisely because he wants to show that both that onefold and these six domains are sheltered and protected from the metaphysical intrusion of *essence* and *essentia.* When in rendering *wesentlich* and *Wesensbereich* we use the word *essential,* we are not at all interested in subordinating them to *essence* and *essentia.* Rather, with *essential* we seek an *approximate* rendering of *wesentlich* and *Wesensbereich* since, after all, the English word *essential* also has connotations such as "original," "elemental," and "primary."

If we restrict our understanding of the word *essential* to its etymological connection to *essence* and *essentia* and take this connection as our guide, then we fail to understand the self-supplying and self-mediating naming that reverberates in the words *wesentliche Einheit* and *Wesensbereich*. It is important to keep in mind that Heidegger's term *Wesen*, which appears in these two key words of *Contributions to Philosophy*, has nothing to do with essence. The essential domain of that which enowning names is not the domain of essence or of *essentia-existentia* for the simple reason that enowning and consequently *der Wesensbereich* of "that which enowning names" have neither an "essence" nor an "existence." Accordingly, it would be a gross misunderstanding to take the words *essential onefold* and *essential domain* as implying that enowning has an essence or an existence.

Because the transformed basic structure of *Dasein* lies in Heidegger's purview—however unthematically articulated—he abandons the transcendental-horizonal thinking, divides *Contributions to Philosophy* into "joinings" rather than "parts," and in addressing these "joinings" speaks of their essential onefold and their essential domains. All this he has in his purview thanks to be-ing's turning relation as a turning *unto his* thinking. It is instructive and illuminating to note that when Heidegger speaks of "[t]he riches of the turning relation of be-ing" as a turning "to Da-sein, which is en-owned by be-ing" (*Contributions*, 6), he is focusing on the sustaining power of this turning relation.

Thus prepared to understand how "Leap" and "Grounding" reveal the transformed basic structure of *Dasein*, let us now turn to these two "joinings." In doing so, we understand Heidegger's proviso according to which "only by way of what Heidegger I has thought does one gain access to what is to be thought by Heidegger II."

III

The concern that dominates and permeates "Leap" is to provoke and thus to invite thinking to respond to the subtle and easily ignored claim that calls on thinking to use philosophy's 'first beginning' as a "leap-off" to leap into the 'other beginning.' The concern that dominates and permeates "Grounding" is the founding or grounding of *Dasein* in the light of what transpires in the 'other beginning.'

Although it is subtle and ignorable, the claim that calls on thinking to take a leap into the 'other beginning' is so thoroughgoing and penetrating that when the leap is enacted, the basic structure of *Dasein* emerges as transformed. Thus the very enactment of the leap suffices to transform "projecting-open" and "throwness." In section 122 of "Leap," Heidegger demonstrates the very enactment of the leap as sufficient for transforming "projection-open" into an en-owned projecting when he notes that the leap "is the enactment of projecting-open . . . in the sense of shifting into the open, such that the thrower of the projecting-open experiences itself as thrown—i.e., as en-owned by being" (*Contributions*, 169). The key to understanding this transformation lies in what Heidegger says about the thrower of projecting-open. If the thrower of projecting-open experiences itself as thrown into and en-owned by be-ing, then projecting-open itself is also thrown into and en-owned by be-ing, that is, is transformed. Thus the transformation of "projecting-open," the basic structure of *Dasein*, manifests itself as en-ownment of this structure by be-ing.

Given its details, this transformation consists of shifting into the open. Since the open into which projecting-open shifts is one that en-owns, the transformation of this basic structure of *Dasein* consists in its being en-owned by the open. Accordingly, the one who enacts this projecting-open—Heidegger calls it the thrower of projecting-open—experiences itself as thrown into and en-owned by the open, that is, by be-ing. In this vein we can say that Heidegger retains the basic structure of projecting-open in being-historical perspective as one transformed in accord with an openness that en-owns this projecting.

Since this basic structure initially appears in the thought of Heidegger I, and since this very same structure appears transformed in the thought of Heidegger II, we understand why Heidegger can say that "only by way of what 'Heidegger I' has thought does one gain access to what is to be thought by 'Heidegger II.'" For only by grasping what Heidegger I has thought, namely, the structure called projecting-open, do we gain access to the enactment of a transformed, en-owned projecting-open that is thought by Heidegger II.

So far I have addressed only the manner in which projecting-open appears transformed in "Leap." What about the other basic structure, the so-called throwness? We know from the fundamental ontology of the transcendental-horizonal perspective that projecting-open occurs equally-originally (*gleichursprünglich*) with "throwness." Accordingly, if in the being-historical perspective projecting-open emerges transformed, then "throwness"—given its equal-originality with "projecting-open"—must also emerge transformed in this perspective. That this is exactly what happens can be seen in the fact that in *Contributions to Philosophy* Heidegger retains "throwness" but abandons its transcendental-horizonal determination in terms of facticity. Instead of focusing on facticity in order to determine "thrownness," he focuses on the counter-resonance of be-ing's enowning-throw and *Dasein*'s en-owned and transformed projecting-open. To understand the novel determination of "thrownness" that hereby emerges, we must take a close look at that counter-resonance.

To approach this counter-resonance we must set out from the relationship between be-ing and man that Heidegger describes by saying: "Be-ing needs man in order to hold sway; and man belongs to be-ing so that he can accomplish his utmost destiny as Da-sein" (*Contributions,* 177). In short, the relationship between be-ing and man consists of being's need of man and man's belonging to be-ing. And this relationship reveals a counter-resonance in which the transformed basic structure of thrownness comes to the fore. This is the counter-resonance of being's en-owning-throw (which mirrors be-ing's need) and *Dasein*'s en-owned projecting-opening (which mirrors man's belonging). In view of this counter-resonance, Heidegger in *Contributions to Philosophy* shows the equal-originality of projecting-open and thrownness. Occurring within the counter-resonance of be-ing's en-owning-throw and *Dasein*'s en-owned projecting-open, thrownness no longer indicates thrownness into the facticity of disclosedness *(Faktizität der Erschlossenheit)* but means being thrown into and being en-owned by be-ing.

Focusing on the transformation of thrownness in the sense of one en-owned by be-ing's en-owning-throw, Heidegger formulates his proviso. Because in Heidegger II thrownness as thought by Heidegger I in terms of facticity of disclosedness reappears as en-owned by be-ing's enowning-throw, Heidegger states in the preface that the thought of Heidegger I (thrownness into facticity of disclosedness) becomes possible as contained in the thought of Heidegger II (thrownness as en-owned by be-ing's en-owning-throw).

As I indicated earlier, the concern that dominates and permeates "Grounding" is to ground *Dasein*. In view of what I have said so far about be-ing's en-owning-throw, it should be clear that this grounding is not primarily and exclusively the affair of an individual and up to his discretion, because it entails be-ing's enowning-throw. This throw enowns not only projecting but also thrownness. Thus the grounding of *Dasein* begins with the en-owning of thrownness by be-ing's enowning-throw. (Heidegger has this enowning-throw in mind when he tells Richardson that he did not invent be-ing's turning relation and that this turning does not concern merely his thinking.)

The results of this brief excursion into "Leap" and "Grounding," suggest that as he abandons the transcendental-horizonal perspective, Heidegger works with the transformed basic structure of *Dasein* within the being-historical perspective. The counter-resonance of be-ing's en-owning-throw and man's en-owned projecting-opening lets the transformed basic structures of *Dasein* emerge in the being-historical perspective. Since projecting-opening and thrownness as thought by Heidegger I in terms of the facticity of disclosedness emerge in Heidegger II as en-owned by be-ing and as thrown into its enowning-throw, in the preface Heidegger can say that the thought of Heidegger I becomes possible as contained in the thought of Heidegger II.

IV

If we have succeeded in elucidating the transformation of the basic structure of *Dasein*, we can say that *Contributions to Philosophy* is the work that contains an elucidation of the proviso under which Heidegger places Richardson's "Heidegger I, Heidegger II" distinction. In elucidating this proviso, I have drawn on specific sections of *Contributions to Philosophy* to demonstrate that in the being-historical perspective Heidegger works with the transformed basic structure of *Dasein*. If the preceding analyses of those sections are tenable, then we must focus on be-ing's en-owning-throw to understand the relationship between transcendental-horizontal thinking and being-historical thinking. If we do so, we realize that this relationship should be understood neither as a simple continuity nor as a break but rather as a passage entailing a constant "back and forth."

I advisedly choose the words *passage* and *back and forth* because in speaking, as I frequently have, of Heidegger abandoning the transcendental-horizonal perspective, I may have inadvertently created the impression that there is a break in Heidegger's thought. If there were such a break, then the emerging of the basic but transformed structure of *Dasein* in being-historical thinking would be inexplicable. It is more appropriate to speak of a passage that entails a constant "back and forth" between the transcendental-horizonal and the being-historical thinking.

There is no break between the transcendental-horizonal and the being-historical thinking because there is no break between the transcendental-horizonal and the being-historical determination of projecting-open and thrownness. Heidegger does not discard the transcendental-horizonal determination of projecting-open and thrownness in favor of their being-historical determination but passes "back and forth" from the one to the other. More specifically, there is no break between the transcendental-horizonal and the being-historical determinations of this structure because the former determination is contained in the latter.

It is interesting to note that this passage and this "back and forth" are already foreshadowed in the path of thinking that Heidegger traverses in *Being and Time*, which is also the path to which he alludes in the introduction to this work. In the preliminary remark *(Vorbemerkung)* to the 1953 edition of *Sein und Zeit*, Heidegger also characterizes this path as one that "still today remains a necessary one if our *Dasein* is to be moved by the question of being."[104] To say that this path remains necessary today is to say that a thoroughgoing familiarity with transcendental-horizonal thinking is still necessary. For this reason the relationship between the transcendental-horizonal and the being-historical thinking should be grasped as a relentless passage and "back and forth" from the basic structure of *Dasein*—already worked out in the transcendental-horizonal perspective—to the basic but transformed structure of *Dasein* that operates in the being-historical perspective.

In the introduction to *Being and Time*, which was written after the completion of this work but precedes it in the published volume, Heidegger points ahead to the division "Time and Being."[105] In this introduction Heidegger envisions what lies ahead and takes a retrospective look at what he has accomplished in *Being and Time*. The look into what lies ahead takes its orientation from be-ing's en-owning-throw, that is, from the en-owning turning relation of be-ing. It goes without saying that the words *en-owning turning relation* do not appear in the introduction to *Being and Time*. But their absence does not mean that the path Heidegger's thinking traverses throughout this work is not already open to the passage and the "back and forth" that occur between the transcendental-horizonal and the being-historical thinking. To assume the contrary is to suggest that the thinking that shapes *Being and Time* does not receive be-ing's throw, that is, to assume that this thinking is not exposed to be-ing's turning relation. But this assumption is completely untenable since it ignores be-ing's turning relation, the sole impetus behind the writing of *Being and Time*.

In this sense this introduction is also no ordinary and familiar introduction; in its own way it too is a "pre-view." Heidegger's unwavering return to *Being and Time* throughout *Contributions to Philosophy*, his undiminished resolve to emphasize from within the being-historical perspective the major achievements of *Being and Time*, for example, "being unto death," are clear evidence that the path of thinking he traverses throughout *Being and Time* is already open to that passage and that "back and forth."

Although Heidegger does not use the words *enowning turning relation* in the introduction to *Being and Time*, he alludes to that passage and that "back and forth" when he points to the division "Time and Being" and says in the Richardson preface that turning "belongs to the dynamics that is named by the titles 'Being and Time,' and 'Time and Being.'"[106] If the enowning turning relation of be-ing is already operative as the dynamics in the move from "Being and Time" to "Time and Being," then this move reveals a passage and a "back and forth" between the transcendental-horizonal and the being-historical thinking. But such a passage and such a "back and forth" should not be construed as originating from within the innovative "acts" of Heidegger's thinking. To subordinate this passage, this "back and forth," to the innovative "acts" of his thinking is to overlook the occurrence called be-ing's turning relation. The passage and the "back and forth" between the transcendental-horizonal and the being-historical thinking do not come about because Heidegger suddenly decides to become innovative. They come about mainly because be-ing's turning relation occurs independently from Heidegger's thinking at the same time as this occurrence *needs* the active engagement of his thinking. That independent occurrence and this engagement sustain the dynamics named "Being and Time" and "Time and Being." The fact that be-ing's turning relation is an enowning relation makes clear that this passage and this "back and forth" occur within the domain of enowning.

Furthermore, the assumption that the passage and the "back and forth" come about because Heidegger suddenly decides to become innovative overlooks the revolutionary discovery that resides at the very heart of *Contributions to Philosophy* and reverberates in its six "joinings." This is the discovery that be-ing as enowning resonates within the counter-resonance of be-ing's enowning-throw and man's opening up this throw, mutatis mutandis, resonates within the counter-resonance of projecting-open and thrownness. The immediate implication of this revolutionary discovery is that thinking *(Dasein)* experiences itself as thrown into be-ing's enowning-throw. Henceforth thinking opens up be-ing's enowning-throw, that is, projects it open, because thinking is en-owned by this throw. Seen in the phenomenologically accessible and hermeneutically explicable context of this counter-resonance, thinking proves to be constrained by its thrownness (its finitude) even as think-ing continues to be exposed to and experience the immeasurable near-ness of be-ing's enowning-throw.

In contrast to the death-bound and finite occurrence of thinking understood as projecting-open, be-ing's enowning-throw is eternal—*ewig*—in the sense not of a selfsame and self-perpetuating eternity but of an ongoing self-sustaining throw that does not cease with *Dasein*'s passing. As long as *Dasein* is, it experiences the nearness to be-ing's enowning-throw as occurring independently from *Dasein*'s own end. This end as the possibility of death comes to *Dasein* thanks to be-ing's enowning-throw.

When we consider be-ing's enowning-throw in conjunction with thinking, thinking appears in a new light. Thinking can no longer be identified with what epistemology calls a faculty of the mind; rather it appears as the mystery through which be-ing resonates within the counter-resonance of a finite projecting-opening and be-ing's ongoing and self-sustaining throw.[107] Heidegger refers to *this* thinking—*not* to the epistemological notion of thinking as a faculty of the mind—when he speaks of thinking as a serenity that is aware of itself (*die wissende Heiterkeit*) and as such is the gate to what is ongoing self-sustaining ([*das*] *Tor zum Ewigen*).[108]

Assuming that be-ing's enowning turning relation is the sole "guiding star" of all thinking of being, I question whether after the pub-lication of *Contributions to Philosophy*, Richardson's "Heidegger I, Hei-degger II" distinction is an appropriate and guiding one. Although Heidegger did not reject this distinction offhand, he did subject it to an important proviso. Once this proviso is fleshed out in the light of the passage and the "back and forth" between the transcendental-horizonal and the being-historical thinking, and once one realizes that this passage and this "back and forth" take place in response to be-ing's enowning-throw—borne out by a careful reading of *Contributions to Philosophy*—how useful is Richardson's distinction? Do we need this distinction to appreciate the revolution in thinking that announces it-self in Heidegger's *Contributions to Philosophy*? Here I raise a question to which Richardson has offered an interesting response.

V

Richardson has addressed my question by reiterating his initial posi-tion that the "Heidegger I, Heidegger II" distinction is not only use-ful but also justified in light of what Richardson has established in

"Conclusion," the last part of his *Heidegger: Through Phenomenology to Thought*. He presents this reiteration in an essay titled "From Phenomenology through Thought to a *Festschrift*: A Response."[109] It is therefore incumbent upon me to deal with Richardson's response in some detail and in this way show how important it is to grasp properly the proviso under which Heidegger places Richardson's "Heidegger I, Heidegger II" distinction.

Let me begin by noting that in his response Richardson does not explicitly reject my analyses and discussion through which I show that in *Contributions to Philosophy* Heidegger retains the basic but transformed structure of *Dasein*. Moreover, he does not reject the results of my analyses and discussion concerning the fact that this transformed basic structure is the locus of the passage and the "back and forth" that transpire between the transcendental-horizonal and the being-historical thinking. Put slightly differently, in his response Richardson does not question my suggestion that there is neither a simple continuity nor a break in Heidegger's thought but a relentless passage and "back and forth" between the transcendental-horizonal and the being-historical thinking. Rather, speaking in an autobiographical context of his experiences in the years he spent in Louvain and Freiburg, he formulates a response in which he essentially reiterates the two closely interconnected theses that he advances in "Conclusion," the last part of his *Heidegger: Through Phenomenology to Thought*. The first thesis is that there is a shift of focus in Heidegger from *Dasein* to being. The second thesis contends that Heidegger II is more original than Heidegger I.

What do these two theses say that might shed light on Heidegger's proviso: "The distinction you make between Heidegger I and Heidegger II is justified only on the condition that this is kept constantly in mind: only by way of what Heidegger I has thought does one gain access to what is to-be-thought by Heidegger II. But [the thought of] Heidegger I becomes possible only if it is contained in Heidegger II."[110] It goes without saying that to respond to this question I must address Richardson's two interrelated theses.

Regarding the first thesis, I must ask whether, considering what transpires in "Leap" and "Grounding" in *Contributions to Philosophy*, there is any justification for Richardson's thesis according to which in Heidegger there is a "shift of focus from There-being [*Dasein*] to Being"?[111] When I consider the transformation of "thrown projecting-open" as manifest in these two "joinings" of *Contributions to Philosophy*, I find no justification for this thesis, for Heidegger equally and forcefully addresses both be-ing and the basic structure of *Dasein* (thrown projecting-open) in the transcendental-horizonal perspective *and* in the being-historical perspective. Richardson's thesis of a shift of focus could be maintained only if he could demonstrate that transcendental-horizonal thinking focuses solely on *Dasein*, without having much to say about being, while being-historical thinking focuses more on being and less on *Dasein*. But this is impossible, for transcendental-horizonal thinking (Heidegger I) does not focus solely on *Dasein* and being-historical thinking (Heidegger II) does not relinquish this focus in favor of exclusively focusing on be-ing. That transcendental-horizonal thinking focuses on being can be seen in the fact that it understands being as the horizon of *praesens* within which the transcendence of beings takes place. That being-historical thinking focuses on *Dasein* can be seen in the fact that *Dasein*'s basic but transformed structure is manifest in "Leap" and "Grounding" of *Contributions to Philosophy*. What gives rise to being-historical thinking is not a shift of focus from *Dasein* to being but an immanent transformation within the matter named be-ing that shows its historicality. Being-historical thinking acquires predominance not because Heidegger shifts his focus from *Dasein* to be-ing but because be-ing's turning relation reveals, first, that there is such a thing as be-ing's en-owning-throw and, second, that this throw is through and through historical.

Regarding the second thesis, I shall begin by addressing the thrust of Richardson's formulation for it. After surveying the entire course of the analyses and discussions in his *Heidegger: Through Phenomenology to Thought*, Richardson asks: "What else is there to conclude than that Heidegger II is *more original than Heidegger I*, went before him along the way?" (Richardson's emphasis).[112] But on what ground does Richardson take Heidegger II to be more original than Heidegger I? The answer to this question lies in Richardson's first thesis. If this thesis is acceptable, then Heidegger II must be more original than Heidegger I because Heidegger II makes good what Heidegger I fails to do; Heidegger II shifts his focus from *Dasein* to being. But how could Heidegger II be more original than Heidegger I when the very originality of Heidegger II depends on the originality of what Heidegger I accomplishes in his fundamental ontology by uncovering the basic structure of *Dasein*? To claim that Heidegger II is more original than Heidegger I is to cast a negative light on transcendental-horizonal thinking, thereby overlooking the fact that it is this thinking that uncovers the basic structure of *Dasein* as a structure without which Heidegger II would remain inexplicable.

What Richardson calls Heidegger II would remain inexplicable without consideration given to the retaining of the basic but transformed structure of *Dasein* in being-historical thinking. Such a consideration shows why, as being-historical thinking unfolds, Heidegger in *Contributions to Philosophy* virtually reexamines all the questions and issues of the fundamental ontology of transcendental-horizonal thinking, instead of discarding those questions and issues. Heidegger's explicit and decisive quest that runs through and shapes the entirety of *Contributions to Philosophy*—the quest concerning the grounding of *Dasein*—can be carried out only if all the questions and issues of fundamental ontology are grounded being-historically. The deciding issue is not whether, compared to Heidegger I, Heidegger II is more original, but rather whether be-ing's turning relation is a hermeneutically-phenomenologically demonstrable turning that en-owns Heidegger's thinking and lets this thinking "see" the basic but transformed structure of *Dasein*. In short, the deciding issue is not a shift of focus from *Dasein* to be-ing but be-ing's turning relation to Heidegger's thinking.

Heidegger alludes to the primacy and decidedness of be-ing's turning relation when in the preface he places at Richardson's disposal one of his most illuminating and instructive directives for understanding the turning. This directive reads: "The turning [relation of be-ing] is above all not a procedure adopted by the thinking that questions [being]. . . . I did not invent it, nor does it concern merely my thinking."[113] If we follow this directive, we realize that turning, as Heidegger understands it, is not a procedure adopted by *his* thinking. It would be so only if with turning he had in mind a "reversal" that would occur in the course of his thought at the moment that he *supposedly* decides to "reverse" the shift of focus of his thinking from *Dasein* to being. But given the preceding analysis of the turning, is there any justification for interpreting the turning in the sense of a reversal? What Heidegger calls *die Kehre* could be interpreted as a "reversal" only if with the term *die Kehre* he sought to capture the change of course—the shift of focus— that supposedly occurs in his thought. But Heidegger's explicit statement that turning *is not* a procedure adopted by *his* thinking makes clear that turning is an occurrence not that his thinking brings about but that comes to pass *in* and *as* be-ing. Put slightly differently, with his characterization of turning, Heidegger speaks of an occurrence that is *not* brought about by *his* thinking ("turning," he says, "is not a procedure adopted by the thinking that questions being") since, as he notes, turning is neither invented by him nor does it concern only his thinking.

Considering this characterization of turning, I must conclude that only when we fail to understand that be-ing's turning relation means be-ing's turning *unto* thinking—a turning to be distinguished from a procedure adopted by Heidegger's thinking—can we claim with Richardson that "Heidegger I takes a turn in his way in order to become Heidegger II."[114] However, Heidegger does not take a turn; instead, be-ing, in its turning relation, turns *unto* Heidegger's thinking. This is another way of saying that the turning that occurs as be-ing's turning relation ipso facto excludes the interpretation of this turning as a turn in Heidegger's course of thought, that is, as a procedure adopted by Heidegger that Richardson calls "reversal."

Heidegger's thinking is distinguished not by altering its focus from *Dasein* to being but in its hermeneutic sensitivity and responsibility, which prompt Heidegger to project-open all the issues and questions of transcendental-horizonal thinking by relentlessly passing "back and forth" between the transcendental-horizonal and the being-historical thinking. Given the primacy of be-ing's turning relation, we must understand the relationship between transcendental-horizonal thinking (Heidegger I) and being-historical thinking (Heidegger II) as a relentless passage and "back and forth." The result of this relentless "back and forth" is Heidegger's revolutionary discovery in *Contributions to Philosophy* that ultimately be-ing is none other than the counter-resonance of an en-owning-throw and an en-owned projecting-opening.

If the relationship between transcendental-horizonal thinking (Heidegger I) and being-historical thinking (Heidegger II) is understood as a relentless passage "back and forth" wherein the counter-resonance of an en-owning-throw and an en-owned projecting resonates as enowning, then all efforts to interpret Heidegger according to the chronology of his writings—all attempts "to start with Heidegger from the start"—are doomed to failure and should be abandoned as misleading. What is at stake is not a piecemeal interpretation of his writings according to chronology but a "leap" by which thinking leaps into the counter-resonance of an en-owning-throw and an en-owned projecting-opening.

It remains to be seen whether the so-called Heidegger literature—following the "Heidegger I, Heidegger II" distinction—understands be-ing's turning relation as one that does not concern Heidegger's thinking alone. It remains to be seen whether this literature will flourish from within the counter-resonance of be-ing's enowning-throw and thinking's en-owned projecting-opening, that is, from within the counter-resonance that resonates as enowning, or whether it will continue to be mired in the track of "subjectivity" without any awareness of that counter-resonance. As far as I can see, a few exceptions notwithstanding, the Heidegger literature continues to be unaware of be-ing's turning relation and of that counter-resonance.

Notes

Bibliography

General Index

Index of Greek Terms

Notes

Preface

1. Alexander Solzhenitsyn, *Cancer Ward*, trans. Nicholas Bethell and David Burg (New York: Farrar, Straus & Giroux, 1974), 105–6.

2. *Briefe 1925 bis 1975: Und andere Zeugnisse / Hannah Arendt, Martin Heidegger*, ed. Ursula Ludz (Frankfurt am Main: Vittorio Klostermann, 1998), 54.

Introduction

3. For approaches based on the assumption of deconstructability of the thinking of being, see note 32 in this volume; for an instance of the hunt for the "genesis" of this thinking, see note 58; for the abuse of the criteria of comprehensibility/incomprehensibility, see note 57. In connection with the criteria of comprehensibility/incomprehensibility, I deliberately characterize their use as an abuse, because properly understood, these criteria always *follow*, rather than *precede*, the thrust of hermeneutic phenomenology.

4. I address this returnership in some detail in the fifth and seventh essays in this volume. Also regarding returnership, see *Contributions*, 319.

5. I address the relationship between machination and Nietzsche's will to power in the seventh essay in this volume.

6. See "Drei Briefe Heideggers an Karl Löwith," in *Zur philosophischen Aktualität Heideggers*, ed. Dietrich Papenfuss and Otto Pöggeler, vol. 2 of *Im Gespräch der Zeit* (Frankfurt am Main: Vittorio Klostermann, 1990), 37. For a perceptive interpretation of this letter, see Kalary, *Das befindliche Verstehen und die Seinsfrage*, 70–74.

7. "Drei Briefe Heideggers an Karl Löwith," 37.

8. For an instance of such a dismissal, see note 58 in this volume.

9. For this characterization of Marina Tsvetayeva, see Fédier, "Hölderlin und Heidegger."

10. Pasternak, Tsvetayeva, and Rilke, *Letters*, 221.

11. Regarding "There-being," cf. William J. Richardson, *Heidegger: Through Phenomenology to Thought*, 34, 44–46, 73–74, hereafter referred to as *Heidegger*.

12. *Rainer Maria Rilke und Marie von Thurn und Taxis: Briefwechsel*, vol. 1 (Frankfurt am Main: Insel Verlag, 1986), 44.

Translating Heidegger's *Contributions to Philosophy* as a Hermeneutic Responsibility

13. Throughout this essay all italics within quotations are Heidegger's. My interpolations are enclosed in brackets.

14. Cf. F.-W. von Herrmann, *Hermeneutische Phänomenologie des Daseins: Eine Erläuterung von "Sein und Zeit,"* vol. 1 (Frankfurt am Main: Vittorio Klostermann Verlag, 1987), 132–33, and *Subjekt und Dasein: Grundbegriffe von "Sein und Zeit,"* 3rd ed. (Frankfurt am Main: Vittorio Klostermann Verlag, 2004), 92.

15. Heidegger, *Identität und Differenz* (Pfullingen: Neske Verlag, 1982), 25.

16. I used the word *enowning* for the first time in my essay "The Place of the Pre-Socratics in Heidegger's *Beiträge zur Philosophie.*"

17. Heidegger, *Beiträge zur Philosophie* (*Vom Ereignis*), ed. Friedrich-Wilhelm von Herrmann (Frankfurt am Main: Klostermann Verlag, 1994), 379.

18. The rendering of *Ab-grund* as "abyss" and the hyphenation of "abyss" are proposed by J. Sallis. See his "Grounders of the Abyss," in Charles E. Scott et al., *Companion to Heidegger's Contributions to Philosophy,* 181–97. For a perceptive critique of Sallis's essay, see Kalary, "Hermeneutic Pre-conditions for Interpreting Heidegger (Part Two)."

19. For the account of "de-cision" and its eleven shapes, see sections 43 and 44 of *Contributions.* On "de-cision," see also "'De-cision' in *Contributions to Philosophy* and the Path to the Interpretation of Heraclitus Fragment 16" in this volume.

20. See *GA* 12:27, 204, 241.

21. Heidegger, *Hölderlins Hymne "Der Ister," GA* 53:76.

22. John Felstiner, *Paul Celan: Poet, Survivor, Jew* (New Haven, Conn.: Yale University Press, 2001), 20.

23. For a discussion of the "Nachbarschaft vom Denken und Dichten," see *GA* 12:173.

24. On the relationship of Heidegger and Paul Celan, see Gerhart Baumann, *Erinnerungen an Paul Celan* (Frankfurt am Main: Suhrkamp Verlag, 1985), 58–81; Otto Pöggeler, *Spur des Wortes: Zur Lyrik Paul Celans* (Munich: Verlag Karl Albert Freiburg, 1986), 248–49, 259–71.

25. Felstiner, *Paul Celan,* 133.

On "Echo," the First Part of *Contributions to Philosophy*

26. My translation is from Heidegger's revised version of a sentence in the 1951 edition of this work. Cf. marginal note marked "a" in *GA* 4:38.

The Place of the Pre-Socratics in "Playing-Forth," the Second Part of *Contributions to Philosophy*

27. Jean Beaufret, "Heraclitus and Parmenides," in Kenneth Maly and Parvis Emad, eds., *Heidegger on Heraclitus: A New Reading* (Lewiston, N.Y.: Edwin Mellen Press, 1986), 70.

28. Heidegger, *Frühe Schriften* (Frankfurt am Main: Klostermann Verlag, 1978), 438.

29. See F.-W. von Herrmann, *Heideggers Philosophie der Kunst*, 2nd ed. (Frankfurt am Main: Klostermann Verlag, 1994), 2, 7, 8. See also von Herrmann, *Wege ins Ereignis*, 55–56 and 67–68.

30. *Martin Heidegger—Elisabeth Blochmann Briefwechsel, 1918–1969* (Marbach am Neckar: Deutsche Schillergesellschaft, 1989), 54.

31. On the relation of "thrownness," "projecting-open," and "being-along-with" to *Rede*, see F.-W. von Herrmann, *Subjekt und Dasein: Interpretationen zu "Sein and Zeit,"* 2nd ed. (Frankfurt am Main: Klostermann Verlag, 1985), 92–114, as well as Parvis Emad, "The Significance of the New Edition of *Subjekt und Dasein* and Fundamental Ontology of Language," *Heidegger Studies* 2 (1986): 141–51.

32. In *Grundfragen der Philosophie: Ausgewählte "Probleme" der "Logik"* (*GA* 45), a lecture course text written at the same time as *Contributions to Philosophy*, Heidegger renders explicit the interconnection between ἀλήθεια in early Greek thinking and τὸ ἀληθές. Given this fact we must consider unwarranted J. Sallis's attempt to deconstruct Heidegger by suggesting that he fails "to demonstrate a certain solidarity between the Platonic dialogues and the writings of the early Greek thinkers." Cf. J. Sallis, "A Wonder that One Could Never Aspire to Surpass," in Kenneth Maly, ed., *The Path of Archaic Thinking: Unfolding the Work of John Sallis* (Albany: SUNY Press, 1995), 262. The lesson that Sallis fails to learn is that in this lecture course text (*GA* 45) Heidegger establishes the interconnectedness of the unconcealed, τὸ ἀληθές, and unconcealment, ἀλήθεια, and thereby does precisely what Sallis accuses him of not doing: Heidegger demonstrates a certain solidarity between Plato and the early Greeks.

"De-cision" in *Contributions to Philosophy* and the Path to the Interpretation of Heraclitus Fragment 16

33. See Emad, "Heidegger's Originary Reading of Heraclitus—Fragment 16."

34. Von Herrmann, *Wege ins Ereignis*, 2.

35. For what follows, see *GA* 55:44–160.

36. For two reasons I translate *Vorrang* as "preeminence" and not as "priority." First, in the word *preeminence* the prefix *pre-*, which calls to mind the German *Vor-*, comes together with *eminence*, which calls to mind the German *-rang*. Second, the English word *priority* has a strong epistemological connotation that I wish to avoid.

37. For an overall, comprehensive approach to Heidegger's interpretation of Heraclitus, see De Gennaro, *Logos—Heidegger liest Heraklit*. For a careful analysis of Heidegger's interpretation of Heraclitus from within the field of classical philology, see Hans-Christian Günther, *Grundfragen des griechischen Denkens* (Würzburg: Königshausen & Neumann, 2001).

38. Heidegger, *Denkerfahrungen* (Frankfurt am Main: V. Klostermann, 1983), 172.

On the Last Part of *Contributions to Philosophy,* "Be-ing," Its Liberating Ontology, and the Hints at the Question of God

39. For the English renderings of the keywords of *Contributions to Philosophy* as used in this essay, see the translators' foreword to this work.

40. In addition to Heidegger's own account of the "turning" dealt with in this discussion, see von Herrmann, *Wege ins Ereignis,* 55–56, 64–84; idem, "Wahrheit-Zeit-Raum," in *Die Frage nach der Wahrheit,* ed. Ewald Richter, vol. 4, Martin Heidegger Gesellschaft, Schriftenreihe (Frankfurt am Main: Vittorio Klostermann, 1997), 243–56; Emad, "A Conversation with Friedrich-Wilhelm von Herrmann"; and Coriando, *Der letzte Gott als Anfang,* 33–34.

41. Cf. the preface to W. J. Richardson, *Heidegger,* xvii, xix, xxi. It should be noted that my renderings of the crucial terms of this preface differ significantly from Richardson's in his translation of Heidegger's letter to him. To make this point clear I shall include in the text the German original of what I quote from the preface. Heidegger's letter to Richardson appears in *Heidegger: Through Phenomenology to Thought* as a *Vorwort,* or a preface, without any indication that originally it was a letter. On this point, see "Vorwort: Brief an P. William J. Richardson von Martin Heidegger," *Philosophisches Jahrbuch* 72 (1965): 397–402.

Regarding the matter of "turning," it should be noted that by interpreting Heidegger's "it worlds" *(es weltet)* from his 1919 war emergency course *(GA 56–57)* as a "turning before the turning," Hans-Georg Gadamer obfuscates the threefold characterizations of the "turning" and unleashes an avalanche of misunderstandings. See his *Gesammelte Werke,* vol. 3 (Tübingen: J. C. B. Mohr, 1987), 423. This obfuscation determines T. Kisiel's understanding of the "war emergency course of 1919." See his *Genesis of Heidegger's "Being and Time"* (Berkeley: University of California Press, 1993), 3, 16. This obfuscation also determines Manfred Riedel's interpretation of the "turning"; see his "Die Urstiftung der phänomenologischen Hermeneutik: Heideggers frühe Auseinandersetzung mit Husserl," in *Phänomenologie im Widerstreit: Zum 50. Todestag Husserls,* ed. Christoph Jamme and Otto Pöggeler (Frankfurt am Main: Suhrkamp, 1989), 215–33. Further, this obfuscation shapes J. van Buren's understanding of Heidegger's early Freiburg lecture courses; see his *Young Heidegger: Rumor of the Hidden King* (Bloomington: Indiana University Press, 1994), 136–37. For a thoroughgoing criticism of these misunderstandings, see Kalary, *Das befindliche Verstehen und die Seinsfrage,* 70–73.

42. Richardson, *Heidegger,* xix, translation modified.

43. Ibid., xvii.

44. For more on "projecting-opening" and the inadequacies of "project" and "projection" as possible renderings of *entwerfen* and *Entwurf,* respectively, see the translators' foreword to *Contributions to Philosophy,* xxvii–xxx.

45. Regarding metontological turning, see Heidegger, *Metaphysische Anfangsgründe der Logik im Ausgang von Leibniz* (Frankfurt am Main: Vittorio Klostermann, 1978), *GA* 26:199–201. For a detailed discussion of "metontological turning," see Friedrich-Wilhelm von Herrmann, *Heideggers "Grundprobleme*

der Phänomenologie": Zur "Zweiten Halft"' von "Sein and Zeit" (Frankfurt am Main: Vittorio Klostermann, 1991), 53–55.

46. For this transformation, see von Herrmann, *Wege ins Ereignis*, 17, 55–58.

47. See *GA* 2:178–239.

48. For a more detailed account of turning in enowning, see sections 135, 136, 137, 140, 141, and 142 of *Contributions to Philosophy*. Here I use the phrase "for the first time" to remind the reader that in characterizing the "turning" as a "turning point in his thinking," Heidegger has in mind what happened *for the first time* in his thinking.

49. What Richardson calls "mittence" (*Heidegger*, 20–21, 434–36) is not entirely the same as this "enowning-throw." In the first place, mittence is Richardson's rendition of Heidegger's *Geschick*, and second, unlike enowning-throw, the word mittence does not explicitly indicate that it stands for a manner of enownment by be-ing.

50. For *Zuwurf* as *Zuruf*, see von Herrmann, *Wege ins Ereignis*, 92: "den Zuruf, den wir auch als Zuwurf fassen können."

51. The hyphenating of *abyss* also will not do. In contrast to the hyphenating of *ab-ground*, which contains the English word *ground*, the hyphenated word *a-byss* does not give any meaning to the construct *byss*, which does not constitute a word and is meaningless. Concerning the proposal to hyphenate *abyss*, see J. Sallis, "Grounders of the Abyss," in Scott et al., *Companion to Heidegger's Contributions to Philosophy*, 197. For a thorough critique of Sallis's essay, see Kalary, "Hermeneutic Pre-conditions for Interpreting Heidegger (Part Two)."

52. If we lose sight of this belonging, we might make the erroneous assumption that in *Contributions to Philosophy* thinking *become*s "a dimension of time and space" (publisher's book jacket description of *Contributions to Philosophy*). Since Heidegger's account of "time-space" in *Contributions to Philosophy* is in no way an account of time and space as they are usually understood, this claim is unfounded.

53. Regarding this expression, see von Herrmann, *Wege ins Ereignis*, 18, 22, 24, 30, 36, 40, 56, 59, 61, 92, 95, 106, 200, 241, 362, and 384.

54. Regarding a being that belongs to the epoch of machination and unfolds from within the 'first beginning,' see the second "joining" of *Contributions to Philosophy*, "Echo," where Heidegger characterizes the epoch of machination as one in which "'beings' . . . are dis-enowned by be-ing" (*Contributions*, 84). Regarding a being that shelters be-ing, see the fourth "joining" of *Contributions to Philosophy*, "Grounding," where Heidegger addresses the possibility of such a being (see esp. *Contributions*, 271–73).

55. The expression "most-ownmost-most-remote" is a translation of Paola-Ludovika Coriando's *das Eigenste-Fernste*. See her "Die 'Formale Anzeige' und das Ereignis: Vorbereitende Überlegungen zum Eigencharakter seinsgeschichtlicher Begrifflichkeit mit einem Ausblick auf den Unterschied von Denken und Dichten," *Heidegger Studies* 14 (1998): 32.

56. Regarding the concept of theological difference, see von Herrmann, *Wege ins Ereignis*, 39, 61, 97, 350, 366, and 385.

57. Burt Hopkins, ed., *Phenomenology: Japanese and American Perspectives* (Dordrecht: Kluwer Academic, 1999), 313.

On the Inception of Being-Historical Thinking and Its Active Character, Mindfulness

58. It would seem that in light of Heidegger's lecture course texts that precede *Being and Time*, T. Kisiel, with his *Genesis of Heidegger's "Being and Time"* (Berkeley: University of California Press, 1993), either prepares for an appropriation of this work or actually appropriates it. A closer look at this book, however, shows that Kisiel achieves neither. His search for the genesis of *Being and Time* misleads him into believing that the question of being is an "ethereal question," and his historical theorizing prevents him from grasping transcendental-horizonal thinking. Kisiel takes *Being and Time* to be the patchwork that Heidegger puts together from the texts of his Marburg lectures. Because of this false assumption, Kisiel cuts himself off from hermeneutic-phenomenological access to *Being and Time*. By historicizing the notion of transcendence, he confuses it with what Husserl and Kant say about it and fails to understand that transcendence in Heidegger means surpassing beings within the horizon of presence. With regard to transcendence in *Being and Time* as well as in Husserl and Kant, see Heidegger's stricture in "Zum Einblick in die Notwendigkeit der Kehre," in *Vom Rätsel des Begriffs: Festschrift für Friedrich-Wilhelm von Herrmann zum 65. Geburtstag,* ed. Paola-Ludovika Coriando (Duncker & Humblot: Berlin, 1999), 1–3. For a thorough and perceptive criticism of Kisiel's book, see Kalary, "Towards Sketching the 'Genesis' of *Being and Time.*"

59. Regarding "immanent transformation," see von Herrmann, *Wege ins Ereignis,* 17, 55–58.

60. See ibid., 6, 59, 90.

61. Regarding Richardson's intimation that I "tout" *Contributions to Philosophy* as Heidegger's second major work, see his "From Phenomenology through Thought to a *Festschrift:* A Response," 27.

62. Paola-Ludovika Coriando, "Zu Hölderlins Wesensbestimmung des Menschen," in Coriando, *Vom Rätsel des Begriffs,* 185–86.

63. Cf. Hans-Georg Gadamer, *Gesammelte Werke,* vol. 3 (Tübingen: Mohr, 1987), 418. See also Kalary, *Das befindliche Verstehen and die Seinsfrage,* 70–73.

Mastery of Be-ing and Coercive Force of Machination in Heidegger's *Contributions to Philosophy* and *Mindfulness* and the Opening to His Nietzsche Interpretation

64. Von Herrmann, *Wege ins Ereignis,* 4, 6, 17, 30, 51, and 55.

65. In this essay the word *perspective* has nothing to do with Nietzsche. In Nietzsche perspective is the indicator of the intensification and the unfolding of the "will to power," which shows that the meaning and function of a perspective in Nietzsche are already decided by the "will to power." However, in the present essay the word *perspective* suggests the openness that still echoes in its Latin roots (*per,* "through," and *specere,* "to see") and thus comes close to what the German word *Blickbahn* indicates. Central to hermeneutic phenomenology and composed of *Blick* (glance) and *Bahn* (path), *Blickbahn* brings to mind the Latin *per* and *specere* and thus fits as a designation of the twofold paths of

hermeneutic phenomenology, that is, its transcendental-horizonal and being-historical perspectives.

66. Von Herrmann, *Wege ins Ereignis*, 1, 6, 17, 23, 26, 30, 32, 35, 37, 40, 55, 65, 72, 75, 78, 83, 95, 104, 200, and 226.

67. Regarding the expression *ereignender Zuwurf*, here rendered "enowning forth-throw," see von Herrmann, *Wege ins Ereignis*, 18, 24, 30, 33, 36, 40, 56, 59, 62, 70, 77, and 92.

68. On this point, see also *GA* 40:174–200.

69. Regarding the expression *enteignender Zuwurf*, here rendered "dis-enowning forth-throw," see von Herrmann, *Wege ins Ereignis*, 34, 59, and 94.

70. Regarding these three concealments, see *Contributions*, 83.

71. It should be noted that Heidegger returns to various "joinings" of *Contributions to Philosophy* not only in *Mindfulness* but also in *Geschichte des Seyns* (*GA* 69). Regarding "power" as the issue he addresses in *Mindfulness*, Heidegger finds, after a careful analysis of "power" in *GA* 69:69, that the word mastery *(Herrschaft)* is inappropriate in reference to be-ing.

72. Cf. Nietzsche's *Zwei Jahrtausende beinahe und nicht ein einziger neuer Gott!* (Almost two thousand years and not a single new god), in his *Werke in drei Bänden*, ed. Karl Schlechta (Munich: Carl Hanser Verlag, 1961), 2:1178.

73. See *Contributions*, 271.

74. Heidegger, *Nietzsche*, vol. 1, in *GA* 6.1:416.

75. Nietzsche, *Werke in drei Bänden*, 2:819.

Heidegger and Christianity: A Look at His Correspondence with Bernhard Welte

76. One such work is the lecture titled "Des heiligen Augustinus Betrachtungen über die Zeit," which Heidegger delivered in the abbey of Beuron before its monks, clerics, and novices in gratitude for their welcoming him there for quiet philosophical reflection. For more on this, see Friedrich-Wilhelm von Herrmann, *Augustinus und die phänomenologische Frage nach der Zeit* (Frankfurt am Main: Vittorio Klostermann Verlag, 1992), 16.

77. For more on Heidegger's friendship with other theologians such as Heinrich Ott and Paul Hassler, see Heinrich Wiegand Petzet, *Encounters and Dialogues with Martin Heidegger, 1929–1976*, trans. Parvis Emad and Kenneth Maly, with an introduction by Parvis Emad (Chicago: University of Chicago Press, 1993), 124–28.

78. Heidegger sometimes speaks of the "flight of gods" and sometimes of the "flight of god." But this should not be taken in terms of the plurality of the many gods or the singularity of a single god. As he notes in *Contributions to Philosophy*, "the talk of 'gods' here does not indicate the decided assertion on the extantness of a plurality over against a singular but is rather meant as the allusion to the undecidability of the being of gods, whether of one single god or of many gods" (308).

79. It is important to note that already in *Contributions to Philosophy* Heidegger distances himself from theism, monotheism, polytheism, pantheism, and atheism (cf. 289 and 308).

80. For more on "being-historical-enowning thinking," see von Herrmann, "*Contributions to Philosophy* and Enowning-Historical Thinking."

81. *Briefe und Begegnungen / Martin Heidegger, Bernhard Welte,* ed. A. Denker and H. Zaborowski (Stuttgart: Klett-Cotta, 2003), 17–18, hereafter cited in the text as page numbers enclosed in parentheses.

82. Heidegger, *Wegmarken,* ed. F.-W. von Herrmann (Frankfurt am Main: Vittorio Klostermann Verlag, 1976), 427, hereafter referred to as *GA* 9 followed by page number(s).

83. For the spelling of "being" *(Sein)* and "be-ing" *(Seyn),* see the translators' foreword to *Contributions to Philosophy,* xxii–xxiii. For more on these four questions, see *Contributions to Philosophy,* 5; and *Grundfragen der Philosophie: Ausgewählte "Probleme" der "Logik" (GA* 45), ed. F.-W. von Herrmann (Frankfurt am Main: Vittorio Klostermann, 1984), 122, 130.

84. For more on "enowning" as a translation of *Ereignis,* see the translators' foreword to *Contributions to Philosophy,* xix–xxii, as well as the translators' foreword to *Mindfulness,* xxii–xxiii.

85. For "beings in a whole" as the appropriate translation of *das Seiende im Ganzen,* see the translators' foreword to *Mindfulness,* xxxiii–xxxiv.

86. For a pioneering discussion of how Heidegger in *Being and Time* assesses the Aristotelian finding that the generality of being is not the same as the generality of the genus, see F.-W. von Herrmann, *Hermeneutische Phänomenologie des Daseins: Eine Erläuterung von "Sein und Zeit,"* vol. 1 (Frankfurt am Main: Klostermann Verlag, 1987), 3–36.

87. Regarding the publication of *Ausgewählte Briefe,* see *Mindfulness,* 385.

Questioning Richardson's "Heidegger I, Heidegger II" Distinction and His Response in Light of *Contributions to Philosophy*

88. See William J. Richardson, "Heideggers Weg durch die Phänomenologie zum Seinsdenken," *Philosophisches Jahrbuch* 72 (1965): 385–96. The English version of the résumé appeared in *Heidegger: The Man and the Thinker,* ed. Thomas Sheehan (Chicago: Precedent, 1981), 79–93, hereafter cited as Résumé followed by page number(s).

89. Résumé, 79.

90. Richardson, *Heidegger,* viii, xvi.

91. Ibid., xxii.

92. Résumé, 93.

93. On the "turning relation of be-ing," see *Contributions,* 6. Translation of the phrase *das Seiende im Ganzen* should take its orientation from the preposition *im,* which does not mean "as" and also refers to the preposition *in* in "being-*in*-the world," which is a *Ganzes,* or a "whole." Given this reference and considering the fact that Heidegger does not say *das Seiende als Ganzes,* the phrase *das Seiende im Ganzen* should be rendered as "beings in a whole." (I also address this point in the introduction and some of the essays in this volume.) Richardson is the first and, I might add, the last who is aware of the philosophical significance

of this preposition *im* since he translates the phrase *das Seiende im Ganzen* as "beings-in-the-ensemble." (Cf. *Heidegger*, 197.) However inadequate the word *ensemble* is for the rendering the German *Ganzes*, it is to Richardson's credit that he correctly translates the preposition *im* and thus avoids confusing *das Seiende im Ganzen*, "beings in a whole," with *das Seiende als Ganzes*, "beings as a whole."

94. O. Pöggeler gravely misunderstands Heidegger's analysis of *die Rede/* discourse in *Being and Time* in that he takes *die Rede* as the third existential structure of *Dasein*. See O. Pöggeler, *Der Denkweg Martin Heideggers* (Pfullingen: Neske, 1963), 209–10. To this date Pöggeler's misunderstanding continues to determine most if not all interpretations of the relationship in *Being and Time* between "discourse," "thrownness," "projecting-open," and "being-along-with." Regarding Pöggeler's misunderstanding, see F.-W. von Herrmann's discussion of this relationship in his *Subjekt und Dasein: Interpretationen zu "Sein and Zeit,"* 2nd ed. (Frankfurt am Main: Klostermann, 1985), 92–114. See also Parvis Emad, "The Significance of the New Edition of *Subjekt und Dasein* and the Fundamental Ontology of Language," *Heidegger Studies* 2 (1986): 141–51.

95. See *Martin Heidegger, Elisabeth Blochmann: Briefwechsel, 1918–1969*, ed. J. W. Storck (Marbach am Neckar: Deutsche Schillergesellschaft, 1989), 35.

96. Heidegger, *Die Metaphysik des deutschen Idealismus: Zur erneuten Auslegung von Schellings "Philosophische Untersuchungen über das Wesen der menschlichen Freiheit und die damit zusammenhängenden Gegenstände,"* GA 49:40.

97. *Martin Heidegger, Elisabeth Blochmann*, 54.

98. F.-W. von Herrmann, *Heideggers Philosophie der Kunst*, 2nd ed. (Frankfurt am Main: Klostermann, 1994), 6.

99. See von Herrmann, *Wege ins Ereignis*, 1, 6, 17, 30, 51, 55, 67, 70, 89, 93, 216, 227, and 331.

100. *Wegmarken*, GA 9:313.

101. Ibid.

102. For Richardson's rendering of this important passage, see his *Heidegger*, xviii. For Heidegger's original German, see xix. Although Heidegger's letter to Richardson does not fully use the language of *Contributions to Philosophy*, what he obviously means here with turning is what he calls in this work the "turning relation of be-ing." Cf., *Contributions to Philosophy*, 6.

103. Richardson, *Heidegger*, xxii.

104. "Vorbemerkung zur siebenten Auflage 1953," in *GA* 2:vii.

105. In this respect, see F.-W. von Herrmann, *Hermeneutische Phänomenologie des Daseins: Eine Erläuterung von "Sein and Zeit,"* vol. 1, "Einleitung: Die Exposition der Frage nach dem Sinn von Sein* (Frankfurt am Main: Klostermann, 1987), 12–19; see also his *Heideggers "Grundprobleme der Phänomenologie": Zur Zweiten Hälfte von Sein and Zeit* (Frankfurt am Main: Klostermann, 1991), 21–30.

106. Richardson, *Heidegger*, xix, translation altered.

107. I do not hesitate to say that thinking in Heidegger is not the same as a faculty of the mind. Even a rudimentary familiarity with Heidegger is enough for one to grasp that thinking as he understands it is not the same as what epistemology designates as a faculty of the mind. Strictly speaking, *Dasein* and thinking in Heidegger do not substitute for what epistemologists call mind and

its faculty, respectively—pace today's verbosity regarding "Heidegger's Philosophy of Mind."

108. Heidegger, *Aus der Erfahrung des Denkens, GA* 13:90.

109. Appeared in *Heidegger Studies* 13 (1997): 17–28. This essay will be referred to hereafter as "Response."

110. Richardson, *Heidegger*, xxii.

111. The term "There-being" is Richardson's rendering of *Dasein*, hence my interpolation. Cf. Richardson, *Heidegger*, 624, and "Response," 20.

112. Richardson, *Heidegger*, 632, and "Response," 24.

113. For Richardson's English rendering of this passage, see his *Heidegger*, xviii. For the German original, see xix.

114. In "Conclusion," the final part of Richardson's *Heidegger*, this quotation reads: "if Heidegger I reverses his perspective to become Heidegger II." Cf. Richardson, *Heidegger*, 632, and "Response," 24.

Bibliography

Brokmeier, Wolfgang. "Der Andere Anfang im Ersten oder das Finden des Eigenen im Fremden der Frühe: Heidegger und Anaximander." *Heidegger Studies* 10 (1994): 111–26.

———. "Heidegger und die Suche nach dem Eigenen—Heidegger und wir." *Genos* 1 (1988): 61–95.

Cooper, David E. "Martin Heidegger, *Contributions to Philosophy* (*From Enowning*), trans. Parvis Emad and Kenneth Maly." *Times Literary Supplement*, August 25, 2000, 12–13.

Coriando, Paola-Ludovica. *Der letzte Gott als Anfang: Zur ab-gründigen Zeit-Räumlichkeit des Übergangs in Heideggers "Beiträge zur Philosophie."* Munich: Wilhelm Fink Verlag, 1998.

———, ed. *Vom Rätsel des Begriffs: Festschrift für Friedrich-Wilhelm von Herrmann zum 65. Geburtstag.* Berlin: Duncker & Humblot, 1999.

David, Pascal. "From Fundamental Ontology to Being-Historical Thinking." *Heidegger Studies* 17 (2001): 157–68.

———. "New Crusades against Heidegger: On Riding Roughshod over Philosophical Texts (Part One)." *Heidegger Studies* 13 (1997): 69–92.

———. "New Crusades against Heidegger: On Riding Roughshod over Philosophical Texts (Part Two): The Genealogy of a Mystification from Ernst Krieck to Victor Farias." *Heidegger Studies* 14 (1998): 45–64.

———. "A Philosophical Confrontation with the Political." *Heidegger Studies* 11 (1995): 191–204.

———. "Sur les *Wege zur Aussprache* de Heidegger." *Heidegger Studies* 5 (1989): 173–79.

De Gennaro, Ivo. "Heidegger on Translation—Translating Heidegger." *Phänomenologische Forschungen* 5 (2000): 3–22.

———. *Logos—Heidegger liest Heraklit.* Berlin: Duncker & Humblot, 2001.

Emad, Parvis. "*Beiträge zur Philosophie.*" In *Encyclopedia of Philosophy Supplement*, 55–56. New York: Macmillan, 1996.

———. "A Conversation with Friedrich-Wilhelm von Herrmann on Heidegger's *Beiträge zur Philosophie.*" In *Phenomenology: Japanese and American Perspectives*, edited by Burt Hopkins, 145–166. Dordrecht: Kluwer Academic, 1999.

———. "A Conversation with Friedrich-Wilhelm von Herrmann on *Mindfulness.*" *The New Yearbook for Phenomenology and Phenomenological Philosophy* 6 (2006): 1–20.

———. "De-cision: Hermeneutic Pre-conditions of Heidegger's Interpretation of Heraclitus." In *Heidegger und Antike,* edited by Hans-Christian Günther and Antonios Rengakos, 115-32. Munich: Verlag C. H. Beck, 2006.

———. "The Echo of Being in *Beiträge zur Philosophie—Der Anklang:* Directives for Its Interpretation." *Heidegger Studies* 7 (1991): 15-35.

———. "Martin Heidegger-Bernhard Welte Correspondence Seen in the Context of Heidegger's Thought." *Heidegger Studies* 22 (2006): 197-207.

———. "Heidegger I, Heidegger II and *Beiträge zur Philosophie (Vom Ereignis)."* In *From Phenomenology to Thought, Errancy, and Desire,* edited by B. Babich, 129-46. The Hague: Kluwer Academic, 1995.

———. "Heidegger's Originary Reading of Heraclitus—Fragment 16." In *Heidegger on Heraclitus: A New Reading,* edited by Kenneth Maly and Parvis Emad, 103-20. Lewiston, N.Y.: Edwin Mellen Press, 1986.

———. "Introduction: Elements of an Intellectual Portrait in H. W. Petzet's Memoirs." In *Encounters and Dialogues with Martin Heidegger 1929-1976,* by Heinrich Wiegand Petzet, xi-xxxi. Chicago: University of Chicago Press, 1993.

———. "Mastery of Being and Coercive Force of Machination in Heidegger's *Beiträge zur Philosophie* and *Besinnung."* In *Vom Rätsel des Begriffs,* edited by Paola-Ludovica Coriando, 73-90. Berlin: Duncker & Humblot, 1999.

———. "Nietzsche in Heideggers *Beiträge zur Philosophie."* In *Verwechselt mich vor allem nicht: Heidegger und Nietzsche,* edited by Hans-Helmuth Gander, 179-96. Frankfurt am Main: Klostermann Verlag, 1994.

———. "On 'Be-ing': The Last Part of *Contributions to Philosophy (From Enowning)."* In Scott et al., *Companion to Heidegger's Contributions to Philosophy,* 229-45.

———. "On the Inception of Being-Historical Thinking and Its Unfolding as Mindfulness." *Heidegger Studies* 16 (2000): 55-71.

———. "The Place of the Pre-Socratics in Heidegger's *Beiträge zur Philosophie."* In *The Pre-Socratics after Heidegger,* edited by David Jacobs, 55-71. New York: SUNY Press, 1999.

———. "Poetic Saying as Beckoning: The Opening of Hölderlin's *Germanien."* *Research in Phenomenology* 19 (1989): 121-37.

———. "The Question of Being: Foremost Hermeneutic Pre-condition for Interpreting Heidegger." *Enrahonar: Quaderns de Filosofia (Heidegger 75è aniversari de la publicació d'Èsser i temps)* 34 (2002): 11-29.

———. "The Question of Technology and Will to Power." In *Kunst und Technik: Gedächtnisschrift zum 100. Geburtstag von Martin Heidegger,* edited by Walter Biemel and F.-W. von Herrmann, 125-40. Frankfurt am Main: Klostermann, 1989.

———. "Translating Heidegger's *Contributions to Philosophy* as an Hermeneutic Responsibility." *Studia Phaenomenologica* (May 2006): 347-68.

Fédier, François. "Hölderlin und Heidegger." In *Voll Verdienst, doch dichterisch wohnet / Der Mensch auf dieser Erde,* edited by Peter Trawny, 51-70. Frankfurt am Main: Klostermann Verlag, 2000.

———. "Traduire les *Beiträge zur Philosophie (Vom Ereignis)."* *Heidegger Studies* 9 (1993): 15-33.

Gander, Hans-Helmut. "Grund- und Leitstimmungen in Heideggers *Beiträge zur Philosophie.*" *Heidegger Studies* 10 (1994): 15–31.

Guest, Gérard. "The Turning of *Ereignis:* Situating 'Deconstruction' in the Topology of Being." *Heidegger Studies* 15 (1999): 19–35.

Ionescu, Christina. "The Concept of the Last God in Heidegger's *Beiträge:* Hints toward an Understanding of the Gift of *Sein.*" *Studia Phaenomenologica* 2, nos. 1–2 (2002): 59–95.

Iyer, Lars. "*Contributions to Philosophy (From Enowning),* by Martin Heidegger, trans. Parvis Emad and Kenneth Maly." *Journal of the British Society for Phenomenology* (January 2002): 95–96.

Kalary, Thomas. *Das befindliche Verstehen und die Seinsfrage.* Berlin: Duncker & Humblot, 1999.

———. "Hermeneutic Pre-conditions for Interpreting Heidegger: A Look at Recent Literature (Part One) General Introduction to Heidegger's Thought and Its Place in Western Philosophy." *Heidegger Studies* 18 (2002): 159–80.

———. "Hermeneutic Pre-conditions for Interpreting Heidegger: A Look at Recent Literature (Part Two) Focusing on, and Thinking *after Beiträge.*" *Heidegger Studies* 19 (2003): 129–57.

———. "Towards Sketching the 'Genesis' of *Being and Time.*" *Heidegger Studies* 16 (2000): 189–220.

Kovacs, George. "Difficulties and Hazards of Dealing with the Question of Being: Examining Recent Heidegger Literature and the Richardson-*Festschrift.*" *Heidegger Studies* 15 (1999): 155–70.

———. "Heidegger in Dialogue with Herder: Crossing the Language of Metaphysics toward Be-ing-historical Language." *Heidegger Studies* 17 (2001): 45–63.

———. "An Invitation to Think through and with Heidegger's *Beiträge zur Philosophie.*" *Heidegger Studies* 12 (1996): 17–36.

———. "The Leap (*Der Sprung*) for Being in Heidegger's *Beiträge zur Philosophie (Vom Ereignis).*" *Man and World* 25 (1992): 39–59.

Maly, Kenneth. "Soundings of *Beiträge zur Philosophie (Vom Ereignis).*" *Research in Phenomenology* 21 (1991): 169–83.

———. "Translating Heidegger's Works into English: The History and the Possibility." *Heidegger Studies* 16 (2000): 115–38.

———. "Turning in Essential Swaying and the Leap." In Scott et al., *Companion to Heidegger's Contributions to Philosophy,* 150–70.

Müller, Christian. *Der Tod als Wandlungsmitte: Zur Frage nach Entscheidung, Tod, und letztem Gott in Heideggers "Beiträge zur Philosophie."* Berlin: Duncker & Humblot, 1999.

Neu, Daniella. *Die Notwendigkeit der Gründung im Zeitalter der Dekonstruktion: Zur Gründung in Heideggers "Beiträgen zur Philosophie" unter Hinzuziehen der Derridaschen Dekonstruktion.* Berlin: Duncker & Humblot, 1997.

Pasternak, Boris, Marina Tsvetayeva, and Rainer Maria Rilke. *Letters: Summer 1926,* edited by Yevgeny Pasternak, Yelena Pasternak, and Konstantin M. Azadovsky, translated by Margaret Wettlin, Walter Arndt, and Jamey Gambrell. New York: New York Review of Books, 2001.

Richardson, William J. "Dasein and the Ground of Negativity: A Note on the

Fourth Movement in the *Beiträge*-Symphony." *Heidegger Studies* 9 (1993): 35–52.

———. "From Phenomenology through Thought to a *Festschrift:* A Response." *Heidegger Studies* 13 (1997): 17–28.

———. *Heidegger: Through Phenomenology to Thought.* The Hague: Martinus Nijhoff, 1967.

Schalow, Frank. "How Viable Is Dreyfus's Interpretation of Heidegger? Anthropologism, Pragmatism, and Misunderstanding of Texts." *Heidegger Studies* 20 (2004): 17–33.

———. "The Question of Identity and Its Recollection in Being's Historical Unfolding." *Heidegger Studies* 11 (1995): 151–65.

———. "Questioning the Search for Genesis: A Look at Heidegger's Early Freiburg and Marburg Lectures." *Heidegger Studies* 16 (2000): 167–86.

Scott, Charles, et. al., eds. *Companion to Heidegger's Contributions to Philosophy.* Bloomington: Indiana University Press, 2001.

Sena, Marylou. "The Phenomenal Basis of Entities and the Manifestation of Being according to Sections 15–17 of *Being and Time:* On the Pragmatist Misunderstanding." *Heidegger Studies* 11 (1995): 11–31.

von Herrmann, Friedrich-Wilhelm. "Besinnung als seinsgeschichtliches Denken." *Heidegger Studies* 16 (2000): 37–53.

———. "*Contributions to Philosophy* and Enowning-Historical Thinking." In Scott et al., *Companion to Heidegger's Contributions to Philosophy,* 105–26.

———. "The Flower of the Mouth: Hölderlin's Hint for Heidegger's Thinking of the Essence of Language." *Research in Phenomenology* 19 (1989): 27–42.

———. "Heideggers Grundlegung der Hermeneutik." In *Kultur—Kunst— Öffentlichkeit: Philosophische Perspektiven auf praktische Probleme,* edited by Annemarie Gethmann and Elisabeth Weisser-Lohmann, 143–55. Munich: Wilhelm Fink Verlag, 2001.

———. "Sein und Zeit und das Dasein." *Enrahonar: Quaderns de Filosofia (Heidegger 75è aniversari de la publicació d'Èsser i temps)* 34 (2002): 47–57.

———. *Wege ins Ereignis: Zu Heideggers "Beiträge zur Philosophie."* Frankfurt am Main: Vittorio Klostermann, 1994.

Ziegler, Susanne. "Hölderlin unter dem Anspruch der ἀλήθεια?" *Heidegger Studies* 10 (1994): 163–83.

General Index

Proper names appearing in the endnotes are not included in the general index.

Index of Greek Terms

Fragments

ἁρμονίη ἀφανὴς φανερῆς κρείττων (Heraclitus Fg. 54), 92
τὸ μὴ δῦνόν ποτε πῶς ἄν τις λάθοι (Heraclitus Fg. 16), 91, 106
φύσις κρύπτεσθαι φιλεῖ (Heraclitus Fg. 123), 92

Words and Phrases